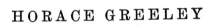

HORACE GREELEY

Yours
Horace Greeley

HORACE GREELEY

FOUNDER OF
The New York Tribune

By

DON C. SEITZ

Illustrated

AMS PRESS

NEW YORK

Reprinted from the edition of 1926, Indianapolis
First AMS EDITION published 1970
Manufactured in the United States of America

Library of Congress Catalogue Card Number: 74-112297
SBN: 404-00210-2

AMS PRESS, INC.
NEW YORK, N. Y. 10003

To
The Memory of
J. A. Seitz, My Father

FOREWORD

For forty years Horace Greeley was the busiest and boldest editor in America. He pried under and tipped over with pitiless pertinacity, to become and remain our greatest polemist. Other men have risen high in New York journalism, but mainly on the shoulders of those less agile than themselves. Mr. Greeley climbed alone. He and no one else made the New York *Tribune,* by pure force of brain and pen. No rival American journalist ever created an influence that penetrated so deeply. The New York *Tribune* was Horace Greeley. Far and wide men and women followed his guidance in great causes. No matter of moment escaped him, no fears ever made him pause. He gave neither himself nor the nation rest.

To tell what he did, how he did it, and what manner of man he was, to a new generation is the purpose of this volume.

D. C. S.

CONTENTS

HORACE GREELEY

HORACE GREELEY

CHAPTER I

THE MAN

OUTWARDLY there was about Horace Greeley little suggestion of force, although few men ever developed more of it. This was a mild-mannered, baby-faced personage who was to break shackles, wreck parties and do as much as any one person to bring on civil war. No stranger-looking figure appeared among the noted men of his day. He was rather tall in stature, five feet ten and a half, with a frame badly set and a large queer-shaped head. It was round as a ball. The forehead bulged, betokening brain power behind it, while on the edge of the dome the blue eyes gazed unblinkingly at mankind. The eyes had no sparkle; indeed were mild and pale. The complexion was white—so white as to be startling, though there was nothing unhealthy in the pallor. This whiteness was set off by a crown of thin silky hair, so light as to suggest the albino, which in middle life came to extend around the face and under the chin, framing the baby countenance. Indeed the whole aspect was infantile. And infant Greeley was, *enfant terrible*. He had no graces. His voice was high and shrill. There was no charm of

1

flowing periods or sonorous appeal. He screeched until hearers put fingers in their ears, but the speech bored through to the protected tympanums; there was no stopping its pervasive penetration.

His dress, if disheveled, was scrupulously neat and clean. His linen was of the choicest and always fresh from the laundry. He liked linen clothes, and in the summer wore a fresh suit daily, covered with a long "duster."

Men of that day wore boots, with the exception of an effeminate few who affected "Congress" gaiters, a shoe with woven elastic fixed in the sides that kept the footgear in place and allowed it to be easily drawn off and on. The boots were formidable affairs, with leather tops reaching to the knees. It was somewhat difficult to adjust the trousers legs smoothly over these leather cylinders and coax them down to the bridge of the feet. Greeley seldom tried thus to perfect his toilet, with the result that one leg or the other of the trousers was usually snagged somewhere on a boot-top. This became a fixture in his costume, and, once he became famous, was eagerly seized upon by the cartoonists to the end of exaggerating his eccentricities, of which disarranged unmentionables were not the least. The blue eyes were weak and had early to take to spectacles. Pince-nez were not of that day, and, if they had been, the small and rather puggy nose would not have afforded safe lodgment for them. Instead, their owner peered through glasses large and round, mounted in a frame that clung for safety to the ears. These glasses gave him an owl-like aspect, much appreciated by the artists. His collar sat around his rather slender neck like the edge of a bowl, and over it the

silken whiskers flowed. A string necktie, that worked
easily round toward one ear or the other, usually completed his adornment. For headgear he liked a broad-
brimmed hat of straw or felt, usually white. Indeed,
white was his favorite garb, it would appear, so that
his picture is always pale in toto. The broad brims
were mainly for the farm. His pet public topper was a
tall white hat, built on the model of the ancient beaver,
but of plain felt. This became his trademark.

He usually carried a fat umbrella that bulged a
good deal, due to the fact that its ribs were whalebone.
These were stout and wore well. Indeed, an umbrella
of the 'fifties had endurance enough to become an heir-
loom. It will be seen that this combination of hat,
spectacles, necktie, boots and umbrella made a figure
not to be easily overlooked.

Besides this, the man was everywhere. The present-day editor seldom makes a public appearance. He
is the slave of the lamp. Greeley covered all outdoors.
He missed few public occasions, spoke much, lectured
more, took part in conventions, either as delegate or
reporter, conferred constantly with the great and near
great, led in party counsels, and went to church. No
editor does any of these things in modern times.

According to Justin McCarthy, the eminent Irish-
English journalist, who became well acquainted with
him and loved him much, Greeley's appearance presented "a great shiny broad forehead, his eyes adorned
by a vast pair of spectacles; a large, almost entirely
bald head, a clean-shaven, fleshy face—a face that, including baldness, spectacles, good-natured smile and
keen shrewd humor of expression, reminded me in an
odd sort of way of Count Cavour, the famous Italian

statesman. Greeley was a much worse dressed man
than even Count Cavour. Cavour was quite aware of
his own unconquerable indifference to dress, and had
therefore provided that his tailor must furnish him at
stated intervals with a new suit of clothes made exactly after the same pattern as the old suit. But
Horace Greeley disdained any such prudent precau-
tion; he simply ordered a new garment when the old
one was falling to pieces.''

McCarthy also observed a temper of cheerful kindliness under an ''occasional asperity of criticism and
manner.'' The fact is that underneath the asperity
and kindliness alike, and giving deeper point to the
short savage thrust of his pen, integrity was the quality in Greeley that impelled people to think over what
he had said. He had no interest in running a newspaper to make money. He was indeed totally unmer-
cenary.

Greeley might have become as rich through the
New York *Tribune* as the elder James Gordon Bennett, his contemporary, did through the New York
Herald. That he did not become rich through it was
not due to any incapacity. From a state of extreme
poverty he reached a point where he earned large sums
of money—for that day—with voice and pen, yet he
kept but little. Indeed, he shaved his interest in the
paper finally down to ten shares. His partner, Thomas
McElrath, made a fat fortune. So did Gordon L.
Ford, of Brooklyn, father of Paul Leicester Ford, who
''farmed out'' the *Tribune's* advertising. The paper
had no coherent business system, but a money-flow
flooded its treasury from all over the North and West.
The weekly was a gold mine and held place next to the

family Bible in the respect of its subscribers. The daily approached nearer the London *Thunderer* than anything we have ever had in American journalism. Bennett sold gossip and news; Joseph Pulitzer combined news and opinion for the market. Greeley proclaimed, pursued and punished like an avenging angel. He sought no profits, and coveted power only for public purposes. The mean-minded have said he was jealous of political preferment. Perhaps he was— momentarily. Hercules probably coveted the golden apples, but he gave them to King Eurystheus. Greeley's great labors, his money and his life were swallowed up in matters of public concern. He chased rascals, not dollars. The chief profiteers by his endeavors were penniless, helpless and black.

His early poverty and that of his parents before him did not lead Greeley to care about money, but rather to feel strongly that work alone deserved money as a reward. He thought money should be earned, not made, as is the modern method. "The darkest day," he observed, "in any man's earthly career is that in which he first fancies that there is some easier way of gaining a dollar than by squarely earning it. He has lost his way through the moral labyrinth and henceforth must wander as chance may dictate." He also learned to feel a horror of debt, growing especially out of the seven years' financial struggle with the *New Yorker*. "I would rather be a convict in a state prison," he wrote in his *Recollections*, "a slave in a rice swamp, than to pass through life under the harrow of debt. . . . Hunger, cold, rags, hard work, contempt, suspicion, unjust reproach, are disagreeable; but debt is infinitely worse than them all. . . . If you have but fifty cents and can get no more for a week, buy a peck of corn, parch it, and live on it, rather than owe any man a dollar. . . . I speak of real debt, that which involves risk and sacrifice on one side, obligation and dependence on the other.''

Clear expression was given by Greeley to what newspapers should and should not be: ''Newspapers,'' he once wrote, ''are (or ought to be) printed for the information and entertainment of the whole community; but when they are mere advocates of petty or even of ponderous private interests, the advertisers of personal schemes, and puffers of men, who, whether connected with them or not, have a large amount of axes to grind, they must lose all independence, manliness, and, in fact, all substantial patronage. Their insolvency must come in time; should they have employed upon them writers disposed to speak their mind, and indisposed to submit to dictation, they must lose those writers in time. The consequences must be shiftlessness, inequality of management, and frequent surrenders of the ghost.''

Junius Henri Browne, one of the ablest and most adventurous of the *Tribune's* staff, once observed:

''If it was Mr. Greeley's fate to be misapprehended, much of this misapprehension arose from his own waywardness, moodiness and determination not to set himself right. Assured of the rectitude of his conduct, he was careless of the impression formed of it, except in instances where temper about trifles got the better of his native judgment. He would be patient and reticent under a serious accusation, when a petty paragraph in an obscure journal would drive him to exasperation. He would declare his supreme unconcern as to the opinions expressed of some policy he had chosen, and an hour later would write a card, bitterly personal, upon a matter too trivial to be noticed. His friends could not be certain of him, for he could not be certain of himself. His growing up wild, so to speak, left a certain trace of social savagery in his nature that could not be eradicated subsequently, even had he made an effort to that end. After every attempt to explain his eccentricities and reconcile his inconsistencies, something of the unintelligible will adhere to his character, which was unquestionably unique. He was not only unlike other men—he was unlike himself often. General rules fail to apply to him on account of numerous exceptions, which, in his case, might almost have been bound into a rule.''

Henry Clapp, Jr., editor of the *Saturday Press* and leader of New York's brief Bohemia that used to gather in George Pfaff's beer saloon in the basement of 647 Broadway, once described Greeley as ''a self-made man who worships his Creator''—a cruel jest, and untrue. A. Oakey Hall, the blithe personage who became William M. Tweed's Mayor of New York, was a better psychologist. He put out in 1862 a clever pamphlet, *Horace Greeley Decently Dissected*. While aiming to be ironic, it is not unjust, and admiration peeps out often between the criticisms. ''Horace Greeley,'' wrote Hall, ''possesses native genius, but . . . has contracted . . . a marked self-consciousness'' that ''destroys his fidelity to friends, his magnanimity to enemies, his devotion to country, and his regard for social tranquillity.'' The *Tribune* Hall described as Greeley's ''glass to reflect self-consciousness in; his viaduct of gossip and his engine of intermeddling.''

There is no doubt that the *Tribune* showed his hand on every page. For Greeley was not just the editor engaged in writing editorials, he was the editor who knew how to edit his paper, and did, through and through. He possessed an equipment for the metropolitan newspaper field not duplicated in that day or this.

Junius Henri Browne believed that "Mr. Greeley's memory was as retentive as Pascal's. His mind was a marvelous storehouse of facts, dates and events. He seemed to forget nothing worth remembering. He was a political encyclopedia, of the best revised edition and entirely trustworthy, of the last forty years. He was every hour of the day what the *Tribune Almanac* is at the close of December. It was hard for him to understand how any member of his profession could be ignorant or oblivious of ten thousand things, which few besides himself held in recollection. He thought every journalist should have at least contemporaneous political facts and data in immediate command."

Besides his remarkable ability as a writer of editorials, Greeley was a first-class reporter. His paper bristled with important news, much of it as provocative as the editorial. He was also master of the printer's art. The *Tribune* was a model of compactness and good editing, set in very small but clear-faced type and extremely well printed.

His editorial habits were pretty regular. Usually he reached the *Tribune* office, following late hours of work, shortly after noon, coming in with pockets bulging with papers he had picked up on the way. These he dumped out on the floor beside his desk and was at once engrossed in his work, having wasted no time saluting the staff. Blunders in fact and style called for a severe "dressing down" for the offenders, while typographical errors roused his deepest ire. "Type-setters," he is quoted as saying, "are not expected to know anything; but we employ the best talent that money and good prices can command for proof-readers, and there is nothing to be said in extenuation of their shortcomings." He read the *Tribune* relig-iously—every word of it—and was intolerant of fail-ures to get all the news. According to Charles A. Dana, he would "scold like a drab, as ferocious as a baited bear." He would go out to dinner around five o'clock in the afternoon, returning, as a rule, and staying as long as there was anything to do or be interested in. Beman Brockway, long editor of the Watertown *Times,* who was intimate with Greeley in the younger days, dating from his work in western New York, and who worked two years on the *Tribune,* in his *Reminiscences* testifies to having seen him fall asleep, pen in hand, and credits him with the ability to sleep only thus when very tired. The same rule ap-plied to meals. Like the man in the comic song, he ate when he was hungry and drank when he was dry, but had no system about it. When he ate meat, as he sometimes did, despite his vegetarian theories, Brock-way says he usually devoured three or four times as much as others would. Like Napoleon, "He ate, as he did everything else, in a hurry; he worked with all his might; ate the same way." Brockway goes on to say:

"Horace used to stop with me when I was in Chau-tauqua—never for any great length of time, for he was always in a prodigious hurry. He called to get a look at the latest papers, which he perused with avidity and care. One evening he took tea at my house. Some ladies happened to be present. He was given an introduction, but he exchanged no words with them; he was too busy talking politics to notice the visitors. I remember that my wife addressed to him the customary inquiry, 'How will you have your tea, Mr. Greeley?' and received in response, 'I will have a little milk and water and sugar and no tea.' He talked incessantly; there was no let-up, even for an instant. In eating he seemed to go for some particular article, and make a meal of it. On one occasion, finding a plate of gingerbread on the table which suited his taste, he took the liberty of helping himself, and made way with nearly the whole of it—in fact, ate little else."

Another hostess at an evening party where Greeley had dropped in late, passed him a plate of doughnuts. Deeply lost in thought, he ate away unconsciously until the doughnuts were gone, and then accepted a plate of cheese, continuing to eat until the last cube had vanished. He then went home, and there is no record of any disaster.

Absent-mindedness became one of his notorious traits. Daniel Frohman, once his office boy, recalls his writing at his desk, oblivious to all but his editorials, while the water dripped down upon him from a leaky pipe above. The *Tribune* office had no heating system, but warm air was coaxed up through wooden boxes from the boiler room in the basement. These flues had slides in them that opened into the floors. One cold Sabbath the editor came in from church, and, pulling off his boots, opened a slide and thrust his stockinged feet into the slot, while he was soon immersed in the

Sunday papers. The day foreman, prowling about, noted his employer's posture and observed:

"There's no heat coming up from down-stairs, Mr. Greeley. The boiler is being fixed."

"You damned fool," retorted Horace, "what did you want to tell me that for? I was just getting nice and warm."

This trick of abstraction caused him to disregard the comfort and convenience not only of himself but of others. In July, 1861, as the war-tide was getting under way, Senator Charles Sumner called on Greeley, who invited him to breakfast the next morning, the meal coming later than with most people, following night hours at the *Tribune* office. Sumner came according to appointment. "I went up there," Sumner said to Moncure D. Conway, "a long distance, and Greeley talked and talked more than an hour about politics. At last it occurred to him that I had not breakfasted. He called up the cook and asked her if there was anything for breakfast. She said there was some milk and bread and cold meat. On that I had to breakfast."

Conway comments on this in his *Memoirs* as follows: "The amusing thing was the serious disgust manifested by the Senator in telling it. It rather increased my respect for Greeley that he should be so absorbed in the state of the country as to forget breakfast, and I probably made that apology for him."

Tobacco was a pet aversion with Greeley. Offered a good cigar, he waved it away with: "No, I thank you. I haven't got so low down as that yet. I only drink and swear."

But while he swore with vigor, he could not be considered profane. It was a style he used in emphatic exclamations. Rum was always "damned" rum, so were other vexations or problems. Brockway came in one Sunday evening from Plymouth Church and asked if he might write something about Beecher's sermon. "I guess so," replied Greeley. "We have done nothing lately but puff the damned theaters; it's about time we did something for religion."

As with some of the inhabitants of Maine, to whom all liquors are "rum," teetotalism with Greeley limited his knowledge of liquid nomenclature. He was much laughed at once for writing, on behalf of temperance, a denunciation of the well-to-do who drank their Clicquots and champagne—not knowing that the excellent widow was a personage rather than a beverage.

When some one in the *Tribune* shop called his attention to the error he replied aptly: "I'm the only editor here who could have made that mistake."

It is part of our national history that editors of that era took themselves and one another seriously. The pen was a lance, the sheet a shield, behind which they jousted merrily on what were not always mimic fields. Brother-editor James Watson Webb, of the horrendous *Courier and Enquirer,* who was a good deal of what was known in that day as a "lady-killer" and Beau Brummel, sneered editorially, for example, at Greeley's ill-worn clothes. Just before indulging in this persiflage, Webb had been indicted, convicted and sentenced for acting as a second to Henry Clay in a duel with Tom Marshall. The term of duress was two years in Sing Sing, but Governor William H. Seward pardoned him before he went behind the bars, in return for which Webb named one of his sec-

William Cullen Bryant

ond-growth sons William Seward Webb, a name that sticks in the family, implying relationship rather than gratitude. The pardon incident gave Greeley a fine chance. He had worn, he observed, better clothes than Webb could wear if he paid his debts, and further: "That he ever affected eccentricity is most untrue; and certainly no costume he ever appeared in would create such a sensation in Broadway as that which James Watson Webb would have worn, but for the clemency of Governor Seward."

"You lie, you villain! You know you lie!" Greeley once hurled at William Cullen Bryant, in capital letters. The author of *Thanatopsis* nearly choked with rage. Greeley had pilloried him in a purely Pickwickian sense, quite unconscious of the fact that he had made use of an offending idiom. Besides, Bryant had not lied. He had merely said something in a way to annoy the editor of the *Tribune*.

Although he could thus objurgate the grave "Thanatopsian," Greeley was broad enough in 1855 when party conditions were still chaotic and a state ticket was being planned on independent lines, to urge Bryant's nomination as secretary of state, "in case we concede that office (as I think best) to the Democracy. . . . You know I don't like him personally, nor he me, but I can't think of any man of greater mark; and I think he is thoroughly honest and capable. Depend upon it, there are a good many of all parties who would gladly and proudly vote for him. If we can only keep off the ticket all the men who want to be put on I think we must succeed. . . . Don't make us swallow Ben Butler, if there is any help for it. He would go very hard."

Butler was the distinguished Benjamin F. Butler, of New York, father of William Allen Butler, and was swallowed, despite its "going hard."

Greeley never hesitated to antagonize. Thoreau has this note in his journal; it might serve as reminder that not all of the controversy was bitter: "Horace Greeley found some fault with me in the world, because I presumed to speak of the New Testament, using my own words and thoughts, and challenged me to a controversy. The one thought I had was that it would give me real pleasure to know that he loved it as sincerely and intellectually as I did."

The *Tribune* sanctum had many callers, for in those days access to an editor was easier than it is now. No respecter of persons, Greeley treated them all alike, that is to say, with curt understanding of all they had to say and a quick dismissal.

There is a story that in the process of doing as he pleased with his own money, Greeley advanced sundry sums to Cornelius Vanderbilt, Jr., the rather unstable eldest son of the great Commodore. This fact reached the ears of the New York Central and Hudson River magnate, and he called at the *Tribune* office. Steered to the sanctum in the usual informal newspaper fashion, he stood on the threshold of the coop in which the editor sat amid a wallow of discarded journals, bent over a desk. The entrance of a caller did not induce him to turn around.

"I am Commodore Vanderbilt," the visitor announced, clearing his throat after a moment.

The engrossed editor did not look up. A little annoyed, the millionaire raised his voice:

"I understand you are lending money to my son,

Cornelius. I wish you to know that if you expect me to be responsible for it you are mistaken. I will not pay one cent.''

"Who the hell asked you to?'' squeaked Horace, not ceasing his labors or taking eyes from paper. The discomfited parent departed. He was true to his word, however, and never did pay a cent. The reckless son died. After the Commodore's own death, William H. Vanderbilt, to his great honor, paid it back, principal and interest, to Greeley's daughters.

Charles Henry Webb ("John Paul") relates how, as a callow youth, he braved the great editor of the *Tribune* to proffer some poetry, and how, to prove that others had thought well of his work, he brought along a copy of *Harper's Weekly* containing an example of it. He found the editor seated at his desk, "his nose nearly touching the paper upon which he was writing,'' owing to his affliction of near-sightedness. "Ah,'' said Greeley reaching for the *Weekly*, "I used to write poetry myself, but it was very long ago.'' He read the poem half aloud, then remarked: "These are fair verses, but they are not well-printed. The alternate lines should have been indented more.'' He then proceeded to show how the compositor should have set up his lines. The style suggested made "a great improvement'' in their presentation. Something about the youngster, who was much scared, interested Greeley, and he laid aside his pen and drew the lad out with engaging conversation. The visitor unbosomed his desire to locate in the city and lead a literary life.

"The great mistake young men make,'' commented the editor, "is in leaving the country and coming to the city.''

"But you came to the city, Mr. Greeley," countered young Webb.

"Yes," Webb responded, "and"—slowly—"sometimes I think it was a very great mistake. But if I could have got a half-dollar a week more I should never have left the country." And he added, "Why, if I were to advertise in my paper to-morrow for fifty men to go on a pirate ship and for five men to work on my farm, there would be five hundred applications for the situation on the pirate ship and not one for the farm. Would you believe that?"

"Yes, sir," responded the young man. "I think I had rather sail on a pirate ship than work on a farm."

Webb, under the encouragement received, turned in a poem very dark in tone, *Colored People Allowed in This Car,* feeling for the negrophile trend of the editor.

It was accepted, and he was told to come back in the spring, when there might be a job on the *Tribune.* He didn't come, but never hearing more of the poem after months of weary waiting, which is the poet's usual reward, wrote to find out what had happened to his verses. He got this tart reply:

"New York Tribune Office,
"May 5th, 1867.

"My dear Sir: In the first place a young man who writes to a busy editor, who has no time to consult gazetteers, without giving the state as well as the village from which his letter is dated, does not deserve an answer. Besides you misspell my name, for which there is no excuse. But I will answer you: Your verses are neither lost nor forgotten. If used now, they would simply be printed—not published. I am

New York,
Sept. 23, '55.

Dear Sir:

George E. Waring Jr.
of Westchester Co. N. York,
will deliver your Address
on Thursday of this week
unless you forbid it. He
will come up to Hillsdale,
N.Y. on the Harlem evening
train of Wednesday the 26th,
and will expect to meet
there some word from you about
getting over. He wants to be
allowed to speak on Thurs-
[day.]

I have told him
you would pay him $30 in-
cluding his traveling expenses.

Yours,
Horace Greeley.

fr Sedgwick, Esq.

Facsimile of Mr. Greeley's Handwriting

waiting an opportune moment to publish them. It is likely a case will soon appear in the courts which will give them a point.

"Yours truly,
"HORACE GREELEY."

To C. H. Webb, Esq., Champlain (I suppose) N. Y.

The illegibility of the Greeley handwriting has become a tradition. It is often cited as being the worst ever known in an editorial room. This is exaggeration, like much other matter current about Greeley during and since his lifetime. In common with all fast thinkers, he wrote rapidly, with lines aslant and creeping up toward the right-hand corner of the page. Probably, when greatly hurried, the writing might not have been clear to the uninitiated. The specimen here reproduced is plain enough—a letter recommending Colonel George E. Waring, Jr., as a good lecturer to some one of the Westchester neighbors. Greeley wrote in a Spencerian age when bookkeeping fixed the standard of penmanship, and, accordingly, his style suffered in comparison with elegancies mechanically produced. Old New York printers still talk of the "one man" in the *Tribune* office who could read the editor's writing. The *History of Typographical Union No. 6*, by George A. Stevens, ascribes this accomplishment to John C. Robinson, who in 1854 "entered the proof-room of the New York *Tribune* and during the first six months of his stay showed himself to be a marvel in deciphering illegible manuscript. To the surprise of his new colleagues he read Richard Hildreth's, Horace Greeley's, Count Gurowski's, Gerrit Smith's, and other notoriously crabbed manuscripts at a glance. Time and again when Horace Greeley acknowledged himself unable to read his own handwriting, he referred it to Robinson, who would examine it steadily for a minute, and then read it off like print.''

Stevens further relates that one night in October, 1866, a letter came to the night editor of the *Tribune* from an up-town hotel, signed, ostensibly, by Greeley, and containing an editorial warmly endorsing a Republican who was running on an independent ticket. It was put in type, but when it reached the proof-room Robinson glanced at the copy which always accompanies proof. It seemed strange to his eye. ''That's not the old man's handwriting,'' he said. The editorial was held out and proved to be a forgery. Robinson was a phenomenal proof-reader. He could and did regularly articulate six hundred and ninety-six words a minute, all proof being read by copy, which he held while another compared it with the proof and presumably caught the errors.

Edgar Allan Poe in *A Chapter on Autography* cited the script to analyze the man:

''Mr. Horace Greeley, present editor of the *Tribune* and formerly of the *New Yorker,* has for many years been remarked as one of the most able and honest of American editors. He has written much and invariably well. His political knowledge is equal to that of any of his contemporaries—his general information extensive. As a *belles lettres* critic he is entitled to high respect. His manuscript is a remarkable one—having about it a peculiarity that we know not how better to designate than as a converse of the picturesque. His characters are scratchy and irregular, ending with an abrupt taper—if we may be allowed this contradiction in terms, where we have the facsimile to prove that there is no contradiction in fact. All abrupt manuscripts, save this, have square or concise terminations of the letters. The whole chirography puts us in mind of a jog. We can fancy the writer jerking up his hand from the paper, at the end of each word, and, indeed, of each letter. What mental idiosyncrasy lies *perdu* beneath all this, is more than we can say, but we will venture to assert that Mr. Greeley (whom we do not know personally) is, personally, a very remarkable man.''

Curiously, Greeley's writing closely resembled that of another furious thinker and rapid producer of copy, Theodore Roosevelt. Both chased their words up-hill and their formation is remarkably alike.

The so-called "illegibility" led to many legends. In one case a man was said to have used a letter from Greeley declining to aid him as one of reference, and to have repeatedly secured good jobs on the strength of it. Compared with the handwriting of the average individual to-day, Greeley's script does not suffer. For one thing he knew how to spell and punctuate. Besides, there was never any lack of clarity in what he had to say. His style was curiously crisp. He used the shortest of words, and these fell like hail upon paper. Any one copying his writing on standard folio sheets will find that he runs usually sixteen words to the line, whereas with many practised editorial writers the average is about twelve. This remarkable terseness was one reason for his power to hold the attention of readers, once he had caught it.

Greeley was a much pestered man, among other things, for his autograph. Adrian H. Joline, in *Meditations of an Autograph Collector,* observed: "Everybody remembers how Horace Greeley answered an application, sputtering in his most characteristic and illegible hand, to the effect that he never, under any circumstance, wrote an autograph for anybody.''

Public speaking and lecturing, usually on political topics, became features of Greeley's activity, but neither of these rivaled his pen. Beman Brockway in his *Reminiscences* testifies that the editor ''was no orator; was not a good speaker, even, but the matter was in him, and he could not speak without saying something, without interesting his auditors. He was a magazine of facts and robust thoughts, and he never spoke but to enlighten and instruct. He was a great wit, though he probably never undertook to say a smart thing in his life.''

Aware of his long-drawn-out tendencies in the public-speaking line, Greeley, as a rule, only spoke where he was especially wanted and not always then. George E. Baker, biographer of William H. Seward, asked him to make a short speech on the Fourth of July, 1852, and received this response:

''I can't make a pyrotechnic ten-minute speech. I can't say anything worth hearing unless I have time to say it in my own way. I was over in Williamsburg last fall and tried to say something, but the chairman put me down as speaking too long, which, I presume, was the fact. You must therefore excuse me as unfit for this sort of business and call in boys who can melt the Fourth of July into Lundy's Lane and serve it up with Chapultepec for gravy. I am nothing in that line.'' (The reference is to General Scott, Whig candidate for president, and his military feats.)

As a speaker Justin McCarthy thought Greeley

resembled Thiers, whom the auditors found "positively bad," but they could never bring themselves to leave the room while he was talking.

Henry Ward Beecher fell in often with his friend Greeley as they traveled over the country filling lecture dates, and once asked him what he called "success" in a lecture. "Well," replied Horace, "where more folks stay in than go out."

The Spruce Street building sheltered, besides the *Tribune, Yankee Doodle,* a comic sheet, constructed on the lines of the new London *Punch.* Its ribald conductors were not above taking a crack now and then at their landlord, who was much beset by an increasing number of rural readers to find opportunities for them to share his fame and fortune in the growing city. Wearied with importunities, Greeley one day broke out in this fashion: "A Personal Explanation—I have long ago avowed my determination to have no part in encouraging removals from the country to the city with a view of finding employment here. In spite of repeated avowals, I am almost daily solicited, by letter or otherwise, to find or make a place for some one who thinks New York is just the sphere for him. I can not conscientiously aid any such effort, unless in some very peculiar case, believing that the city is extremely overcrowded now; that a newcomer can hardly find business here except at the expense of the many already here who need it, so that the tide of emigration ought to set strongly from the city and not to it. Erroneous these opinions may be, but they are firmly fixed and can not be easily put aside."

The editor of *Yankee Doodle* solemnly avers that on the Saturday morning following the publication of this tart "explanation" the whole town seemed to be transformed into one huge May day, everybody following Greeley's fervid advice. Later he discovered "a fine-looking head, with flaxen locks, thrust out of an upper window, and the owner shouting at the top of his lungs." It was the editor beseeching his subscribers to come back and take the paper: "At this request," *Yankee Doodle* observed, "the whole body of people wheeled in mass" and returned. "Mr. Greeley was much amused, but looked melancholy."

The humorists, as a rule, touched Greeley tenderly. The cleverest of the war-time satirists, Robert H. Newell, who wrote as "Orpheus C. Kerr," now and then introduced a good sidelight. Here is one: He, Kerr, was in company, in the lines of the Army of the Potomac, with Captain William Brown of the celebrated Mackerel Brigade, when suddenly the sound of a rich manly voice swelled up from the bosom of the valley.

" 'Hush,' says William, sternly eying the band who had just hiccupped—' 'Tis the song of the contrabands.'

"We all listened, and could distinctly hear the following words of the singer:

" 'They're holding camp meeting in Hickory swamp,
    O, let my people go;
De preacher's so dark he carry um lamp.
    O, let my people go;
De brethren am singing dis jubilee tune,
    O, let my people go,
Two dollars a year for the *Weekly Tribune,*
    O, let my people go;'

"As the strains died away, the adjutant slapped

MR. GREELEY IN 1846
(*From "Yankee Doodle," Dec. 13, 1846*)

his left leg. 'Why,' said he dreamily, 'that must be
Greeley down there!'

" 'No,' says William solemnly. 'It is one of the
wronged children of tyranny warbling the suppressed
hymn of his injured people.' "

Greeley could scarcely be called a religious man,
but the church interested him. His faith was that of
the Universalist denomination, described by Henry W.
Longfellow's witty brother-in-law, Thomas G. Apple-
ton, as that of those who "believed God was too good
to damn them," in contrast with the Unitarian conceit
that "they were too good to be damned." Greeley first
attended in New York the Orchard Street Church, of
which the Reverend Thomas J. Sawyer was pastor.
Another eminent Universalist of the day was Phineas
Taylor Barnum, builder of the Greatest Show on
Earth. The two were great friends. Barnum lived in
Bridgeport, but when in New York over Sunday, worshiped at the Universalist church on Broadway, near
Prince Street, where the Reverend Edward Hubbell
Chapin, D. D., preached. Here Greeley also became a
pretty regular attendant. Doctor Chapin ranked with
Henry Ward Beecher as one of the great pulpit orators
of his day. Indeed he was the better speaker, but there
was less sparkle of the offhand in his talk. He built up
magnificent periods and thrilled his hearers with his
sonorous voice. By and by Doctor Chapin's church became that of the Divine Paternity and stood long at
the corner of Fifth Avenue and Forty-fourth Street,
until it was sold and pulled down to make way for
Sherry's. He was as much of a church magnet in New
York as Beecher was in Brooklyn, and had no equal for
eloquence among his city fellows. People went to his

church quite as much to get a glimpse of Greeley and Barnum as they did to hear Chapin. Politicians often attended to hunt Greeley in his pew.

When the editor, the showman and the parson foregathered together, as they often did, the talk was worth listening to. Barnum and Greeley both had high piercing voices. Both believed in temperance. Barnum got so fanatical that he would not let a man travel with his show who did not swear off when it took the road. Chapin rivaled Greeley and Beecher in the lecture field, where all three were very popular. Barnum lectured occasionally on temperance and was strong against slavery. Little Cordelia Howard, with her mother as Topsy, packed the theater in Barnum's American Museum at Broadway in *Uncle Tom's Cabin,* where Father Howard played Uncle Tom, and little Eva joined the angels several times a day. The play and the *Tribune,* a couple of blocks down Park Row, were the greatest anti-slavery factors at work, even though many were busy, including Mr. Sharp's celebrated rifles.

Chapin, Barnum and Greeley were interesting contrasts. The preacher was broad and burly, with a square face and huge head. His aspect was rather, though not intentionally, severe. Out of the pulpit he was somewhat silent and reserved. Barnum was a plump red-faced man, who bustled and cackled continually. Greeley became a frequent visitor at the Barnum home in Bridgeport where a special room was always reserved for him, known as "Mr. Greeley's."

The editor and the showman first met in the office of the *Christian Messenger,* a Universalist publication, where their conversation ended in an election bet,

Greeley borrowing enough money to cover his stake. Barnum was much amused by the episode, and the two became lifelong friends. Like Barnum, Greeley was a master of the great art of attracting public attention. With Barnum it was artificial, the result of calculation, invention and careful planning; with Greeley it was automatic. He had only to appear to make a stir, only to speak to be heard. What he wrote was more widely read than anything that ever came from a journalist's pen. "What does Greeley say?" was the natural query on every tongue in times of crisis and in the development of events.

Colonel Thomas Wentworth Higginson records that in the 'fifties the two men most in the public eye were Horace Greeley and Henry Ward Beecher. Theodore Parker stood third. People were intensely interested in seeing and hearing all three.

When Greeley went to church he usually had his overcoat or duster pockets packed with newspapers, and, apparently, at once fell asleep in a comfortable corner of his pew. In reality he only closed his eyes, but kept his ears wide open, listening most alertly to the sermon, and could always give a most accurate summary of the preacher's words.

In his *Recollections* Greeley has this to say, specifically, of his denominational creed:

"Perhaps I ought to add that, with the great body of the Universalists of our day (who herein differ from the earlier pioneers in America of our faith), I believe that 'Our God is one Lord,'—that though there be that are called gods, as there be gods many and lords many, to us there is but one God, the Father, of whom are all things, one Lord Jesus Christ, by whom

are all things,' and I find the relation between the
Father and the Saviour of mankind most fully and
clearly set forth in that majestic first chapter of He-
brews, which I can not see how any Trinitarian can
ever have intently read, without perceiving that its
whole tenor and burden are directly at war with his
conception of 'three persons in one God.' Nor can I
see how Paul's express assertion that 'when all things
shall be subdued unto him, then shall the Son himself
also be subject to Him that put all things under him,
that God may be all in all,' is to be reconciled with the
more popular creed. However, I war not upon others'
convictions, but rest satisfied with a simple statement
of my own.''

His broader faith is well shown in this excerpt
taken from *The Ideal of a True Life* published in the
Printer's Book for 1849:

"A true life must be genial and joyous. Tell me
not, pale anchorite, of your ceaseless vigils, your fastings, your scourgings. These are fit offerings to
Moloch, not to our Father. The man who is not happy
in the path he has chosen, may be very sure he has
chosen amiss, or is self-deceived. But not merely
happier—he should be kinder, gentler and more elastic
in spirits, as well as firmer and truer. 'I love God and
little children,' says a German poet. The good are
ever attracted and made happier by the presence of
the innocent and lovely. And he who finds his religion
adverse to, or a restraint upon, the truly innocent
pleasures and gaieties of life, so that the latter do
not interfere with and jar upon its sublimer objects,
may well doubt whether he has, indeed, 'learned
Jesus!' ''

For some reason Greeley was easy prey for beggars and borrowers. Henry Ward Beecher once wrote
of this phase: "Greeley was forever imposed upon by

the base and the undeserving. Yet no man was shrewder. He was a great character, and he looked quite through the deeds of men. But he thought that to be born with a burden of lazy shiftlessness, or of a mean cunning, was almost the heaviest curse of heaven, and that those of us who came into life better equipped, through no desert of our own, owed these incurables something in the way of help. Moreover, he had a sunny belief that each new loan would be the lever of a vast prosperity to the especial pirate who obtained it. And the number of these beseeching brigands was legion. But his kindness did not stop there. No needy creature appealed to him in vain for assistance; no charity lacked his good help.''

An undeserved repute for piety made him a special victim of church beggars. One persistent caller, on being curtly refused, asked in mild surprise: "But, Mr. Greeley, don't you want to save sinners from going to hell!" "No," replied Horace. "It isn't half full enough of them now.''

It is difficult to understand the extraordinary animosity generated against Greeley in the South. Resentment there seemed to concentrate upon his head. The *Tribune* was anathema in southern post-offices. It was unsafe to be a subscriber and dangerous to represent the paper in any way. Men suspected of being *Tribune* agents or correspondents had to run for their lives and seek safety in deep disguise; Albert D. Richardson, the paper's best reporter, traveled under an assumed name through the states and took elaborate precautions against discovery. Other papers said much the same things as Greeley's paper, but none of them said it in the same way. Murat Halstead, whose ancestors were from North Carolina, though

he fulminated from Cincinnati, Ohio, could assail the
South like the glorious young swashbuckler he was,
without any one putting a price on his head. James
G. Birney could advocate absolute abolition and create
no such aversion as Greeley did. The fact that both
had southern backgrounds may have tempered the
views of their opponents. Greeley was a Simon-pure
"Yankee" and a "black Republican." He epitomized
in his person and paper all that was baleful and
threatening, yet was fairness itself in giving room to
the views of his foes. The irritating effect of his
writing was not that of invective or insult. It possessed a penetrating quality, a certainty in reaching
sore spots, that no other writer before or since his
day has duplicated. The northern Democrats regarded with equal venom a man who could pointedly
expose their own weaknesses, which were glaring. "I
never said all Democrats were saloon-keepers," he
averred. "What I said was that all saloon-keepers
were Democrats." His knowledge of politics was so
thorough that no man could escape his own past, and
this produced a good share of the trouble.

John Greenleaf Whittier, in an enthusiastic moment, once described Horace Greeley as a "second
Franklin." He was far from that, save in being a
poor boy and a printer who commanded success.
Franklin was consistently constructive; he both invented and improved. The placid Franklin uniting
the discordant elements around him is a far different
person from the Greeley who attacked, scolded, and
everywhere aroused antagonism. Horace Greeley has
his own place in history but it is not beside Benjamin
Franklin.

CHAPTER II

THE mild blue eyes first opened at Amherst, New Hampshire, February 3, 1811. Horace was the third child of Zaccheus Greeley and Mary Woodburn. Zaccheus was the third of his name and line, the first having come to America from England in 1640. In all, the family counted seven children, the death of two born before his birth leaving Horace the eldest. The father and mother were intellectual people, who ground out their lives fighting the climate and soil.

Amherst was a typical New Hampshire town, with unfertile farm lands thinly settled, with poor markets and small chance for making money. For three years before the birth of Horace, Zaccheus and his fine young wife had struggled on a forty-odd acre farm, where granite boulders occupied most of the soil and the ax found more work than the plow. To make the task of getting on more difficult, Zaccheus had no capital and the farm was well laden with a mortgage. The growing family lived in a small one-story house of the common type, heated, if the term can be used truthfully, by fireplaces with vast appetites for fuel, the warmth from most of which went up the chimney. Both parents worked hard. Mary Woodburn, with fast-coming children, cooked, nursed and spun. She

even raked hay and "picked up" about the place.
That she did a man's work, as claimed by some biographers, is denied by her descendants. There was
enough to do without that.

Things did not thrive on the forlorn farm. Such
surroundings may breed stupidity or precocity in
about equal proportions. With little Horace precocity
was marked. He could read almost as soon as he
could talk, and had the uncanny gift of being able to
visualize a page and absorb its contents from any
angle—sidewise or upside down. When he was three
it was decided his education must begin. The farm
was two miles from a schoolhouse. So the child was
sent, at that ripe age, to the residence of his grandfather Woodburn at Bedford, next door to an institution of learning, and thus took his first step into the
world.

Soon he was "teacher's pet" in the company of
hobbledehoy boys and sweet New England girls. The
boys had to be beaten into submission, and the teacher's lot was hard. No wonder, then, this wise infant
was dear to the heart of the instructress. He had a
phenomenal fancy for the spelling-book. No word
could stump him and he "spelled down" all competi-
tors at the spelling bees.

Becoming something of a champion, the boy was
at first made captain of his "side" at a spelling bee,
with the duty of selecting the "team," but it was soon
found that while he could spell well himself he was
poor at picking out others, his eye rather than his
brain operating in making a choice of associates. That
is, he chose the best-looking girls, who were apt to be
less intelligent than the homely lassies, so he lost this

part of the leadership under the stern requirements of competition.

"Speaking pieces" was a favorite school exercise, and in this exhibition of talent Horace likewise led, piping out with spirit lusty lines learned by heart from *The Columbian Orator.*

The infantile prodigy found school easy and entertaining. His taste for reading cleared the way for lighter tasks in other studies, and he was omniverous, devouring all the printed food he could find. Fancy a child "eating up" the Bible, *Pilgrim's Progress, The Arabian Nights, Robinson Crusoe,* and all sorts of stuff besides, to satisfy his intellectual cravings. Horace, indeed, had finished the Bible at the age of five!

Rather delicate, and burdened with a weighty brain, he was not active physically. He did go fishing occasionally, but most of the time his face was wedged between the pages of a book. Temperamentally he was timid and afraid of physical risks, although morally he was bravest of the brave.

The school at Bedford was outside of the Greeley district, and to educate an outsider, whose parents paid no taxes, was a serious matter. The prize pupil, however, won even the heart of the school trustees, who waived his intrusion, but protected the taxpayers by prescribing that "no pupils should be received from any other town, except Horace Greeley alone."

His talents attracted such attention that some well-to-do gentleman in the town offered to see him through Phillips Exeter Academy, and thence through college. The thought of charity did not appeal to Zaccheus. He declined the kindly proffer and Horace remained at home. Times were hard. The Jefferson embargo had choked New England. Zaccheus Greeley "lost" his farm, which means it was foreclosed. Besides, he was deep in debt, and the law of that day allowed creditors to jail debtors. To save himself from the sheriff he fled by night to the hospitable state of Vermont, which had been peopled by the out-of-luck who had not lost sympathy with their kind.

The family remained, wondering, behind. "Father lost everything he possessed," relates his daughter Esther (Mrs. John F. Cleveland). "After he left, his furniture was attached and sold. I remember strange rough men in the house, who pulled open all the trunks and chests of drawers, and tossed about the beautiful white bed and table linen that mother had wrought before her marriage. Another picture, too, is impressed indelibly upon my mind—how mother followed the sheriff and his men from room to room with the tears rolling down her face, while Brother Horace, then a little white-haired boy, nine years old, held her hand trying to comfort her, telling her not to cry—he would take care of her."

The mother cared for her brood as best she could during three months, until Zaccheus Greeley had earned enough cutting wood at fifty cents a day in Vermont to call them to him. They went in winter by wagon over the mountains a hundred miles, to West Haven, Vermont, near Lake Champlain, and lodged in a little cabin on what was known as the Minot estate, where the father was employed.

Two milk pans were the only utensils in their possession at first. The children ate their "mush" out of one, in common—each had a spoon—and the father

HORACE GREELEY'S BIRTHPLACE

and mother out of the other. Things improved, but slowly. They soon had enough to eat and wear. Money was the scarce commodity. Zaccheus was clearing a fifty acre lot of its timber. The whole family labored at the task—father and mother, boys and girls. Horace and his brother Barnes used the ax. The others gathered slashings and kept the fires going. The beautiful hard-wood trees were burned to make way for profitless husbandry.

Expanding a little, Zaccheus Greeley operated a saw-mill on shares, but lost more than he made. The boys were kept out of school in summer to aid in the land-clearing and the saw-mill enterprise. "When Brother Horace was thirteen years old," recites Esther, "he was taken out of school, as the teacher could instruct him no longer. I was kept at home also, and brother taught me, giving me lessons in arithmetic and penmanship, which studies had been prohibited me at school. As there were two children, Barnes and sister Arminda, between us, our difference in years had hitherto kept us somewhat apart, but after brother had been for several months my instructor, we were from that time the nearest."

The lives of the Greeleys in Vermont were pleasant, if not prosperous. They "got along" if they did not "get ahead." The mother, freed from child-bearing, became brisk and cheerful. The odd Horace gave the family distinction, even though he preferred poetry to play, and sat in the corner with Byron, Campbell and Shakespeare for companions. The other Greeley children were normal.

Horace could, however, be sociable, if he cared. His sister relates that when he was thirteen a dance was to be held in West Haven, and "much speculation was excited among our young friends as to whether Horace would dance at this ball, and especially if he would fetch a partner with him. It was the general opinion that he would not, as he did not bear a high reputation for gallantry. Great, then, was the astonishment of all present when Horace entered the ballroom with Annie Bush, the prettiest girl in the neighborhood, upon his arm. He opened the ball with her, and his deportment quite silenced those who had questioned his appearance."

Annie Bush was a year younger, "extremely pretty," according to Esther Greeley, "a slender figure, cheeks like roses, blue eyes, dark hair and very gentle, ladylike ways." Two other girls met with her brother's boyish favor—Cornelia Anne Smith and Rebecca Fish. Cornelia was older, and so attracted the bookish boy more than the others. They would work over their lessons together. He kept up his acquaintance with these two all his life, corresponding with them and visiting them on occasions after both had married and set up homes. "He clung to his early associations," says his sister, with "tenacity."

Horace liked girls, but as friends and intellectual companions. "He used to correct their grammar when they conversed," recites Esther, "and gravely lecture them upon the folly of wearing stays."

This dislike for corsets, or stays, was one of his pet aversions when he grew up to be an all-round reformer. "The corsets which aroused his ire," his sister said, "were quite different from those of the present day [1873]. At that time, you must know, the Empire dress, that you have seen in portraits of the time of the first Napoleon, was all' the fashion; no crinoline, skirts so extremely scant and gored that they clung to the figure like drapery upon a statue, and waists a finger and a half in depth, with inch wide bands instead of sleeves. This style of dress was very graceful and becoming when worn by a woman of slender figure, and those who were not favored by nature made the best of their thin figures by wearing what we then called 'busks' or more popularly 'boards.' The corsets did not clasp in front; merely laced behind, and inserted in the lining of the front was the 'busk,' a piece of steel or wood two inches wide and the depth of the corset. This 'busk,' with the addition of very tightly drawn lacing strings, was supposed to give great symmetry to the figure. No village belle ever liked to own that she laced tightly, or that she wore a board, as it was a tacit admission that her figure could not bear unaided the test of the Empire dress; consequently, brother's remarks would be received by his young friends with an injured air, and a vehement protest against such a false accusation. Brother would then test their truth by dropping his handkerchief and requesting them to pick it up; if they wore a 'board' stooping would be impossible, or, at all events, very difficult. The ordeal would cover them with confusion, when the philosopher of thirteen years would resume his moral lectures upon the laws of hygiene and the follies of fashion.''

Life began young with the New England children in the 'twenties. Horace, who had no mind for farming as a means of livelihood for himself, though strong in commending the occupation to others, decided to become a printer at the age of eleven. He persuaded his father to take him to Whitehall, New York, six miles from West Haven, where he applied for a place in the local printing office. The proprietor, though needing a boy, rejected him as too small for the work. The hand-presses of the period required height and muscle, whether to "roll" or "pull" the forms. Four years later he tried again, this time with better fortune. Amos Bliss, who managed the *Northern Spectator* at East Poultney, a dozen miles distant, advertised for an apprentice. Horace answered and was accepted. The initiative in both instances was his own. Neither parent desired to part with their eldest child, who, though but a little lad, was so wise and seemed so old. The terms were fair. He worked six months for his board alone. After that a stipend of forty dollars per annum was added to his "keep." He was indentured for five years. Departure from home came easy to the self-centered lad, who was soon deeply happy in the printing office. The family was near and could be visited at will.

The hard-worked Zaccheus, now approaching forty and making no headway, decided to try another move. He was a man of high type, cramped by the limited opportunities about him, and made somber by unrequited toil; he was largely self-educated, but a superior mathematician, and wrote a fine hand—gifts which he failed to hand down to his eldest son. He possessed a most musical voice, that often took the place of an instrument at farm dances, where he would sing the measures to which the feet kept time. Pride and dignity were his chief characteristics, and these now impelled him to flee from a scene of failure, and make for another forest in northwestern Pennsylvania where he would attempt to carve out something of his own, and shake off the odium of being a "hired man," which was his part in Vermont. So the family girded up its few belongings and rode away west, the mother tearful at leaving familiar social surroundings and her precocious boy. Four children went west too, Barnes, Esther, Arminda and Margaret.

Beman Brockway, who had met all the Greeleys, says: "I knew Zack Greeley, the father of Horace, a small, sandy-haired, sandy-whiskered man, with light eyes and colorless eyebrows; likewise his mother, a stout, hearty, fair-skinned woman." Of the other members of the family the same friend observes: "Neither the sisters nor the brother possess extraordinary talents. They are a good sort of people, but lack energy and vigor. They are not thrifty."

All the "energy and vigor" were concentrated in Horace, it would appear. Thrifty he was not, although he thought he was. "Mrs. Greeley," according to Mr. Brockway, was "the brains of the family," but "she was easy-going and very much such a housekeeper as Horace was farmer. . . . Things had a fearfully slip-shod look both in Wayne, Pennsylvania, and at Chappaqua, New York."

Horace was strongly tempted to go with the family to Wayne. His heart was heavy when he bade them good-by and turned toward Poultney. "A word from my mother," he wrote long afterward, "at the critical moment might have overcome my resolution, but she did not speak it and I went my way." The family adventure resulted in much improvement of their fortunes, eventually. The year was 1826, and the journey was made by road and the new Erie Canal.

Land was cheap in Erie County and Zaccheus was able to acquire two hundred acres. Two of his brothers, Benjamin and Leonard, had preceded him to the new country and broken a hole in the wilderness. The two hundred acres in time were nearly doubled. But at the start the family found, on their arrival, only a single-room log hut, at the barren sight of which Mary Greeley gave way to tears. They were soon dried, and in time all the disadvantages were comfortably overcome. Venison and wild fowl provided abundant food until the soil gave a return and the barn was filled with cattle and stores.

Horace made two visits to the new home during his period of apprenticeship, staying a month at a time. He was not destined to serve out his indenture in the *Northern Spectator* office. The paper died in June, 1830, and he left the Green Mountains to make his way to Wayne and seek his fortune in new fields.

There was genuine sorrow in Poultney over the boy's departure. He had come to fill a large place in the little town. There was a local "forum" which met in the schoolhouse, and here he shone. No orator, but a profound controversalist and bubbling with information, he lent luster to the debates, confounding elders and gaining no small fame for himself. So, when he departed, his landlady presented him with a Bible, and his employer gave him a second-hand overcoat to cover clothes all too shabby and poor. With little or no money he started away on foot, and by picking rides on the road and getting lifts on canal boats, he at last reached the log cabin in Wayne, four hundred miles from his starting point. To handicap him on his journey, he was lame. Chancing to strike his leg on an overturned box in the *Northern Spectator* office, he had received a cut below the knee and had neglected it, with the result that it became infected and caused him much trouble. Indeed, he limped for three years. This dragging of the foot created an appearance in his garb as if one leg of his trousers was shorter than the other, and biographers have lent currency to the tale of his going clad in misfits.

Working around the farm soon palled on the apprentice. A few days' employment were picked up on the *Journal* at Jamestown, in Chautauqua County, New York, just over the border, and at Lodi, in Cattaraugus County. Between these intermittencies Horace plied an ax at home. Then, feeling that he must go on as he had begun, he walked to Erie, a substantial town in the home county on the lake shore, and sought work in the shop of the Erie *Gazette*. The owner of the paper, John H. Sterrett, was not enthusiastic at first, but a good word from a family friend secured a place for the boy at fifteen dollars per month. He boarded with the Sterretts, that being included in the terms, and sent most of the money home to Zaccheus. An old lady in the town gave him an embrocation that cured the lingering lameness.

Erie was unpromising as to the future, and at the end of seven months the apprentice concluded to call himself a journeyman and venture forth into the world. He had twenty-five dollars and carried his possessions in a very small bundle. After a short stay at home he headed for New York, there to begin his amazing career. Lightly equipped, he tramped to Buffalo, where the canal offered a water route the rest of the way. He "beat" his passage on various boats, walked the tow-path, and somehow got to Albany. Thence he went to New York on a slow-moving tugboat, that spent twenty-four hours going the one hundred and forty-six miles from the capital to the metropolis.

The date of arrival in New York "was, if I recollect aright," wrote Greeley in his *Recollections of a Busy Life,* "August 17, 1831. I was twenty years old the preceding February, tall, slender, pale and plain; with ten dollars in my pocket, summer clothing worth as much more, nearly all on my back, and a decent knowledge of so much of the art of printing as a boy will usually learn in the office of a country newspaper. But I knew no human being within one hundred miles, and my unmistakably rustic manner and address did not favor that immediate command of remunerative employment which was my most urgent need. However, the world was before me, my personal estate tied up in a pocket handkerchief did not at all encumber me."

Even then New York was a big town, holding two hundred and twenty thousand very busy people, and fronting a harbor filled with ships, which were already pouring immigrants into the country. The boat landed him at Old Slip, still a canal-boat port, near the foot of Broad Street, up which wide thoroughfare he strolled, looking for a lodging. He first called at a boarding-house, the site of which is now covered by the modest quarters of J. P. Morgan and Company, but the price of its hospitality being six dollars per week, he passed on in search of something cheaper and found it at 168 West Street, where room and meals were offered at two dollars and fifty cents per week. There was a saloon on the ground floor, but the place was quiet, and Edward McGoldrick, the landlord, was a decent sort of man, though one of the chief patrons of his own bar.

For several weeks young Greeley sought work, but either it was scarce or his appearance was against him. He landed nowhere. The great David Hale, then head of the *Journal of Commerce,* thought he had run away from some apprenticeship and ordered him out of his office. It began to look as if he would have to return to the woods, when a fellow boarder steered him to an opening in the printing office of John T. West, at 85 Chatham Street. West did the printing for McElrath and Bangs, publishers, who had the ground floor of the building. Greeley and McElrath were destined to become close associates in after years.

So eager was the young man to get at something that he perched on the steps of the printing office at five thirty A. M., to be the first in line at seven when the shop opened. A journeyman, coming early, questioned him. The man was from Vermont, and the kinship of a common home caused him to take the tow-head to the foreman and persuade him to give the applicant a tryout. This the foreman did by giving him the job of setting up a Testament in twelve em agate lines, with four em notes in pearl—one of the hardest tasks that could be given even a typesetter of experience. Greek letters and sundry signs had to be inserted. Paid by the piece for this perplexing composition, Greeley could barely earn a dollar per day. The job lasted some time and nearly ruined his eyesight. When it ended he was laid off, but with good repute in the shop. He next worked on a young monthly that died before it had paid its help. Another

Bible job turned up at West's, *Notes on Genesis* by Doctor George Bush. This carried him toward the end of the year, when a spell of idleness set his mind again toward the Pennsylvania forests. Then luck turned. The foreman at West's, who had given him the much needed chance, was William T. Porter, who, on January 1, 1832, started, as his own venture, a weekly sporting paper, *The Spirit of the Times.* Porter achieved some fame as a semi-humorous writer of hunting adventures, such as *The Big Bear of the Arkansas.* Cholera demoralized the city and made life hard for *The Spirit of the Times.* It survived, however, and gave Greeley a job until fall. Then he found a situation with J. S. Redfield, who set up books and turned the type into page plates by the then new process of stereotyping. Mr. Redfield, in season, became a somewhat successful publisher himself.

Landlord McGoldrick drank too much, and the boarding-house had too liquorish an air for the temperate printer. It was also far from Chatham Street. So he found quarters at Chatham and Duane Streets. He began to know the city and to take an interest in things and the way they were run. The protective doctrine of New England already had become his own. He had seen poverty made poorer, he thought, by the import of manufactured articles from abroad, and he ascribed economic conditions to the lack of protection, whereas it was the long embargo, which protected the country with a vengeance, that had caused the hardships he had viewed as a little boy, destroying our commercial income, and causing over-production at home. The believers in protection held a tariff convention at the American Institute, of which Greeley was to live to become president, and he spent an idle week profitably attending its sessions. He got a little time at "the case" in the office of the *Evening Post,* but was turned out because it desired only "decent-looking men about," a meticulousness which it never lost. The *Commercial Advertiser* gave him a "show at subbing." He had made friends with the foreman of *The Spirit of the Times,* Francis V. Story, and the pair essayed to establish a printing business. Between them they possessed about two hundred dollars. With this they tackled the job of getting out a *Bank Note Reporter,* that was more truly an organ of the then flourishing lottery business. They made some money and looked about for more trade.

Doctor H. D. Shepard, who had done some medical publishing, decided to issue a *Morning Post.* The young pair took the contract, George Bruce, the type founder, staking them with equipment. The new daily came out on January 1, 1830, in a big snowstorm that chilled the enterprise at its birth. It lived three weeks, by which time its promoter's slender capital was gone. The *Bank Note Reporter* brought in a good deal of lottery printing, to which was added the *Constitutionalist,* tri-weekly, also a lottery organ, the publication of drawing numbers giving it circulation and life. The lottery magnate was Dudley S. Gregory, who liked Greeley and kept the wolf from getting past the door. Unhappily Story was drowned while swimming in the East River, on July 9, 1833. Jonas Winchester took his place in the firm, but no one ever filled it in Greeley's affections. Story was a rare and fine young man.

In his easier getting on, Horace did not forget the

family in the Wayne woods. On his first visit home his sister Esther "was much impressed . . . with a marked change in brother's taste and character—a change indicated as much by his reading as by his external appearance. His trunk was now filled with standard works and volumes of poems, instead of treatises upon science, and he appeared in a perpetual rose-dream. He seemed to me the embodiment of romance and poesy, and now, as I think of him, with his pure unselfish nature, so early devoted to what was noblest and best, I can only compare him to the high-minded boy saint, the chaste seraphic Aloysius."

CHAPTER III

THE printing business prospered and soon the firm of Greeley and Winchester was well known. One day James Gordon Bennett came in with a small handful of ready money, which he exhibited, and invited Greeley to join him in establishing the New York *Herald*. The opportunity was declined. Instead, on March 22, 1834, the young printers began to publish the *New Yorker,* a weekly literary journal which Greeley edited himself. It was a handsome, well-printed and neatly made sheet, that soon found a solid clientele, though it began with less than a dozen subscribers. The paper was issued on Saturdays in two forms, a four-page folio and a sixteen-page quarto. The folio seems to have been used for local distribution and the quarto for the mail subscribers. One edition sold annually for three dollars and the other for four dollars. In time the circulation rose to 7,500. Both were made up usually of the same matter, except that the last page of the quarto was filled by a sheet of music. This made it very popular and was a feature of the paper as long as it existed. The music was mainly of the tum-tum variety and the songs sentimental, such as the prim misses of the day might be expected to appreciate.

The contents were chiefly literary, but the editor gratified his bent for politics by making his paper an
authority on political facts and election figures. Most
of the matter was culled. His own contributions were
editorials and news items reshaped with crisp comment. Park Benjamin was for some time the critic, and
later Charles Fenno Hollman, both men of conspicuous
attainments. For active assistant he took on Henry J.
Raymond, who was to be an important rival as editor
and founder of the New York *Times*. Raymond was
barely of age and began work for a small sum. An
offer made to him to go south as a teacher forced a
"raise" from Greeley, who had little to give. Raymond worked indefatigably, as did his employer.

A fire in 1835 damaged the plant and pocketbook of
the firm, but the job business and the *New Yorker*
easily made up for it. Indeed, matters moved so pros-
perously that young Greeley felt able to marry and
set up a comfortable home at number 124 Greenwich
Street, then a fairly fashionable neighborhood.

Beman Brockway, looking for a printer's job, met
Greeley first in the office of the *New Yorker;* he
was "sitting at a small table at one side of the
little composing-room, writing furiously, and had
barely time to look up when I was introduced to him.
He was not yet twenty-five years old, and the greenest
specimen of an editor I had ever looked at."

Another caller knocked in those days at the *New
Yorker* portals; a strange young man named Edgar
Allan Poe, who wrote poetry, came around occasionally and once borrowed fifty dollars, which he did not
return. Greeley was later besought by an autograph
collector to contribute some rareties from his corre-

spondence. He offered the Poe I. O. U. at its face value, but the proffer was not accepted.

In writing his share of the *New Yorker,* the editor sometimes descended to verse, but disowned any private relationship with the Muse.

Once, in after life, when asked to furnish some specimens of his verse for an anthology, Greeley declined rather curtly, saying that while he had written some lines he was not a poet, and did not want to be advertised as such. The poets pressed hard upon the *New Yorker,* which printed a good many poems, many of them pretty long, despite the editor's frequent calls for brevity. Contributors found their respective merits discussed at the top of the page where much of the editor's own comment appeared. Some examples follow:

"*The Orphan Girl's Lament* is declined. It is quite too defective."

"The *Shooting Star* does not please us."

"*Dangers* (F. S.) will probably appear, though the writer has done slender justice to himself in the conclusion. Smartness, especially when allied to levity, is entirely out of place in the termination of a poem."

"*The Incentive* is most imperatively declined."

"*Stanzas* is declined. The author will not take the time to perfect his versification—and we can not."

"*Friendship's Wreath* seems deficient in ideas."

"The *poet* who stole *Sir Cupid* from an old magazine and imposed it upon us as an original production, is informed that we hope to be favored with no more of his efforts in the pilfering line."

"*Crede Byron* we should be forced to decline on account of its length, if it had no other fault. The art of ceasing when you have said enough is one most difficult of attainment in unpractised writers."

"All young essayists would oblige us by studying the rules of metrical composition before they favor us with their attempts at blank verse."

"*Stanzas* are respectfully declined. They are not intolerable, but we have a great deal of barely endurable rhyme marked for publication already."

"*Rhymes to a Dyspeptic* are not pathetic, as the author fancies."

"*A Fragment* is not at all to our liking. The author is even greener than he esteems himself."

"*The Weeper* will probably appear."

"We regret to decline *Soliloquy, or, Complaint of Mary, Queen of Scots*, but really there is no alternative. The Royal Martyr has been executed too often in our columns already."

"We have an utter and unconquerable aversion to the Ossianic School of prose and poetry, whatever it may be considered."

"*Affection* is spoiled by sheer carelessness. For example:

" 'Though splendid seems the golden chain
That does Earth's brightest joys unite,
But touch a link, and *back again*,
To common dross 'twill *vanish quite!*'

"This will never do. There are words to express the sentiment here aimed at."

"We like smooth rhymes, but *O'er* with itself for a couplet, is a little too smooth."

"*The Maiden's Lament* is inconceivably stupid. We entreat the writer to burn his manuscript with all possible expedition."

"*The Grave* is too stiff and statue-like for poetry. The words 'agnition,' 'facinorous,' 'diaphonous,' etc., seem to have been dragged in by the ears."

"*Spring* is too lachrymose. We give the concluding stanza, and trust the writer will excuse the nonappearance of the preceding:

" 'Few lines of noble rhyme I've written,
    And far less of common prose;
Few times with love I have been smitten
    And once I liked to froze my nose.' "
"We would remark that all poetical pieces are generally rejected."

The editor took a fancy to the poetry of Mrs. Caroline Norton, the gifted daughter of Richard Brinsley Sheridan, and republished much of it. Her domestic difficulties were an international topic in 1837, commenting on which in the *New Yorker* for November fourth Greeley wrote: "Mr. Norton, the husband of the distinguished poetess, from whom she was separated some eighteen months since, under the most unpleasant circumstances, has *advertised* her in the papers—warning the public not to trust her on his account! The case is plain that either she is a most abandoned profligate, or he is a pitiful scoundrel." The latter was the fact.

Samuel Woodworth, author of *The Old Oaken Bucket*, fell into adverse circumstances, and was accorded a benefit. The *New Yorker* liberally boosted the affair, the chief part of which was a performance of *Cato* with George Vandenhoff, the elder, in the titular part. Miss Turpin sang *The Old Oaken Bucket* and earned "great applause." The receipts of a "most agreeable evening" were two thousand five hundred dollars, of which two-thirds went into Woodworth's bucket. There was the usual "benefit" row. Edwin Forrest had been solicited to appear by the committee and declined, but sent fifty dollars. This was not appreciated, and the pen of the editor was very sarcastic in dealing with the great tragedian for getting off so cheaply. "Now fifty dollars is a pretty sum—a very pretty sum—we know by experiencing the lack of it and a great deal more at many times, but especially at the present," quoth Greeley, in mocking extenuation of Forrest's refusal to give one night out of thirty offered him to choose from. A later benefit netted Woodworth a thousand dollars.

The editor often discussed his typographical troubles with his readers.

"Errata—A vexatious blunder occurred in the touching ballad of *Madelaine,* which we published last week. The second line of the seventh stanza is printed
'The master bought the same,'
making nonsense. The true reading is—'The *master-thought* the same.' So the first line of the poem should read
' 'Twas a *bright* (instead of light) and golden evening!'
"Such mistakes will happen, though we take pains to prevent them, and are probably as successful as others. All the proof sheets are read by the senior editor, who can not tell where his wits could have been when the more atrocious blunders escaped him, as he had previously interposed the hyphen in 'master-thought' to preclude misapprehension."

Again, when absent, the editor was afflicted by having "Lower Strata" in one of J. C. Neal's *Charcoal Sketches* come out as "Corner Strata"—making "nonsense." In an editorial "erect subtreasuries" became "enact," while the name of "Mr. Janes" appeared twice as "James." The editor was pretty mad about this.

A local item of interest was printed by the *New Yorker* on February 17, 1838:

"The New Alarm Bell. One of the much talked of Spanish bells, weighing 1,705 pounds, has been placed upon the City Hall and is rung by means of a balance wheel. If this bell were properly hung, the sound it makes might, perhaps, be heard at a distance of some 300 yards; but as it is, the inhabitants in the immediate vicinity of the Park get all the benefits of it. The *Star* says it has all the boom of a large Spanish cathedral bell. Fudge! It is more like that of a steamboat or a hotel."

Monday, April 23, 1838, the first cross-Atlantic steamships, the *Great Western* and *Sirius,* under English colors, came into New York harbor and opened a new era. They received an amazing welcome. Greeley reproved Doctor Dionysius Lardner, the Dublin scientist, for his five years' teaching that steam could not span the ocean: "The only point is whether it will pay." Soon he was able to record that the *Great Western* cleared twenty-three thousand dollars on a round trip and the single doubt vanished. The *Sirius* was the first to make the return voyage, with forty-seven daring passengers. Four packet ships sailed a few hours in advance, hoping to beat the kettle into Liverpool. They did not, and their doom was soon sealed. The *Great Western* carried seventy people when she departed a few days later for Bristol.

Amusements were not neglected by the *New Yorker.* "The American Museum" (later Barnum's) was noted as becoming more interesting than ever by the addition to its attractions of "A real Albiness, and his mighty *highness,* the Irish Giant." "The Pink-Eyed Lady," it is observed, "has been favored with an unusual number of calls during the past week, and the giant continues to be quite a lion."

The editor evidently had a pass to William Niblo's celebrated garden. In June, 1838, he describes it as an amusement elysium, and adds: "We shall bid good-by to theaters until fall, and take a nightly stroll through Niblo's paradise." To this diversion he appended the benefits of Leonard and Archer's Broadway Baths, at number 600 on that thoroughfare. "We commend these baths," Greeley wrote. "We are rather fastidious in such matters and can be relied upon. There is your vapor bath for your choleric gentleman, your tepid bath for your easy gentleman, and your hot bath for your phlegmatic gentleman."

During the era of the *New Yorker* the journalists of New York fought one another with exemplary energy, in and out of their columns. James Gordon Bennett was several times assaulted physically by the gigantic James Watson Webb of the *Courier and Enquirer;* and William Cullen Bryant, author of *Thanatopsis* and editor of the angelic *Evening Post,* horsewhipped Colonel William L. Stone of the *Commercial Advertiser* right before the horrified eyes of Mayor Philip Hone, who records the shocking episode in his diary.

Bennett used to chronicle his combats with relish in the columns of the *Herald.* Here is an account of a collision with James Watson Webb, published on May 10, 1835:

"As I was leisurely pursuing my business yesterday in Wall Street . . . James Watson Webb came up to me on the northern side of the street—said something, which I could not hear distinctly, then pushed me down the stone steps leading to one of the broker's offices, and commenced fighting with a species of brutal and demoniacal desperation, characteristic of a fury. My damage is a scratch, about three-quarters of an inch in length, on the third finger of the left hand, which I received from the iron railing I was forced against, and three buttons torn from my vest, which my tailor will replace for a sixpence. His loss is a rent from top to bottom of a very beautiful black coat that cost the ruffian forty dollars, and a blow in the face that may have knocked down his throat some of his infernal teeth, for anything I know. Balance in my favor, thirty-nine dollars and ninety-four cents."

The *New Yorker,* on July 28, 1838, printed this paragraph concerning two eminent journalists of the day: "Mr. William Leggett of our city, ex-editor of the *Evening Post,* has been held in bail in the Public Court for an assault and battery on Mr. David Hale, editor of the *Journal of Commerce.* The provocation consisted of an editorial on Mr. Leggett's presumed authorship of [Edwin] Forrest's Fourth of July oration; the assault consisted of striking Mr. Hale and spitting in his face. Rather a dirty business."

Leggett was really Greeley's predecessor in the modern art of writing spirited leaders. When he died, May 29, 1839, William Cullen Bryant mourned him in the *Democratic Review:*

"The earth may ring, from shore to shore,
    With echoes of a glorious name:
But he whose loss our hearts deplore
    Has left behind him more than fame.

"For when the death-post came to lie
    Upon that warm and mighty heart,
And quench that bold and friendly eye,
    His spirit did not all depart.

"The words of fire that from his pen
    Were flung upon the lucid page,
Still move, and shake the hearts of men,
    Amid a cold and coward age.

"His love of truth—too warm, too strong,
    For Hope or Fear to chain or chill—
His hate of tyranny and wrong
    Burn in the breasts he kindled still!"

These verses well might have been written of Greeley a generation after. He reprinted them in the *New Yorker*.

No brother editor tried to spank Horace Greeley, not because his invectives did not earn castigation, but because his physical appeal was so poor. There could be no glory in assaulting such a whimsical-looking body. So the pen alone was used in castigating him. And with the same weapon Greeley always "came back."

Politics had their milder moments. The *New Yorker* viewed with calm impartiality the presidential election of 1836, when Martin Van Buren with one hundred and thirty-nine electoral votes, won against William Henry Harrison, Whig, with seventy-three, and printed the most intelligent summaries of election figures and of opinion. "If ever our Republican fabric shall be violently destroyed," the editor commented, "the catastrophe will be the immediate consequence of a rupture between the Constitutional authorities and the actual majority of the people."

The pressure of the government to sell public lands, the proceeds of which were being divided among the states then existing, now resulted in much wild speculating and swindling, and in corresponding depression. Things were better in the spring of 1838, and the editor rejoiced in the "return of prosperity." To make this permanent he held it to be the first duty of government "to take care and pursue such a course that every man able to work may certainly have employment." It would be well also, he thought, if the "sickly thousands" clustered in the cities could be "called forth into the green fields and the stout forests."

"Keep out of New York and all cities," Greeley urged. "The times are evil, and the present amount of trade is not sufficient to support those already clustered in the cities. To remove to a city now, without some insured means of getting a living, is madness. There is abundance of land yet untilled which will produce potatoes with proper culture; there is no general insurance from starvation in cities. As General Sam Houston ordered after the victory of San Jacinto: 'Let the people plant corn.'"

Greeley gave much attention to facilities for travel and their development—the rough rivalries among Hudson River steamboats, their fares and accommodations, and plentiful news of railroad progress. He did not consider that three dollars for a steamboat fare to Albany was too high, as some did, and found, as a traveler, the facilities of New York in general to be "many years in advance of her sister states." His chief complaint was want of ventilation in steamer cabins, in which "two hundred passengers are piled on a July night, where half so many swine would suffocate." Vigilant against economic oppression, he proclaimed: "All combinations or bargains to raise prices are exceptionable and contrary to law, just as much on the part of steamboat owners as journeymen shoemakers. Let us have done with them!'' Discussing railroads, September 21, 1839, he looked ''confidently to see the rates of transportation reduced and the amount of travel on them consequently increased, within the next ten years, to an extent now contemplated by few''—all of which came duly to pass. The passenger rate then averaged five cents per mile, while freight was carried at seven and one-half cents per ton mile. Three thousand miles of road were in operation.

The *New Yorker* strongly preached the need of political education in the North, to offset, it may be assumed, that of the South: ''then the people could blame no one but themselves if they found themselves disgraced by a dunce or a blackguard in Congress.'' Greeley also came vigorously to the defense of his friend, D. S. Gregory, the lottery man, who was charged with unfairness in a drawing for the benefit of the city of Alexandria, Virginia. ''Lotteries may be wrong, and the purchase of tickets an act of imprudence or folly; but no one can doubt the prompt payment of their prizes by Messrs. D. S. Gregory and Company, even though their losses were to exceed a million.''

The battle of San Jacinto now made Texas free, and General E. P. Gaines had moved United States troops into the territory, to Greeley's great concern. President Jackson recalled Gaines, and the troubles of Texas were briefly postponed.

Though trusted by publishers, the newspaper subscriber has always been the most unreliable of debtors. Receiving for the cost far greater value than that

given him by any other form of wares, he is careless
about paying and indifferent to the distress caused by
his delinquency. With such the young editor had his
share of bother. "Our own experience," he wrote,
August 31, 1839, commenting on the newspaper business, "leads us to believe that the losses of New York
publishers by unjust subscribers and more villainous
agents amounts to not less than one-fourth of their
entire incomes. The systematic delinquency of a large
portion of those who presume to patronize them destroys all profit or hope of profit with the majority.
Of full one hundred firms engaged in the publication
of periodicals in this city, we doubt if one-half receive
the amount of their unavoidable expenses, though
nine-tenths have patronage enough to support them
adequately, if their subscriptions were punctually
paid. The profitable concerns are almost without exception those which depend mainly upon their advertising, which is substantially a cash business. There
can hardly be one which does not sustain a dead loss
on that portion of its business in which credits are
given. . . . The system of extending credits all over
the country in little amounts from two to twenty dollars must be abolished, or greatly retrenched and
regulated, or it will ruin those who tolerate it. No
other business attempts it and ours can not stand it.
To give credit indiscriminately is to offer a premium
for roguery. It would be an excellent thing if the
world were an honest one, but as it is, it is most ruinous. We speak from a long and bitter experience.

"The penny (daily) papers and their adjuncts
have adopted the right plan—the stern English one of
no credits at all. The publishers sell their papers in

their own office and take their pay for them there—
trusting no one out of their sight. . . . For our own
part we have had 'glory enough.' We commence this
week a thoroughly 'searching operation.' Within the
ensuing month we shall suspend the transmission of
our paper to about one thousand five hundred of our
subscribers who are longest in arrears. . . . To be
just to our creditors we are constrained to be more
strict to our debtors.''

But delinquent subscribers embarrassed the editor
again. March 7, 1840, found him remarking: ''Subscribers to newspapers in this country have been too
apt to regard it as an act of patronage on their part
to take a newspaper. If there is any one word in the
vocabulary for which we have a mortal aversion, it is
'patronage.' It has done more to degrade and em-
barrass the press of the United States than all the
'bribery and corruption' that political machines ever
engendered.''

Offenders were frequently exhorted to pay up in
this personal and pertinent manner: ''Will Mr.
Charles W. Tucker, Waverly, corner of McDougal
Street, call and settle the balance due him on subscription to the *New Yorker?* The amount is three dollars.''
Peter Schermerhorn also was several times invited to
come in and pay up.

Besides keeping close contact with political news,
the young editor revealed his deep interest in journalism by frequent mention of new publications and
changes in that field. Usually he was complimentary;
sometimes curt. To a report that George D. Prentice
was to leave the Louisville *Journal,* he added this:
''Don't believe it.'' It was the correct view. Here is

a sample item in which he introduces Rufus W. Griswold, the biographer of Poe, to the public:

"The *Tattler*: This is the title of a new evening paper, the prospectus of which has just appeared. It is to be rich in entertainment of all kinds and has the original and novel recommendation of being printed at noon. Its editor, Mr. Rufus W. Griswold, is a young gentleman of the finest capabilities and of a correct and chastened taste. Everything that is diverting and important may be looked for in his columns, and we are certain that they will be free from all that ministers to a depraved appetite."

In the same issue he praises the New York *Dispatch*:

"We have been intending for some time to express our good opinion of this little morning paper. It is under the able charge of Mr. H. H. Wild, a gentleman of large experience as an editor. In this, his new enterprise, he has won golden opinions from all sorts of people, and it gives us great pleasure to record the merited success of his labors."

In another instance:

"We have received one number of the ———. We can't print the name, but it is a paper printed in modern Greek at Constantinople by our friend, Demetrius Stamiatiades—by birth an Athenian, we believe, but who has resided many years and acquired a liberal education at Hartford, Connecticut, and this city. We can not read his paper, but we wish it every success."

The *Arkansas Star,* of Little Rock, would be "a fair sheet if it were not so badly printed." The Boston *Nation* was "about as large as all outdoors"—there was a passion for printing gigantic "blanket" sheets at the time—and its publishers dispensed altogether with "editorial talent and industry," using instead "a hogshead of paste and a pair of sheepshears." Greeley had "half a mind to come out with a sheet the size of a turnip field," but decided to give it further thought.

The union of the New York *Gazette* with the *Journal of Commerce* in April, 1840, caused Greeley to note that the *Gazette* was "the oldest daily paper in the city, having been regularly published for upward of fifty years."

The birth of the celebrated Philadelphia *Public Ledger* was announced April 2, 1836, in these terms: "The *Public Ledger,* a highly creditable addition to the large and thrifty family of penny dailies, made its first appearance in Philadelphia on Saturday last [March 26, 1836]. It is published by Messrs. Swain, Abel and Simmons—all, we believe, recently of this city; and we remark with satisfaction that it eschews the grossness of language and sentiment, and the practises of pandering to the evil passions, unjust prejudices, and perverted tastes of the less enlightened, by which some papers of the class have won their way to profitable but unenviable notoriety."

Another newspaper birth met with this greeting: "*The White Mountain Ægis* is a new Whig paper which hails from Lancaster, N. H. A Whig paper in Coos! It is to be hoped the Editor has a taste for spare living."

"Highly encouraging" he heads the report that General Duff Green, in winding up the United States

HENRY J. RAYMOND

Telegraph, found fifty-five thousand six hundred dollars due him from delinquent subscribers.

Greeley's expression of political opinion grew as the *New Yorker's* years extended. Of the Northeastern boundary troubles in 1840 it was "manifest that this controversy must soon either be settled by compromise or result in a war. Who can soberly prefer the bloody alternative?"

The capture of a Spanish schooner, the *Amistad,* with a cargo of African negroes, bound for Cuba and slavery, who had risen and taken the vessel, which was now brought into New Haven, excited "much sympathy" and gave rise "to an infinity of speculation." The *Amistad* negroes, save one, Antonio, proved to have been already enslaved, were set free in time and the decision was reported "to have afforded unbounded delight to the poor negroes when it was told them." The *New Yorker* showed no emotion on this subject, while vigorous in opposition to a further extension of female rights to the control of property that was their own before marriage, as proposed by some pending legislation.

"We repudiate," Greeley wrote, "the doctrines advanced by Frances Wright, and since, in a different form, but resting substantially on the same basis, of Miss [Harriet] Martineau, of the rightful equality of the sexes in political privileges and social conditions. . . . We insist that a tacit compact has ever prevailed and still exists, by which the sphere of action of either sex is marked out and defined. That this apportionment of the duties of life is perfect, or uniformly observed, as it should be, of course, we do not maintain; but that it is right in itself and in the aggregate vastly conducive to the happiness of by far the greater number, we can not for a moment doubt.''

Greeley had been married three years. His comment continues: ''It is best, then, if we are correct in our premises, that the husband and wife should have a perfect community of interests; that the latter should yield in general and cordial, though not servile, deference to the former, and that there should be an apportionment between them of the responsibilities and duties of life.'' He thought ''a thousand evils'' would result from a wife having property apart from her husband, and as tending to result in careless marriages and laxity of domestic morals, concluding: ''We stand resolutely and fixedly opposed to any legislation which shall conflict with those principles, or with the established canons of common law, of social order, and of stern morality.'' He lived to step far off from this stand.

He evidently heard from this, for the next *New Yorker* contained a lengthy tribute to ''Woman,'' endowing her with every attribute of charm and graciousness, using a lecture by Richard Henry Dana as a text.

The *New Yorker* also sounded a note of praise for a lecture given by Caleb Cushing. ''The particular fallacies to which he directed his attentions, were first, that which, setting out with the propositions that all men are born free and equal, and that government derives its just powers only from the consent of the governed, demands that women be admitted to participation in all the rights and duties as well as social equality with men; secondly, the proposition that, since war is always unjustifiable and evil, therefore all defensive preparations and armaments should be abandoned, and the peaceful and good left to the mercy of the violent and unprincipled. Mr. Cushing exposed the absurdity of these doctrines in language by turns earnest and playful, but at all times appropriate and forcible. We have rarely attended a lecture which was listened to with higher or more general gratification.''

In June, 1839, Greeley began to travel about. He left New York on an extended tour that first took in his old home country in Vermont, in a visit to East Poultney. The neighbors were apparently glad to see him, and the new clothes he wore. A brief letter, dated ''on the wing, June 22, 1839,'' records that a few days amid the scenes of his boyhood had glided ''like a blissful dream. . . . In the few hours shared with the friends from whom we have been severed for years, and from whom the setting sun will again divide us, perhaps forever, we live the essence of years past and to come.''

Buffalo was the next stopping point. He had not been there since 1835, when financial speculation was rife and the town buzzing with excitement. He found fewer building lots and more buildings; fewer saloons and more blacksmith shops; fewer bubbles afloat and larger steamboats. Buffalo, he opined, had ''sowed her wild oats'' and entered upon a vigorous, sober, though early prime. He went from the city to his father's house and dated his letter ''At Rest, July 6, '39.'' He had been eight days in the wilderness, in ''a land of hardy health and rude happiness; of industry, thrift, progress; of hill and valley, fertile soil, wholesome water, and abounding streams.''

He had yet to cry: "Go West, young man, go West!" for he concluded: "If I were a farmer without a satisfactory farm, I *might* emigrate to the far West; but I should be quite as likely not to wander beyond the western boundary of Erie County, Pennsylvania."

Detroit was the farthermost point of this journey. The steamer trip took in Cleveland, Sandusky and Toledo. Greeley approved of all three, though times were "hard" in Cleveland. Keen observations of neglected opportunities for canals and railroads pepper his correspondence. His chief discovery was that the ravages of the Hessian fly in Michigan wheatfields had been much exaggerated. Though proposing to write more about the trip, he did not do so.

Returning toward the end of the month to his sanctum he found a "dozen poetical pieces" on his table, "much too good to burn" and far too long to print. "What to do with them puzzles us exceedingly," he remarked, following which he pleaded with the poets, "Why will not the gifted study a briefer measure? The brightest thought may be repeated a dozen times in ten lines. The tenderest one should never swell beyond fourteen, and twenty are as much as most periodical readers will ever go through at a sitting. Why indulge, then, in this immoderate length of 'linked sweetness long drawn out?' A story may be of any length you please, provided it be a good one; but a lyrical piece should always be short enough to be sung—short enough, if possible, to be quoted in conversation—a gem of fancy in setting so compact that people may carry it about with them."

He who was to become a leader in forming opinion

sided with John Quincy Adams in 1840 in denouncing the "Tyranny of Opinion," using the word, however, in the exact modern sense, almost, of propaganda. Adams objected to opinion being thus organized, either for abolition or temperance purposes, though he was active in presenting petitions to Congress on behalf of the former. "The machinery of moral improvement," Greeley observed, "is clicking around us at every turn—the manifestation of opinion is conducted by associations at every corner, and a man, instead of doing his own thinking, may have it furnished to order by companies of one kind or another in every direction. Nay, he is not permitted to do it himself, for these associations, having embarked both industry and capital in their operations, monopolize an almost unquestioned legal right to fashion and form his thoughts, or, at least, his altered sentiments, to any pattern in which they are dealing at the moment."

So it would appear that the great twentieth-century opinion-making machines are not original, but renaissance!

"However desirable," Greeley concluded, "may be the end they have in view—however excellent the individuals who give their unpaid labors to promote that end, they can not but in some shape subserve the growing Tyranny of Opinion."

It is interesting to follow the growth of power in Greeley's pen, as threaded through the *New Yorker*. When the Cherokees shot Elias Boudinot and John Ridge, who signed without authority a treaty that further prescribed their borders after a long course of rascally treatment by the whites of Georgia, and it was proposed to demand their "murderers," Greeley broke out:

"The spirit of vengeance or of outraged justice, as you please to term it, burned like a half-smothered fire in the breasts of the Cherokee people, and Ridge and Boudinot have been made to pay the penalty of the violated law. They sleep in death; the protection of the United States has availed them nothing; and now we hear that General Arbuckle has been instructed by our government to demand their 'murderers,' and is preparing to carry fire and sword into the new Cherokee country, if the demand is not complied with—as, of course, it probably will not be. Is it not best to hesitate and consider? Have we indeed 'stept into blood so deep' that we may better go on than retrace our steps? In the eyes of justice and God, the United States are the real murderers of those poor victims. Shall we wash the blood from our souls by adding many thousands to their number?"

Mormons who had settled in Jackson County, Missouri, were being attacked by squatters, and by state troops, who were supposed to protect them. New York held a mass meeting at National Hall, September 16, 1839, with Charles King in the chair, and the meeting framed resolutions denouncing the conduct of the Missourians, about whom Greeley had this to say: "It is a burning disgrace to civilization and humanity that the outrages of which the poor Mormons were the victims were committed, but a far deeper disgrace that those enormities have not to this day been made the subject of any judicial investigation. The grand juries and prosecuting attorneys of the counties adjacent to the scenes of horror are grossly culpable; but what shall we say of a governor [L. W. Boggs] who officially countenanced the murder of a people whom he was bound to protect? Missouri, until the blood is washed from her garments, is a disgrace to the Union.''

The devious conduct of Nicholas Biddle in his conflict with Jackson and Van Buren over their destruction of the United States Bank, largely owned in Great Britain, failed to find favor with Greeley, though the bank was a Whig baby and kept Daniel Webster on its secret pay-roll. The editor erupted in the *New Yorker,* November 30, 1839: ''We have hitherto had much to say in opposition to the doctrine—preeminently Philadelphian—that banks may suspend the payment of their obligations merely because other banks have done so or in obedience to what they may deem the interests or convenience of the public. To this doctrine we are radically and strongly hostile. We are aware that the practise is not specially of Philadelphia paternity, but the logic by which a justification of that practise has been attempted, is strictly so. . . . Let us be understood. We do not cast blame upon the Philadelphia suspension, for we believe it was strictly necessary; but we condemn the attempt to conceal that necessity, and make the act appear one of policy or mercy. That attempt deceives few or none; and the logic which sustains it is susceptible of very dangerous uses.''

The lack of specie and the resulting use of paper notes kept money values unsteady and securities uncertain. The *New Yorker* printed this jest apropos:

''Have you heard,'' asked a loafer the other day of a brother, ''that the Boston banks have broke?''

''Broke! How can that be? They suspended [specie payments] last May.''

''Yes, but they broke again.''

"How?"

"Why, you fool, they run out of paper."

The disastrous Canadian "rebellion" was on and came to a quick collapse. Many Americans engaged in the luckless affair. Of these Greeley thought a man "as a friend of Liberty and Right" might at some time feel impelled to disregard the "obligations of country for those of humanity" and take the consequences. "His country," he added, "is henceforward that in which he has his lot, and the issue of the struggle must determine whether he is to be celebrated as a patriot or execrated as a rebel." When the rebellion was snuffed out at Prescott and sixteen of the captives, nearly all Americans, were sentenced to die on the gallows, Greeley made a strong plea for mercy.

"It is impossible," he wrote, "that any generous soul should not feel a sympathy for these misguided men, who so periled their lives on the rashest enterprise ever attempted by men. . . . How an American citizen can be guilty of treason against the Queen of England may be the subject of a cavil, but that they were guilty of an aggravated political offense is most certain. But must their lives pay forfeit? . . . We can perceive no reason for severity. . . . Our conviction is strong that the course of mercy is the course of policy and wisdom. We believe clemency shown these men would do more to tranquillize the radical spirit lingering in the Canadas and to remove the irritation that is still felt by the people of our own frontier than any measure of reform or conciliation which could be devised."

Ten of the raiders were hanged and a hundred and

forty-one sent to Van Diemen's Land. There was not much mercy in Lord Durham's heart and he stood firm—especially against the Americans.

Greeley's Americanism at the moment was strictly one hundred per cent. Vide this: "The beautiful leghorn hat intended as a present to [Queen] Victoria, will be exhibited at 265½ Broadway until the sailing of the *Great Western* on Monday next. The public are invited to call and see it. These presents to Victoria have all been made by foreigners, and we trust that no Americans will be in haste to follow the fashion."

A wide eye was always kept on Washington. "A sale of rare old wine took place in Philadelphia, and the average price obtained was about half a dollar per wineglass. (We expect to see the fact duly chronicled in Senator Benton's next speech to prove that there is no pressure or trouble in the land; *i. e.* when three men can pay half a dollar a glass for wine, how can any one want bread or more uniform currency?)"

Burglars who tried to rob the Chemical Bank of New York, then young, got only a few coppers—not worth the tools they left behind. "A bank is about the last place to look for mint-drops nowadays," observed Horace with a grin, noting that the thieves got no more than some rogue took from his own till not long before.

"Too tough" is the heading put over this item: "There is a story going the rounds that Nick Biddle [of the U. S. Bank] has loaned five millions to the Republic of Texas at 10 per cent. per annum. There are two obstacles to our believing it; first, we do not think the bank is in a condition to lend the money; in the next place we do not fancy the security, though Biddle may.''

On crime exploitation the editor expressed this thought: ''We do not care to publish accounts of murders except where they can be made to tell against that infernal scourge of the country—ardent spirits. . . . We hold that no man has a moral, and none should have a legal, right to sell that debasing and maddening poison, Alcohol, to his neighbors. How many think with us? How many are prepared to take an immediate and energetic stand against the destroying traffic? It is time!''

This is one way Greeley culled the sort of murders he liked from the general news field:

''A man by the name of Tibbetts, a short time since, jumped into eternity and the Kennebec River at one and the same time! Cause, intemperance.''

''A young man named Hallett Greenman was murdered at a tavern in Fort Hunter, Montgomery County, New York, by an individual named Noah M. Thomas, on Sunday 1st inst. Greenman was keeper of the tavern and refused to give liquor to the depraved wretch.''

Greeley's early interest in the American Institute, of which he became president in after years, was frequently manifest. In booming the exhibition of 1839 he observed: ''The power of the electro-magnetic machine in operation, with the improvements it has received, will alone be worth a journey to our city.''

Once, in its brisk career, the *New Yorker* indulged in the extravagances of a steel-plate title-page. John Sartain's wonderful engravings had made *Graham's Magazine,* in Philadelphia, the most successful of

American periodicals. This essay was used in introducing Volume 8, September 21, 1840. It was a beautiful print of the Outlet of Lake George, showing the granite outlines of Rogers' Rock in the background. The plate was engraved by D. H. Cushman, after a drawing by I. C. Ward. Incidentally, Greeley disapproved of an attempt (it did not stick) to rename the lucid lake "Horicon," a title invented by James Fenimore Cooper in *The Last of the Mohicans*.

The *New Yorker* began its last volume Saturday, March 13, 1841, with the announcement that it would continue to do business on a cash basis with subscribers, and promised more of Charles Dickens, whose *Master Humphrey's Clock* has been pirated as a feature for some weeks before. The paper had not been as good as previous to Greeley's entrance into political journalism, the story of which follows. The sparkle of his quips was not there, and the miscellany had a heavier tone.

CHAPTER IV

POLITICAL JOURNALISM

IN THE middays of the *New Yorker,* its editor
wrote copy for a daily campaign paper called the
Constitution, which was published during a hot mayor-
alty campaign by A. R. Crane. The *Constitution*
supported Gulian C. Verplanck for mayor of New
York, on the Whig ticket, against Cornelius W. Lawrence, Democrat. Lawrence won, after a furious local
campaign, by three hundred and eighty-four votes.
His name survives on a fire-boat in New York harbor.
The Whigs had, however, a majority of the Common
Council, and their success encouraged them mightily,
including Greeley, who thus had his first taste of blood
in the political arena.

The activities of Greeley were great enough to
secure him the offer of a nomination for assemblyman
on the Whig ticket, which he very sensibly declined,
though he might have been elected. The panic of 1837
reacted upon the party in power, after the fashion of
such commercial cataclysms, and the Whigs won a
great triumph in the fall election, choosing one hundred out of the one hundred and twenty-eight assem-
blymen. This big majority was not able to do much,
as the State Senate, being chosen one-fourth every
year, contained enough Democratic survivors to cir-

cumvent legislation. No state officers were elected, the governorship coming up for contest in 1838. The situation made an opening for Greeley in political journalism.

The panic had put a severe crimp in the prosperity of the *New Yorker*. Half of the subscribers failed to pay their dues—subscriptions being scantily paid in advance. This strained the editor's purse. He increased his personal share in getting the sheet out, writing editorials and articles and setting them up himself—he had become an expert compositor.

In this time of need his talent as a crisp critic of public affairs became conspicuous. The era was the fading one of Andrew Jackson, who had abolished the United States Bank, so earning the credit of bringing on the panic, though the crash fell upon the shoulders of Martin Van Buren, whom Old Hickory had forced into succession. In the resulting reaction toward Whiggery, Thurlow Weed, astute editor of the Albany *Evening Journal,* saw a rainbow of promise. William H. Seward, a young man from Florida, New York, had settled in Auburn in 1823 as the agent of some landowners and had developed into an able lawyer and politician. Weed determined to groom him for governor, seeing a chance for his election in 1838, with a further outlook for Whig successes in the national campaign of 1840. Some sort of state-wide publication was needed, and Greeley's Whig outcroppings in the *New Yorker* attracted Weed's attention. In company with Lee Benedict he came to New York, it having occurred to him "that there was some person connected with the *New Yorker* possessing the qualities needed for our new enterprise. In reading the

New Yorker attentively, as I had done, I felt sure that
its editor was a strong tariff man, and probably an
equally strong Whig. I repaired to the office in Ann
Street, where the *New Yorker* was published, and inquired for its editor. A young man with light hair
and blond complexion, with sleeves rolled up, standing
at the case 'stick' in hand, replied that he was the
editor, and this youth was Horace Greeley.''

Greeley records himself as ''somewhat surprised''
at the visit, being unconscious of any reputation up-
state, but cheerfully accepted an invitation to confer
with Weed and Benedict at their hotel. He came duly
to the rendezvous, and ''the business which brought the
friends to New York was unfolded,'' as he narrates.

One of Weed's first questions was, ''Have you a
family?'' to which Greeley replied: ''I have a wife,
but she keeps school and is no hindrance to the enterprise.''

His own story continues: ''Decided as had been
our triumph in the state, it had been won on a moderate
vote, and quite as much by the failure of Democrats
to exercise their right of suffrage as by their voting the
Whig ticket. The next election would naturally bring
many of these stay-at-homes to the polls, and—there
being a governor and representative in Congress to
be chosen, with a United States Senator in prospect—
would inevitably draw out a heavy vote. To maintain
and confirm a Whig ascendency, it had been resolved
to publish throughout 1838 a cheap weekly journal, to
be called the *Jeffersonian*, which I had been picked
upon as the proper person to edit. I believe Mr. Weed
first designated me for the post, though he knew
nothing of me except by reading my paper, the *New*

Yorker; for, though I had written for several Whig dailies, mainly of the ephemeral type, I had done so anonymously."

Weed, Benedict and Greeley dined together, and before their parting, the editor of the *New Yorker* had agreed to become responsible for the desired organ. Albany was to be the place of publication, which meant the calling of its editor to that city several days a week. Greeley was to be paid one thousand dollars for the campaign. He made the trip in midwinter by sleigh, taking three days for the journey. The sheet had its first issue on March 3, 1838. It made a great impression, with its excellent editorials and concrete political information. The circulation rose to fifteen thousand copies. With its effective aid Seward defeated the popular William L. Marcy for governor; and this done, the *Jeffersonian* ceased to be. It had sold at fifty cents for the period of its life and left no dividends behind. The *New Yorker* suffered from the divided alliance and the continuing hard times, which were not banished by Seward's election. Van Buren's term had two years to run, and no Whig policies could be put through until there was a Whig in the White House.

When Greeley first journeyed to Albany and Weed made him acquainted with Seward, the latter found him "a slender, light-haired young man, stooping and near-sighted, rather unmindful of social usages, yet singularly clear, original and decided in his political views and theories." Thus began their long and consequential relationship.

William H. Seward's ambitions were great, his talents considerable, he stood up for his views. He was opposed to Van Buren on the United States Bank question, and while governor, when the latter was president, refused to attend a reception given the President by the Common Council of New York, on the ground of political differences that forbade him to be sociable. "Our Republican institutions," he said, in extenuation for his refusal, "can never be more safe than when the discussion of public measures, and the character of public men, is so vigorous as to bring into the offices of the general and state governments, individuals whose relations prevent the possibility of combination between them to perpetuate power conferred only for the public good."

Pretty stiff-necked was this young man. (He was thirty-seven.) Yet he was destined to see the despised Martin Van Buren head the first ticket of a party determined to prevent the extension of slavery.

Active entrance into party politics began for Greeley when he reported the Whig National Convention held in Harrisburg, Pennsylvania, December 4, 1839, to nominate a candidate for president, who should run the next year. His first day's impression was that Henry Clay would get the prize, though he was cautious enough to express it as uncertain. The convention was held within the walls of the new Lutheran Church at Harrisburg. Clay had one hundred and three votes on the first ballot, William Henry Harrison ninety-one, and Winfield Scott sixty. All but sixteen of Scott's votes went to Harrison on the next ballot and he was nominated. After this, without division, Governor John Tyler, of Virginia, was named for vice-president, and the year's campaign was begun.

This report Greeley followed up by attending the session of the Legislature at Albany in January, 1840, and sending short summaries of its doings to the *New Yorker*. The first thing he had to chronicle was the taking of the state printing away from Edwin Croswell, publisher of the Albany *Argus,* and giving it to Thurlow Weed of the Albany *Evening Journal,* "the Whigs controlling both Houses and being hungry for spoil." In a notice to his readers Greeley advised them that Charles Fenno Hoffman would be reponsible for the literary opinions of the *New Yorker* during his Albany stay, "while those on political and kindred topics may be attributed, as heretofore, to Mr. Greeley."

This campaign for Harrison was the first contest in which the Whigs took up with popular methods, making appeal to the farm folks as Jackson had done. Harrison was a resident of Ohio, but was Virginia born, descendant of the butcher Harrison who lost his head for voting to take off that of Charles the First. He had lived on the Ohio frontier, been governor of the territory, and a picturesquely successful fighter of Indians and British. Thus he was widely known to the pioneers of the West, and on these a "log cabin and hard cider" canvass made a great impression. The candidate had resided in this type of domicile and presumably knew the taste of the acrid fluid. The Whig campaign picked up speed early in the year. General Harrison's affinity for hard cider and log cabins had been molded into a cause, and "Tippecanoe and Tyler too" into a slogan

The Democrats met in convention in Baltimore, Tuesday, May 5, 1840, and unanimously nominated

Martin Van Buren. They rejected R. M. Johnson, the Vice-President, and adjourned without making a nomination for that post, so Van Buren ran the race without company. The Whigs held a "convention" at the same time in the same city, rather for the purpose of blanketing the discordant Democrats. Some enthusiasts brought a log cabin on wheels from Pennsylvania. Eleven thousand "delegates" came to town and paraded in a procession five miles long. It is doubtful if America ever saw such a fervid demonstration, roused by hard times and resulting unrest.

From this time on the campaign became more of a circus than a political canvass. Log cabins sprang up in every town and at many crossroads. Barrels of hard cider kept them company and were freely tapped. Even the New York Whigs built a big building of logs at the corner of Broadway and Prince Street, which became the local rallying place of the party. Paraders were always marching, and the land seethed with excitement.

During this hectic period the country literally gave itself over to political frenzy. Women and children shared in the excitement, which was pretty nearly all on one side. The dignified Van Buren did not foster novelties like cider, coons and cabins. The battle-field of Tippecanoe, a rather inglorious spot when all the facts are known, became a place of pilgrimage. Old soldiers of the Revolution were rallied to head processions. Halls could not hold the crowds that gathered to hear the Whig orators. The broad fields were turned to forums, and crowds were measured by acres rather than numbers. One of the attractions of the log cabins was the fact that "the latch-string was always out." General Harrison, in bidding his army of 1812 farewell, had told the soldiers they could be certain of this sign of hospitality at his rude house. There were no locks, and security was obtained by pulling in the string that lifted the latch from without.

"It was determined," Greeley said, "in the councils of our friends at Albany, that a new campaign paper should be issued, to be entitled the *Log Cabin;* and I was chosen to conduct it. No contributions were made or sought in its behalf. I was to publish as well as edit it; it was to be a folio of good size; and it was decided that fifteen copies should be sent for the full term of six months (from May first to November first) for five dollars.

"I had just secured a new partner (my fifth or sixth) of considerable business capacity, when this campaign sheet was undertaken; and the immediate influx of subscriptions frightened and repelled him. He insisted that the price was ruinous—that the paper could not be afforded for so little—that we should inevitably be bankrupted by its enormous circulation—and all my expostulations and entreaties were unavailing against his fixed resolve to get out of the concern at once. I therefore dissolved and settled with him, and was left alone to edit and publish the *New Yorker* and the *Log Cabin,* as I had in 1838 edited, but not published, the *New Yorker* and the *Jeffersonian.* Having neither steam presses nor facilities for mailing, I was obliged to hire everything done but the head work, which involved heavier outlays than I ought to have had to meet. I tried to make the *Log Cabin* as effective as I could, with wood engravings of General Harrison's battle scenes, music, etc., and to render it a model of its kind; but the times were so changed that it was more lively and less sedately argumentative than the *Jeffersonian.*"

The *Log Cabin* began its life May 1, 1840, with the intention of existing six months; the subscription price was fifty cents for the period. It became enormously popular. "Its circulation was entirely beyond precedent," Greeley said in speaking of the venture later in life. Indeed, forty-eight thousand copies were sold of the first issue, of which the type had to be reset to fill a resurging demand. No human being ever worked harder than he during those six months. He wrote, edited and set type wtih unceasing energy. The *Log Cabin* almost touched the eighty thousand mark and would have gone higher had it been possible to print and mail more copies.

"With the machinery of distribution by news companies and expresses, etc., now existing," its editor mused later, in 1868, "I guess that it might have been swelled to a quarter of a million."

Besides editing, writing and setting type, Greeley served on the campaign committee, sat in party councils and made many speeches. He became the vital center of the campaign in state and nation. Never did so young a man make so prodigious a stir with his pen. He himself was a teetotaler (indeed he drank neither tea nor coffee) and did not regard hard cider as a temperance drink. He conceded that there were those who liked it and went no farther. But on the issues of the day his pen burned red spots. Presently, Wednesday, August 12, 1840, Governor Seward was renominated and became a sharer in the campaign with Harrison and Tyler.

Hard cider flowed in rivers; miniature log cabins and barrels of the liquid graced processions. Fireworks and oratory drove the country frantic. To all this excitement Greeley in the *Log Cabin* contributed liberally. He departed from the conservative reasoning of the *Jeffersonian* and turned on the loud speaker. The success of the music page in the *New Yorker* led him to fill one in the *Log Cabin* with campaign songs. These added to popular interest in the fight and were shrieked in all keys on all occasions.

"Tippecanoe and Tyler too" lent itself readily as a refrain. Here is a fair sample.

> "What has caused this great commotion,
>   motion, motion,
> Our country through?
> It is the ball a-rolling on
> For Tippecanoe and Tyler too, Tippecanoe
>   and Tyler too!"

As for the lonely Democratic candidate, he was—

> "Van, Van, the used-up man!"

Maine had been solidly Democratic, but at the September election chose Judge Kent, Whig, governor, which inspired another refrain:

> "Maine went hell-bent
> For Governor Kent!"

As a matter of fact, the Judge had about three hundred majority, but it sufficed.

"Our songs," Greeley wrote Weed, "are doing more good than anything else. I know the music is not worth much, but it attracts the attention of even those who do not know a note. Really, I think every song is good for five hundred new subscribers."

At the end of all the oratory and demagogy "Tippecanoe and Tyler too" won, having 234 votes in the Electoral College, while Van Buren had but 50. Harrison's popular majority was 148,315.

"The Great Question Settled" was the *New Yorker's* head-line over the news that on November 6, 1840, Harrison and Tyler had been elected, with Seward again victorious in New York. Golden days seemed to have dawned for the Whigs. Three days later Governor Seward issued a most complacent Thanksgiving proclamation, in which, with proper pride, he inserted this paragraph pertaining to the political result:

"We have exhibited to the world the sublime spectacle of millions of freemen carefully discussing the measures and policy which concern their welfare, and peacefully committing the precious trust of their interest and hopes to their chosen magistrates. While our confidence in the stability of Republican institutions is thus strengthened, their benign operation has been manifested in the sway of mild and equal laws, the enjoyment of equal privileges by all classes of citizens, the security of personal rights, and the intellectual and moral improvement of society."

Greeley had been permitted to perform the giant's share of labor in the campaign, but was not allowed to advise or counsel from the inside. Weed played that part. Greeley thought himself entitled to some share in the rule. He asked Seward, shortly before the campaign ended, for the privilege of "an earnest talk" after election. "I have held in as long as I can," he wrote, "or shall have by that time. . . . I have tried to talk to Weed, but with only partial success.

Weed likes me and always did—I don't think he ever
had a dog about the house he likes better—but he
thinks I know nothing about politics. If there are
any plans for the future, I want to know what they
are, and if there are none, I want to know that fact,
and I will try to form some sort of a plan myself."

The interview was never held.

The victory had the effect of tying Seward, Weed
and Greeley together into a political firm that lasted
until the Republican party came into being. Their
relations were close, but not always harmonious. The
junior partner asserts:

"I was early brought into collision with both my
seniors on the subject of the Registry law. Every
Whig who had been active in the political contests of
this city was instinctively and intensely a champion
of a registration of legal voters; knowing well, by sad
experience, that, in its absence, enormous frauds to
our damage are the rule, and honest and legal voting
the exception. So, in the first legislature of our state
that was Whig all over, a bill was introduced, with my
very hearty assent and active support, which provided
for a registration of voters here; and it had made such
headway before it attracted the serious attention of
Messrs. Seward and Weed, that all their great influence could not prevent the Whig members supporting
and passing it. Yet the measure was so intensely
deprecated by them, as tending to alienate the undistinguished poor, and especially those of foreign
birth, from our side, by teaching them to regard the
Whigs as hostile to their rights, that the purpose of
vetoing it was fully formed and confidentially avowed;
and, though it was at length abandoned, and the bill
signed, Mr. Weed assured me that the Governor would
have preferred to lose his right hand.

"On one important question, Mr. Weed and I were
antipodes. Believing that a currency in part of paper,

kept at par with specie, and current in every part of
our country, was indispensable, I was a zealous advocate of a National Bank; which he as heartily detested,
believing that its supporters would always be identified in the popular mind with aristocracy, monopoly,
exclusive privilege, etc. He attempted, more than
once, to overbear any convictions on this point, or at
least preclude their utterance, but was at length
brought apparently to comprehend that this was a
point on which we must agree to differ.''

The *Log Cabin* did not end its existence with the
close of the campaign. It held some ten thousand subscribers. This considerable following caused Greeley
to continue publication, though poorly prepared financially for the task. He also continued the losing *New
Yorker*. The spring of 1841 found him with his hands
over full. More than once he paid five dollars on
Saturday for the use of five hundred dollars until
Monday to meet his pay-roll and other bills.

Like the western adventurers, who, with their
paper on the verge of bankruptcy, decided to enlarge
it, Greeley now conceived a bold project. He determined to start a daily morning newspaper in New
York, in a field well filled with ''organs,'' and possessing in James Gordon Bennett's *Herald* and Moses Y.
Beach's *Sun* two papers of the popular type. The idea
met with the approval of Dudley S. Gregory, to whom
Greeley was already in debt and whom he now declined to owe more, accepting instead a loan of one
thousand dollars from John Coggshall, which gave
him the means to start. He proclaimed his purpose in
the issue of the *Log Cabin* for April 5, 1841, which
carried also the news that President Harrison was
dead. Horace Greeley was then thirty years of age.

CHAPTER V

THE *Tribune* took the air, to use a present-day phrase, on the morning of April 10, 1841. This was its prospectus:

"On Saturday, the tenth of April instant, the subscriber will publish the first number of a New Morning Journal of Politics, Literature and General Intelligence.

"The *Tribune,* as its name imports, will labor to advance the interests of the people, and to promote their Moral, Political and Social well-being. The immoral and degrading Police Reports, Advertisements, and other matter which have been allowed to disgrace the columns of our leading Penny Papers, will be carefully excluded from this, and no exertion spared to render it worthy of the virtuous and refined, and a welcome visitant at the family fireside.

"Earnestly believing that the political revolution that called William Henry Harrison to the Chief Magistracy of the Nation was a triumph of Right, Reason and Public Good, over Error and Sinister Ambition, the *Tribune* will give to the New Administration a frank and candid, but manly and independent support, judging it always by its acts, and commending those only so far as they shall seem calculated to subserve the great end of all government—the Welfare of the People.

"The *Tribune* will be published every morning on

a fair royal sheet (size of the *Log Cabin* and *Evening Signal*), and transmitted to its city subscribers at the low price of *one cent* per copy. Mail subscribers $4 per annum. It will contain the news by the morning Southern Mail, which is contained in no other Penny Paper. Subscriptions are respectfully solicited by Horace Greeley, 30 Ann Street.''

"My leading idea," Greeley wrote later, "was the establishment of a journal removed alike from servile partisanship on the one hand, and from gagged, mincing neutrality on the other. Party spirit is so fierce and intolerant in this country that the editor of a non-partisan sheet is restrained from saying what he thinks and feels on the most vital, imminent topics; while, on the other hand, a Democratic, Whig or Republican journal is generally expected to praise or blame, like or dislike, eulogize or condemn, in precise accordance with the views and interest of its party. I believed there was a happy medium between these extremes—a position from which a journalist might openly and heartily advocate the principles and commend the measures of that party to which his convictions allied him, yet frankly dissent from its course on a particular question, and even denounce its candidates, if they were shown to be deficient in capacity or (far worse) in integrity. I felt that a journal thus loyal to its guiding convictions, yet ready to expose and condemn unworthy conduct or incidental error on the part of men attached to its party, must be far more effective, even party wise, than though it might always be counted on to applaud or reprobate, bless or curse, as the party's prejudices or immediate interest might seem to prescribe. Especially by the Whigs—who were rather the loosely aggregated, mainly undisciplined opponents of a great party, than, in the stricter sense, a party themselves—did I feel that such a journal was consciously needed, and would be fairly sustained. I had been a pretty constant and copious contributor (generally unpaid) to nearly or quite every cheap Whig journal that had, from time to time, been started in our city; most of them to fail after a very brief and not particularly bright career; but one— the *New York Whig*, which was, throughout most of its existence, under the dignified and conscientious direction of Jacob B. Moore, formerly of the *New Hampshire Journal*— had been continued through two or three years. My familiarity with its history and management gave me confidence that the right sort of a cheap Whig journal would be enabled to live. I had been ten years in New York, was thirty years old, in full health and vigor, and worth, I presume, about two thousand dollars, half of it in printing materials. The *Jeffersonian,* and still more the *Log Cabin,* had made me favorably known to many thousands of those who were most likely to take such a paper as I proposed to make the *Tribune,* while the *New Yorker* had given me some literary standing and the reputation of a useful and well informed compiler of election returns. In short, I was in a better position to undertake the establishment of a daily newspaper than the great mass of those who try it and fail, as most who make the venture do and must. I presume the new journals (in English) since started in this city number not less than one hundred, whereof barely two—the *Times* and the *World*—can be fairly said to be still living; and the *World* is a mausoleum wherein the remains of the *Evening Star,* the *American,* and the *Courier and Enquirer* lie immured; these having long ago swallowed sundry of their predecessors. Yet several of those which have meantime lived their little hour and passed away were conducted by men of decided ability and ripe experience, and were backed by a pecuniary capital at least twenty times greater than the fearfully inadequate sum whereon I started the *Tribune.*"

New York was plentifully supplied with newspapers, and the newcomer was not warmly greeted by its contemporaries. The *Sun* was chief in the penny field, with something like twenty thousand circulation, and Moses Y. Beach, its publisher, took unavailing steps to head the *Tribune* off. Papers were then delivered by carriers whose routes were a sort of franchise. The *Sun,* having the largest list, was naturally a power among the men who took the dailies from house to house. The *Tribune* was a real newspaper, the *Sun* only a thing of clippings and a few police items. As a result the Greeley venture forged ahead. Beach tried to coerce and buy its carriers, and his newsboys drove those of the *Tribune* away from selling points. The *Tribune* hired bigger boys to defend its sellers, and pretty fighting followed, in which Beach had to rescue some of his crusaders in person. The conflict was sharp, short and decisive, ending in defeat of the *Sun,* which took a back seat and stayed there for thirty years.

According to Frederic Hudson's *History of Journalism in America,* the field in New York, as covered in November, 1842, was as follows:

Cash Papers		Wall Street Papers	
Herald, 2 cents	15,000	*Courier and Enquirer*	7,000
Sun, 1 cent	20,000	*Journal of Commerce*	7,500
Aurora, 2 cents	5,000	*Express*	6,000
Morning Post, 2 cents	3,000	*American*	1,800
Plebeian, 2 cents	2,000	*Commercial Adver-*	
Chronicle, 1 cent	5,000	*tiser*	5,000
Tribune, 1½ cents	9,500	*Evening Post*	2,500
Union, 2 cents	1,000	*Standard*	400
Tattler, 1 cent	2,000		
	62,500		30,200

Sunday Papers		Saturday Papers	
Atlas	3,500	*Brother Jonathan* ...	5,000
Times	1,500	*New World*	8,000
Mercury	3,000	*Spirit of the Times*..	1,500
News	500	*Whip*	4,000
Sunday Herald	9,000	*Flash*	1,500
		Rake	1,000
	17,500		21,000

While the physical prowess of the *Tribune's* distributors was distinguished, it did not compare with the editorial energy of the sheet. Greeley kept his word about suppressing low stories of crime, and even excluded theatrical advertising for a time, but relented later in favor of the good shows. The place instantly made for the paper was not due to its moral but to its mental tone. If ever an editorial page was stirring, this one of the *Tribune's* was. Every sentence rang like a bell.

The one thousand dollars in borrowed funds and the scanty income from the weeklies could not keep an all-devouring daily going at the speed engendered by the *Tribune,* which required immediate working capital and some sort of business management. The editor sensibly interested Thomas McElrath, the publisher who had been a tenant in the printing office building where he first found employment. Their co-partnership was announced on July 31, 1841. Greeley proclaimed it in the paper:

"The undersigned has great pleasure in announcing to his friends and the public, that he has formed a co-partnership with Thomas McElrath, and that the *Tribune* will hereafter be published by himself and Mr. M. under the firm of Greeley & McElrath. The principal editorial charges of the paper will still rest with the subscriber; while the entire business management of the concern henceforth devolves upon his partner.

"This arrangement, while it relieves the undersigned from a large portion of the labors and cares which have pressed heavily upon him for the last four months, assures to the paper efficiency and strength in a department where they have hitherto been needed; and I can not be mistaken in the trust that the accession to its conduct of a gentleman who has twice been honored with their suffrages for an important station, will strengthen the *Tribune* in the confidence and affections of the Whigs of New York."

Greeley found his new partner "so safe and judicious that the business never gave me any trouble, and scarcely required of me a thought during that long era of all but unclouded prosperity." Under McElrath's skilful handling, receipts far outran expenditures. In less than two months the sales had touched ten thousand a day, a figure that was soon to be doubled. The real triumph came when, on September 20, 1841, the struggling *New Yorker* and the *Log Cabin* were merged into the weekly *Tribune,* which speedily became the most popular, most widely circulated and most influential journal in the country.

James Gordon Bennett of the *Herald* did not underestimate the speed of the newcomer and at once got up extra steam. The two papers immediately became active rivals in the pursuit of news. Bennett had the most money and the fewest scruples. He usually won in the race, but seldom by more than a head. The rivalry of the pair roused great public interest in their performances. Without cables, telegraph or decent

JAMES GORDON BENNETT

railway connections, it took much ingenuity then to bridge gaps in the news. The Cunard liners made Halifax their first port of call, whence carrier pigeons brought condensed European news under their wings. When the Oregon treaty was pending, the *Tribune, Sun* and *Journal of Commerce*—the germ of the modern Associated Press—formed a combination with Philadelphia, Boston, Baltimore and Washington papers to send the fast pilot boat, *William J. Romer,* to Europe after the news, hoping to beat the Cunarder *Cambria* back with it. The pilot boat made a slow trip over, being delayed by ice floes which it encountered on the way, and Bennett paid the captain of the *Cambria* to force his engines. He made an extra fast run—instead of the usual eighteen days—doing the stretch from Halifax to Boston in thirty-six hours. Thence the *Herald's* despatches went by rail to Allyn's Point, Connecticut, whence a fast steamer took them to Greenport, Long Island. An express engine did the rest over the Long Island railroad—this then being the "fast" way to Boston, no rail line having yet reached New York. Bennett thus beat his rivals five and one-half hours, to Greeley's great chagrin. He tried to prove the *Tribune* was only three hours behind. The *Herald's* exultant crows were worth listening to. Bennett sent Greeley his elaborate compliments on his "enterprise," which had so well served to exalt that of the *Herald.* This was in March, 1846.

There was no all-rail route from Albany. The trip was made by boat. The *Tribune* installed a typesetting outfit on the river steamer, and while the correspondents wrote on the way down, skilled compositors set up their copy. Henry J. Raymond once furnished eight columns of solid nonpareil, written during the eight-hour trip, and the type was ready for the forms when the boat reached her dock.

The defeat of Van Buren by Harrison did not bring in the new era that Greeley had hailed. Harrison himself, far from being a man of might, in any case, held his high office but one month, and died on April 4, 1841. Thus Tyler came into power, to begin a course that was to deprive the Whigs of all advantages and end in their destruction. A party divided against itself could no more stand than a house. One of the fervent factors in the splitting was Horace Greeley with his *Tribune*.

By curious mockery, the despised Martin Van Buren became the first candidate for the Free Soilers, with whom Greeley had finally to align himself. In the splitting of the Whigs, southern domination, of course, weighted the party beyond its power to bear the load. It was to struggle a decade, and win one more presidential election before it went under.

Since the administration of John Quincy Adams, through the arid period of the Jackson era, the Whig party had clung convulsively to the coat-tails of Daniel Webster and Henry Clay. Clay was the elder by five years and came into the arena that much earlier, becoming senator from Kentucky in 1806-7, while Webster entered the House of Representatives from New Hampshire in 1812. Parties were shaping themselves out of the non-partisan Washington-Adams period, when faction, not nation-wide alignments, furnished political diversion. Jefferson's "Republicans," who were to be "Democrats" in time, had become coherent out of the "Democratic Societies" that aped the echoes of the French Revolution. Fragmentary Federalism furnished the opposition. Clay remained but a year in the Senate on his first essay, but returned to Congress in 1809 and shone there most of the time for fifteen years following. He was speaker in 1814, and was one of the commissioners who fashioned the Treaty of Ghent that ended the War of 1812. In 1824 he was in the scramble for the presidency, out of which John Quincy Adams pulled the plum and definitely established the Whigs as a full-grown party. Adams made him his secretary of state. The greatest feat of Clay as a congressman was the Missouri Compromise of 1820, which put up the first bar against the extension of slavery.

Andrew Jackson, who had opposed Adams in 1824, defeated him in 1828 as a Democrat, "Republican" having disappeared as a party name. Running for re-election in 1832, Jackson had Clay for an opponent and easily won. Clay was sent to the Senate by Kentucky in the same year and served ten years more, grooming himself all this time for another try at the presidency. This brings him into Greeley's day.

Webster came to Congress from Portsmouth, New Hampshire, as a Federalist in the election of 1812. Here he remained until 1817, when his removal to Boston took him out of New Hampshire politics. Gaining great repute as a lawyer through winning the Dartmouth College land grant case and other important cases, he was elected to Congress from Massachusetts in 1823. Following four years in the Lower House he was promoted to the Senate, and there remained until a month before the birth of the *Tribune,* when he had become Harrison's secretary of state.

The two, Webster and Clay, had become the twin gods of the Whigs. Both enjoyed an eminence and influence never since acquired by any American statesman. They were at the summit when the young editor of the *Tribune* began stirring up the animals.

In his short inaugural address Tyler had alluded to his administration as elected to correct and reform "errors and abuse," and deprecated the "spirit of faction, which is deeply opposed to the spirit of lofty patriotism," as something that "may find in this occasion for assaults upon my administration." Within three months, or, as Senator Thomas H. Benton expressed it: "Within less time than a commercial bill of exchange has to run, the great party which elected him and the Cabinet officers which he had just appointed with such warm expressions of respect and confidence" were "united in that assault."

Tyler was in hot water, as Benton notes, almost from the beginning of his taking office. An extra session of Congress furnished the immediate cause, with the ghost of the United States Bank as a provocative. The old Biddle following had looked to the Whigs to revive the bank. This they undertook to do by legislation, which Tyler vetoed. In September, 1841, his Cabinet, with the exception of Webster, resigned. It was refilled with new and poorer material. The thunder-clap came when Henry Clay, chafing in the Senate, resigned his seat in March, 1842. He had been defeated by Harrison in the contest for the presidential nomination and now was side-tracked in the Senate by the President's disregard of his policies. Clay, in quitting, delivered a valedictory. "Infirmities and disinclination for public life," as Benton put it, had no share in the reasons. "Disgust, profound and inextinguishable, was the ruling cause." Benton believed the money of the banks had elected Harrison and might have done as much for Clay, and so produced a president who would have been "a reality."

Clay felt that his rule of the party had passed away, and while he placed the blame on Tyler, he well knew that Daniel Webster and Caleb Cushing, then Congressmen from Massachusetts, were responsible for his set-back. He preferred to retire with a grand flourish and did so. The chief elements in the party sustained him and he was able to secure the nomination for president, only to be beaten by James K. Polk in 1844. He came back to the Senate in 1846, to remain there the rest of his years. Cushing turned from Whiggery to the Democracy after Tyler's defection, and was a Democrat from 1851. Webster resigned on May 8, 1843, frozen out by the conduct of Tyler's close friends in the Cabinet, who, linked with John C. Calhoun, Senator from South Carolina, were intriguing for the annexation of the struggling Republic of Texas, as an enlargement of slave territory, and regarded Webster as an obstacle in the way. Abel Parker Upshur succeeded him. Upshur was killed by the explosion of a gun on the man-of-war *Princeton*, February 28, 1844, and to the amazement of the country Calhoun became secretary of state, and the annexation of Texas an accomplished fact.

Thus it befell that the Whig policy, as Greeley and Seward saw it, went to the wall, and Tyler acted as became a pro-slavery president. Death had promoted the cause of bondage and its extension to the unmeasured plains of Texas.

The defeat of Henry Clay by Polk was a keen affliction for Greeley. Seward bore it philosophically. The late Lucian Brock Proctor, of Albany, long Secretary of the State Bar Association, was a student in Seward's law office at Auburn at the time and told once that he carried the delayed news of Clay's defeat to the Governor. Seward was standing in the doorway when young Proctor, coming up the walk, called out: "Mr. Clay is defeated!"

"Mr. Clay is defeated?" repeated Seward slowly: "What a la-men-table thing!"

In the 1844 campaign Greeley not only wrote for Clay, but appeared frequently on the platform in his behalf. Here is his own view of his efforts:

"I have admired and trusted many statesmen; I profoundly loved Henry Clay. Though a slaveholder, he was a champion of Gradual Emancipation when Kentucky formed her first state constitution in his early manhood; and was openly the same when she came to revise it, half a century later. He was a conservative in the true sense of that much-abused term: satisfied to hold by the present until he could see clearly how to exchange it for the better; but his was no obstinate, bigoted conservatism, but such as became an intelligent and patriotic American. From his first entrance into Congress, he had been a zealous and effective champion of Internal Improvements, the Protection of Home Industry, a sound and uniform National Currency—those leading features of a comprehensive, beneficent national policy which commanded the fullest assent of my judgment and the best exertions of my voice and pen. I loved him for his generous nature, his gallant bearing, his thrilling eloquence, and his life-long devotion to what I deemed our country's unity, prosperity and just renown,

Hence, from the day of his nomination in May to that of his defeat in November, I gave every hour, every effort, every thought, to his election. My wife and then surviving child (our third) spent the summer at a farm-house in a rural township of Massachusetts, while I gave heart and soul to the canvass. I traveled and spoke much; I wrote, I think, an average of three columns of the *Tribune* each secular day; and I gave the residue of the hours I could save from sleep to watching the canvass, and doing whatever I could to render our side of it more effective. Very often I crept to my lodging near the office at two to three A. M. with my head so heated by fourteen to sixteen hours of incessant reading and writing, that I could only win sleep by means of copious effusions from a shower bath; and these, while they probably saved me from a dangerous fever, brought out such myriads of boils, that—though I did not heed them until after the battle was fought out and lost—I was covered by them for the six months following, often fifty or sixty at once, so that I could contrive no position in which to rest, but passed night after night in an easy chair. And these unwelcome visitors returned to plague me, though less severely, throughout the following winter.''

He complained constantly of insomnia—the normal period of sleep for Greeley was not more than five or sometimes six hours—but he had the habit of napping, and on the whole enjoyed about the average amount of slumber, until the later days when he became broken in health. He could seemingly drop off at will and yet remain semi-conscious of all that was going on, a form of repose which rested, even if it did not provide the perfect anodyne.

Strong as he was for a protective tariff, Greeley never dreamed of the majestic heights to which its walls were destined to rise. Writing to Beman Brockway, November 13, 1847, concerning the Whig outlook for 1848, he expressed himself as desiring and expecting to see it revised downward: ''The tariff need no longer be in the way, for every year of thrift is placing our own manufactures farther and farther beyond the reach of destruction, and I am confident that ten years hence, the lowest duty that the government can live on will be high enough for the great mass of our iron, woolen and cotton fabrics.''

With respect to the political chances of Seward, Greeley believed ''we couldn't get Seward nominated by our [Whig] party,'' but thought ''he might be named for vice-president,'' instead of which that booby prize fell to Fillmore and chance made him president. Land reform and labor reform, Greeley thought, would be the issues of the next two decades. To these he hoped to add the abolition of the Army and Navy. He said nothing about slavery. The *Tribune* quarters suffered damages by fire on February 5, 1845, but the disaster was energetically overcome. Other papers showed the customary brotherliness and the *Tribune* came out as usual and rose traditionally stronger from the ashes.

These were the days when ''Greeley's paper'' began to attract young writers. Just as the wind blows toward the storm, so talent swept into the *Tribune* office. One of the earliest of arrivals was Bayard Taylor, debonair and young, who, a printer by trade, took to world tramping. He applied for space on the paper when a boy of nineteen, with his plans for a trip to Germany. ''No descriptive letters,'' was the editor's ukase: ''I am sick of them. When you have been there long enough to know something, send to me, and if there is anything in your letters I will publish them." Taylor held off for a year, then sent in seventeen, all of which appeared. In 1848 he became a regular member of the staff. Taylor was treated to many a hard bump, but he stuck to the *Tribune* and the *Tribune* to him. He used to get pretty mad, especially when Greeley once called some verses he had written "gassy stuff." They were. No one of Greeley's associates, according to Taylor, ever wrote a line that Greeley did not critically read.

The *Tribune* office in Greeley's day harbored more real journalists than any newspaper in America ever did, except, perhaps, the *Sun,* and there the number was fewer and the talent less varied. Topped by Greeley himself, the list grew to include, besides Taylor, Charles A. Dana and George Ripley, John F. Cleveland, who married Greeley's sister Esther and became associate editor, as well as being responsible for the *Tribune Almanac,* a job that was no sinecure under Greeley; James E. Mix, who became President Lincoln's bodyguard; Solon Robinson, "farm" editor; Frederick Gedney, Robert W. McAlpine, Nathan D. Urner, George W. Pearce, George H. Stout, Oswald Allen, N. G. Shepard, who wrote good verse; Oliver B. Stout, Curtis F. Gilbert, John Russell Young, John R. G. Hassard, W. W. Denslow, Professor A. J. Schem, foreign editor; Amos J. Cummings, who was to become a headlight for the *Sun;* Albert D. Richardson and Junius Henry Browne, famous as war correspondents and scouts in the South as it was seceding; William Winter, long famous as dramatic critic; Whitelaw Reid, who was to own the paper; John Hay, author of

Pike County Ballads; James Young, John Russell's
brother, a bright reporter who became congressman
from Philadelphia and used to stir the Gridiron Club
by his dramatic singing of *There's a New Coon in
Town;* Margaret Fuller, Samuel Wilkeson, Oliver
Johnson, brother of the Alton martyr; A. H. Byington,
F. J. Ottarson, W. E. (Richelieu) Robinson, Mortimer
M. Thompson (Philander Q. K. Doesticks), E. H. Clements, who was to head the Boston *Transcript;* Zebulon
White, who, with Clements, represented those who
parted their hair in the middle, a practise then
eschewed by all red-blooded Americans; John B.
Wood, who became the famous "condenser" on the
Sun; Clarkson Taber, S. T. Clarke, R. W. Johnson,
who fled from Jamaica with a price on his head for
taking part in the rising led by George William Gordon, and Frank Cahill, once editor of the New Orleans
Picayune.

When Solon Robinson became weighted with years
and retired, N. C. Meeker was made agricultural editor.   He had written much from a model farm he
pretended to cultivate at Dongola, Illinois, affecting to
recite the amazing results of his efforts.   My father,
who always cherished the delusion that money could be
made out of farming, was misled into making a journey to Dongola to view Meeker's wonders with his
own eyes.   He found a meager, miserable apology for
a farm, overrun with weeds and brambles, and not a
trace of the scientific success he had been led to expect.

Amos J. Cummings won his place on the *Tribune*
rather amusingly.   As a boy of eighteen he had tried
to join William Walker's ill-fated filibustering expedition against Nicaragua in 1860.   Shipwreck saved

him from worse consequences. He then entered the Union army, and at the close of his enlistment decided he wanted to work on the *Tribune*. Knowing how to set type, and aware of Greeley's predilection for printers, he braved him in his den, wearing the uniform of his country. The sight enraged the editor, who had been beset by discharged soldiers looking for places on the paper. When Amos made his mission known, Greeley shrieked:

"Do you expect me to hire the whole damned army?"

Amos modestly explained that he wanted a job for himself alone.

"Have you any other reason than that of having been a soldier for asking employment?" the editor demanded.

For reply Amos swung about, and, gracefully parting the long coat-tails of his blue overcoat, revealed a painful absence of fabric from the seat of his trousers.

He was given a chance and made good so quickly that he was soon an active factor in the editorial rooms, remaining until Charles A. Dana bought the *Sun* and took him on as the best managing editor New York ever knew.

Solon Robinson wrote a series of semi-humorous sketches which were put into book form as *Hot Corn; or, Life Scenes in New York*. It is pretty dull stuff now, but sold fifty thousand copies in its day. Charles Graham Halpine (Miles O'Reilly) became a member of the brilliant company. His poem on the retrieval of Anthony Burns, the fugitive slave from Boston, contained this vivid stanza:

"Tear down the flaunting lie!
    Half-mast the starry flag!
Insult no sunny sky
    With this polluted rag!
Destroy it, ye who can!
    Deep sink it in the waves!
It bears a fellow-man
    To groan with fellow-slaves!''

The verses were sent in anonymously and Greeley was given the credit down South for writing them. The blame followed him into his presidential campaign in 1872.

William H. Fry, the musical critic, had a masterly knowledge of his field. George M. Snow, financial editor, was a high authority. Fitz Henry Warren, Washington correspondent, had the toughest assignment, interrupted, as he often was, by Greeley's presence at the capital and his unruly outpourings.

In its career under Greeley the *Tribune* had four managing editors: Charles A. Dana, Sidney Howard Gay, John Russell Young and Whitelaw Reid. Young was credited with inventing the term "Copperhead" as referring to anti-war Democrats.

In addition to the able office staff, the *Tribune* drew into its columns the reflex of the best brains here and abroad. Thomas Hughes (Tom Brown) wrote letters from London, and Emilio Castelar, who was to become president of the Spanish republic, corresponded from the continent. Hughes made America acquainted with the liberal views of John Bright and Cobden, while Castelar's letters were notable reviews of continental complexes. Moncure D. Conway was a regular contributor from abroad, and George W. Smalley began his distinguished London career at Greeley's instance. Margaret Fuller's work attracted great attention. Greeley thought Margaret Fuller "the loftiest, bravest soul that has yet irradiated the form of an American woman," but is also on record as believing that "noble and great as she was, a good husband and two or three bouncing babies would have emancipated her from a good deal of cant and nonsense." He made her acquaintance through Mrs. Greeley, who had met her during a trip to Boston some four years before she became a member of the *Tribune* staff.

Excitement often invaded the *Tribune* office when the editor left town to become outside correspondent for a brief season. Greeley's letters to his managing editor, Charles A. Dana, written from Washington during the Banks speakership fight, teem with anguish. They were put into print some years ago by Joel Benton, an old friend of Greeley. Some of them point to pains of journalism not often revealed to the outer world. The correspondent, away from the office, is ofttimes a keen sufferer from the antics of the blockheads on the copy desk, or even the luminous writers who "interpret" for him on the editorial page. These selections from Greeley indicate that his troubles went deeper than this.

"I hate this hole," he wrote from Washington on December 1, 1855, "but am glad I have come. It does me good to see how those who hate the *Tribune* much, fear it yet more."

January 7, 1856, finds him annoyed at the space given in the *Tribune* to the new Academy of Music at Fourteenth Street and Irving Place. "What would it cost," he asks Dana, "to burn the Opera House?

If the price is not unreasonable, have it done and send me the bill. I think this last is the most unlucky week the *Tribune* ever saw—beaten in the documents and in every way besides. . . . All Congress disappointed at not seeing [Franklin] Pierce and [Caleb] Cushing demolished in the *Tribune*. . . . I began this letter to apologize for taking up three or four columns with a controversy with Dick Thompson, which I shall send you to-day, probably by Adams Express. Considering, however, those XIX columns of Coroner Fry's inquest on the putrefying opera, I won't apologize. This controversy concerns not Dick Thompson only, but the whole breed of Whig Doughfaces, and the room is well spent. You must give it soon—on the outside, of course. Yours soreheadedly.''

The next day found him insisting that Dana "caution your folks not to 'hit out' at everything and everybody here, but consider our position. We must have friends, not only in one party, but in all parties, if we can learn nothing. . . . You remember the Grand Vizier who knocked in the head the Sultan's proposal to exterminate the Infidel Dogs with this sensible demur: 'If we kill all the Rajahs, what shall we do for the capitation tax?' . . . Please think of these things and don't let your people in New York attack persons with whom we are in daily intercourse here, unless there shall be imperative necessity for it.''

In a postscript he observes: "I think it wrong to say Catholics, like slaveholders, are opposed to reading the Bible, when editions are published by them and urgently recommended by their bishops. I dread all meddling with theology.''

He referred to some editorial attack on the Jews,

with this comment: "I have labored for many years to give the *Tribune* a reputation for candor and generosity toward unpopular creeds and races. Stewart will use this up if you will let him. . . . Let us try to cultivate a generous spirit in all things."

Of Hildreth, another editorial writer, he declared: "He is essentially a Timothy Pickering Federalist of fifty or sixty years ago and is always fighting the battles of that class of well-meaning, but shockingly maladroit politicians. He hates slavery mainly because the South turned out old John Adams. You must gradually teach him to let the dead bury the dead."

On the seventeenth he is tired, but "shall see these treacherous scoundrels through the speakership, if I am allowed to live long enough, at all events. Our plans are defeated, our hopes frustrated from day to day by perpetual treacheries on our own side. . . . Since my letters get in somehow, I am less uneasy here, but every traitor and self-seeker hates me with a demoniac hatred which is perpetually bursting out. Lastly your friend, Judge Shankland, General of the Kansas Volunteers, has notified me that he shall cowhide me (for rudeness in refusing to be further bored by him), the first time he catches me in public. Now I am a hater of novelty, and never had any taste for being cowhided, cowhid or cowhidden, or whatever the past participles of the active verb used by General Shankland may be, but he is short of funds and I could not think of putting him to the trouble of chasing me all over the country, so I shall stay here for the present. I trust the man from whom he buys the cowhide will know him well enough not to sell it on tick. I prefer to be the only sufferer by the application."

Friday night, January 25th, 1856, his grief boiled over:

"Dana: I shall have to quit here or die, unless you stop attacking people here without consulting me. You have a paragraph (utterly untrue) from a Boston paper stating that Pennington was in Boston closeted with Governor Gardner, which was interpreted here as an attack on P. Then comes one from an Ohio paper, classing Ball with Moore and Scott Harrison as opposing Banks long after Ball had come back to Banks. And now comes an awful attack on old Brenton, who has been voting steadily for Banks and the Plurality rule for at least two weeks past—certainly since the second nominating caucus. This article will be handed around and read by every shaky man on our side before to-morrow noon, as an evidence of my malignity against every one who ever opposed Banks, and an earnest of what they will all get as soon as Banks is elected. It will hurt us all dreadfully. Do send some one here and kill me if you can not stop this, for I can bear it no longer. My life is a torture to me.
H. G."

The 28th found his anguish at top pressure:

"Dana: If you were to live fifty years and do nothing but good all the time, you could hardly atone for the mischief you have done by that article on Brenton.

"The stupid old dunce had killed himself, and I had decently buried him. After doing all the harm he could, he had come back to us and was voting steadily though sulkily. His power for mischief was at an end, and he could never again have been in a condition to do any. Your savage, blundering attack upon his putrefying carcass has raised it out of the grave and reanimated it with power for mischief. A great testimonial of sympathy and confidence is being got up, and good men are signing it. He is to shine forth a glorified saint tried in the purifying fires of the *Tribune's* malice and falsehood—nay, of mine. I have the whole right side of the House upon me—one down, another come on—and I have had to explain the matter separately to each. I had to go to the old animal himself, apologize humbly, and tell him I had telegraphed a contradiction, which would be in Saturday's paper. But Saturday's paper came and no contradiction. I have it in yesterday's Third Edition, but there is probably not another copy of that in Washington, and I have stood before the House for another day as a liar as well as a libeler. This will go all over the country as an evidence of my bullying falsehood and malignity against any one who ever dared to think of another candidate than Banks. It will injure the *Tribune* horribly, and enable the old mule to throw away his district in the fall.

"Now I write once more to entreat that I may be allowed to conduct the *Tribune* with reference to the mile wide that stretches either way from Pennsylvania Avenue. It is but a small space, and you have all the world beside. I can not stay here unless this request is complied with. I would rather cease to live at all. If you are not willing to leave me entire control with reference to this city, both men and measures, I ask you to call the Proprietors together and have me discharged. I have to go to this and that false creature and coax him to behave as little like the devil as possible (Lew Campbell, for instance), yet in constant terror of seeing him guillotined in the next *Tribune* that arrives—and I can't make him believe that I did not instigate it. So with everything here. If you want to throw stones at anybody's crockery, aim at my head first, and in mercy be sure to aim well."

The folly of an editor attempting to play politics

on the ground reached its high point on February first. Greeley then wrote:

"Dana: For God's sake speak the truth to me. The *Tribune* is cursed all over the House as having beaten us to-day by your most untimely article on Bayard Clarke in yesterday's *Tribune*.

"We lost to-day by two votes, and Lew Campbell wanted to give us the casting vote, but one would not do it. Now, Bayard Clarke had promised to vote for us if his vote would carry it, and in this case it would have done it with Lew Campbell's. But when he was called on he would not do it, and gave as his reason your article of yesterday. Of course, I am not supposing the false knave would have done it at all; but you have given him what served him as an excuse for not doing it, and the *Tribune* has to bear the credit of beating Banks—for to-day certainly, perhaps forever—in spite of your promise never more to attack any one here without consulting me.

"I must give it up and go home. All the Border Ruffians from here to the lowest pit could not start me away, but you can do it, and I must give up. You are getting everybody to curse me. I am too sick to be out of bed, too crazy to sleep, and am surrounded by horrors. I shall go to Pittsburgh on the twenty-second, and I guess I shall not return. I can just bear the responsibilities that belong to me; but you heap a load on me that will kill me.

"That article on War and Insurrection in the South is bad in spirit, and does no good. Such will cause the *Tribune* to be stopped in the South."

Moved by a desire to make the *Tribune* something more than a private possession, Greeley, in 1851, persuaded McElrath into creating a corporation—the Tribune Association—with a capital stock of one hundred thousand dollars. The paper was worth much more. Shares were of one thousand dollars value. At first the stock was mainly held by Greeley, McElrath and various *Tribune* employees—Charles A. Dana, Bayard Taylor, Thomas N. Rooker, foreman of the composing-room; Albert D. Richardson, Stephen T. Clark, Oliver Johnson and Solon Robinson. When Dana left the *Tribune* he sold his stock to Doctor J. C. Ayer, the Lowell, Massachusetts, Cherry Pectoral man. McElrath in season parted with his shares, and Samuel Sinclair became the largest single holder and publisher. Other employees came in and some outsiders. Greeley's proprietary interest dribbled away, but his pen stayed ruler through it all. It is impressive, some persons have even found it inspiring, to realize how little interest at any time this man took in making money.

In 1852 Greeley registered indignation at what he thought was sharp practise on the part of his former helper, Henry J. Raymond, and D. B. St. John, head of the Banking Department, which led to his dubbing Raymond "little villain." Presumably in aid of the *Tribune*, Thurlow Weed had caused the passage of a law requiring the publication of New York bank statements in one daily paper, which was to be paid for the service. This sort of thing was then news, and it was further required that the alternative paper should receive proofs. When St. John took office he switched the business to the *Times*, and the latter "held out" the proofs on the *Tribune*. Greeley wrote St. John some burning letters about it.

"I have a most insolent and scoundrelly letter from

your favorite, Raymond, offering to send me these returns at his own convenience if I will credit them to the *Times* (not the Bank Department, of which only have I asked them), and talking of his willingness to grant favors to those who prove worthy of them, but not to be 'kicked into benevolence,' etc. All this insolence of this little villain is founded on your injustice. I have not written to him; I have asked no favor of him; and I shall not answer him. I am sorry to find one of his falsehoods copied into your letter—that which speaks of my being offended at your selection of the *Times* to print the advertisements! You both know a great deal better—that I have never asked you for advertising of any sort, but solely for the information to publish without charge. Have I not reason to despise alike the author and propagator of this unfounded imputation?''

High and low tariff were fiery issues of the period, and ''bad times'' were traced inevitably to one or the other as a cause. A mild panic took place in 1854, when money rose to a sharp rate of interest and the value of securities dropped, as they always do when there is no demand for investment. ''Greeley,'' Charles A. Dana wrote, ''had to let good lands in Pennsylvania, on which he had paid five thousand dollars, go to the dogs because he could not raise five hundred dollars.'' The gold of California had bred an inflation that was now collapsing, and most of the specie in the land was going to Europe to pay interest, and for imports. This Greeley credited to lack of protection, though it was really lack of business sense. The Democrats were in power, and declined to yield on the tariff. In July three years later a genuine panic began, with many failures. Greeley lined up the facts cogently when he wrote, shortly before the crash came: "We are heavily in debt to Europe. Our city merchants and bankers owe those of Great Britain; the country owes the cities, the farmers owe the merchants—in short, two-thirds of us are in debt." The unemployed in New York were stirred up, as a new election grew near, to demand bread and work. The tariff had been reduced another five per cent., and this Greeley made the most of as against the Democrats, while still upholding Fernando Wood, the Philadelphia printer, whose election as mayor of New York he had abetted. Wood was a Democrat and turned out to be a pretty bad one. By 1860 Greeley had enough of Wood, apparently, yet in 1862, when, after a gap of two years Wood ran again, the *Tribune* was hostile to C. Codfrey Gunther, Union and Tammany candidate, and by no means hurtful to Wood in a campaign that made him mayor during a wartime period when his southern sympathies were a disadvantage to the Union cause. Neither as Whig nor Republican would Greeley be bound by party lines in local matters.

The *Tribune's* balance sheet in 1865 and 1866, as rendered to the Income Tax Department at Washington, is reproduced from Hudson's *History of Journalism,* as an interesting exhibit of its prosperity, as well as of the current costs:

EXPENDITURES

1865		1866	
Printing paper..	$315,162.61	Printing paper..	$418,199.62
Pressmen, repairing presses....	35,255.07	Pressmen, repairing presses ...	46,398.08
Ink	8,420.00	Ink	9,927.50
Glue and molasses, for rollers	869.46	Glue and molasses, for rollers	943.67
Compositors	73,769.71	Compositors	86,609.14

EXPENDITURES

1865		1866	
Editorial expenses	51,884.05	Editorial expenses	81,775.40
Correspondence .	41,073.76	Correspondence..	49,300.57
News by telegraph	22,044.76	News by telegraph	58,776.04
Harbor news ...	1,875.20	Harbor News....	2,112.34
Publishing offices, salaries	19,720.72	Publishing office, salaries	22,841.65
Advertising	7,080.48	Advertising	17,219.07
Mailing, counting and packing papers	35,088.36	Mailing, counting and packing papers	35,005.60
Postage	6,184.23	Postage	11,963.74
Printing and stationery	2,463.16	Printing and stationery	6,198.06
Libel suits	1,390.51	Libel suits	9,876.65
U. S. tax on advertising receipts	8,376.45	U. S. tax on advertising receipts	10,082.19
Gaslight	5,077.15	Gaslight	5,862.50
Expense account, i n c l u d i n g plumbing, gas fixtures, carpenter work, etc.	10,371.48	Expense account, i n c l u d i n g plumbing, gas fixtures, carpenter work, etc.	18,816.57
		Donation of Freedman's Aid Union	1,000.00
		Donation to Union State Committee	1,000.00
		Donation to Portland Sufferers	250.00
Total $646,107.16		Total $885,158.39	
Receipts over expenditures ... 170,429.86		Receipts over expenditures 24,259.50	

The policy of the *Tribune* in the field of foreign affairs was direct and enterprising. Charles A. Dana

was sent to France in 1848 to "cover" the Revolution
that drove Louis Philippe from his throne and brought
on the second republic with the third Napoleon as
president. During the Franco-Prussian War, which
occurred in Greeley's last days, the *Tribune* was easily
first in its reports and comments.

Of the *Tribune* in the popular mind, J. C. Derby,
noted publisher of the day, in his *Recollections* says:
"It seemed to fill a void in the tastes of a class of
readers who were inclined to well-written, original
articles and literary matter selected with great taste
and care, while the current news of the day was sufficient to meet the wants of the general readers of the
paper. The fact that it was so often spoken of as
Greeley's *Tribune* testified to its creator's directing
force, and should testify even further that the force
was generated by a man's power not from without but
from within."

Greeley wrote in his *Recollections of a Busy Life*:

"Fame is a vapour; popularity an accident; riches
take wings; the only earthly certainty is oblivion; no
man can foresee what a day can bring forth; while
those who cheer to-day will often curse to-morrow; and
yet I cherish the hope that the journal I projected and
established will live and flourish long after I shall have
moldered into forgotten dust, being guided by a larger
wisdom, a more unerring sagacity to discern the right,
though not by a more unfaltering readiness to embrace
and defend it at whatever personal cost; and that the
stone which covers my ashes may bear to future eyes
the still intelligible inscription, 'Founder of the New
York *Tribune*.' "

CHAPTER VI

THE decades from 1830 to 1850 were probably the primmest in American history. The female sections of the population almost fainted if any one said "pants" in their presence, and modesty was so complete as nearly to constitute caste. But the men were pretty tough. They drank, fought duels and were most profane. Many gambled for high stakes. They were gallant and obsequious to ladies, but kept mistresses, and were not safe to leave alone in the presence of the fair, though zealous to defend female honor against all males but themselves. Great men like Daniel Webster got drunk. Henry Clay lost fortunes at cards. Yet all masculinity had a high opinion of itself and was strong for social order.

The unconventional in man or woman was sternly rebuked. Men who kept women were shocked at a doctrine called "free love" that came to life out of the prevailing outward austerity. People who opposed slavery were regarded as pestiferous persons to be sternly dealt with. No abolitionist was considered respectable until William Ellery Channing espoused the cause.

One of the first upsetters of convention was Fanny Wright, an English woman of high ideals, who was

114

opposed to slavery, and deeply concerned with women's rights. She essayed in 1825 to found a colony in Tennessee called Neshoba, where she planned to educate negroes, on a two thousand-acre estate, in order to show "that nature had made no difference between blacks and whites, excepting in complexion," as her horrified friend, Mrs. Trollope, put it in a chapter of *Domestic Manners of the Americans*.

As may be imagined, this doctrine did not get very far in Tennessee. Neshoba was persecuted out of existence in 1828. Later Miss Wright took on the "free love" doctrine that a woman's morality might be just as much a matter of her own choosing as a man's. This, of course, capped the sheaf. She was violently assailed, but the Quakers regarded her indulgently, and Greeley eventually became her friend, though his early references to her are scarcely those of intimate regard. After the failure of her Tennessee experiment, Miss Wright took a husband. The editor of the *New Yorker* notes her coming to town on August 4, 1838, in terms that hardly suggest any desire to know her better:

"Mrs. Frances Wright D'Arusmont announces herself as on hand in our city ready to recommence her lectures on the iniquities and oppressions of Christianity, Matrimony, Banks, Corporations, etc., etc. She always favors us with a visit about the time an election is coming on, by accident, of course."

Later the lady was accorded this somewhat ungracious attention:

"There was a slight row at Masonic Hall last Sunday evening. Fanny Wright D'Arusmont delivers lectures there every Sunday night, against Priest-craft, Banks, Whiggery, etc., and in advocacy of the sub-treasury scheme, of which she claims to be the father or mother, we don't know which. She has hired the hall for these evenings and has a right to say what she pleases in it, and those who don't like her notions may stay away. They don't, however, and on her re-marking that she had been disturbed the preceding Sunday by a lot of 'Whig Loafers' (very true, we fancy), the lads made an uproar. Mayor Clark had anticipated some disturbance, and had a band of police in attendance, who soon restored order, and Fanny's eloquence was thus enabled to disembogue itself un-interruptedly—

" 'In one weak, washy, everlasting flood.' "

That the clever, talented, philanthropic woman was going pretty strong for any day, and tremendously so for her own, can well be understood. The lady kept the country more or less stirred up until the mid-'forties, and Greeley's editorial enemies made much of his reception of some of her ideas. Their moral reactions were often diverting. The wicked James Watson Webb was especially shocked at Greeley's as-sociation with "vice," in the person of Fanny Wright. Webb was also racked with horror at Greeley's accept-ance of the vegetarian doctrines of Graham, a Con-necticut man, born in 1794, who invented the flour that bears his name, and that is still popular. The doughty colonel regarded non-meat eaters as white-livered, so to speak, and brutally assailed Greeley, who replied meekly that his diet was "vegetarian, mainly," but as it was a private and personal matter, with which he did not burden his readers, he could not see "why it should concern the colonel."

The full name of the flour faddist was Sylvester Graham. He was a native of Suffield, Connecticut, who became a Presbyterian clergyman and preached long in New Jersey, giving up the pulpit to proclaim his doctrines of health. According to Greeley he tabooed "tea and coffee as well as tobacco, opium and alcoholic potables, cider and beer equally with brandy and gin," and rejected besides all spices and condiments save a little salt. The bolting of meal he also reprobated, teaching that "the ripe, sound berry of wheat or rye, being ground to the requisite fineness, should in no manner be sifted, but should be made into loaves and eaten precisely as the mill stones deliver it." Graham died in 1854, at the early age of fifty-seven, a poor testimonial for his theory. Greeley's own comparatively short life would also appear to testify in favor of meat eaters and bibbers of wine.

The appetite for new ideas, social and religious, at the period was such that Mrs. Trollope wrote with truth when she said: "I sincerely believe that, if a fire-worshiper or Indian Brahmin were to come to the United States, and could preach and pray in English, he would not be long without a respectable congregation." In using the word "respectable" the good lady refers to size, not character. It was not possible to be respectable and unorthodox in that day, unless Unitarian, whom the orthodox held in great awe. It was a Unitarian source that evolved the first great purely American social experiment in the way of communism, at Brook Farm, near West Roxbury, Massachusetts. This was soon to engage Greeley's attention and lead him further.

Unitarianism, having produced Transcendentalism

under the benign guidance of William Ellery Channing, that purest product of liberal perfection, sought some outlet for better things on earth, having nicely arranged affairs in Heaven. Channing expressed his ideas to George Ripley and Doctor John Collins Warren, of Boston, at whose house a meeting was called, where the design took shape. Ralph Waldo Emerson was in the company, and has given a good account of what occurred, as well as the after result. It was a "well chosen company of gentlemen" who enjoyed, besides Channing's address, "an oyster supper with good wines," which was about as far as they got that evening. At first came merely a grouping of kindred souls among the younger Unitarians—Margaret Fuller, Frederick H. Hedge, George Ripley, Orestes A. Brownson, William H. Channing, nephew of William Ellery Channing. These, with many others, met together as students of advanced thought, social and religious. "These persons," quotes Emerson, "became, in the common chance of society, acquainted with each other, and the result was a strong friendship, exclusive in proportion to its heat."

Their first cooperation was in the publication of a quarterly, the *Dial*, edited by Margaret Fuller, which remains a remarkable example of intellectual expression. This was in 1840. A year later the Brook Farm project took shape.

Two hundred acres of land were purchased at West Roxbury and there the Transcendentalists gathered. Emerson does not know how the name came to be applied, or who first used it in describing the unusual company. Some of those who came put in money— others only their labor. Here gathered such young minds as those of Miss Fuller, Charles A. Dana, (not yet of the *Tribune*), George Ripley, Dana's associate in editing the first American Cyclopedia; George William Curtis, who was to be editor of *Harper's Weekly* and of the Easy Chair in *Harper's Magazine* for a generation; Theodore Parker, the great preacher; Orestes A. Brownson, Nathaniel Hawthorne, and others whose names were to rise high and live long in American annals. Miss Elizabeth P. Peabody described the scheme in the *Dial* of October, 1841. Briefly, Brook Farm in its inception was an effort to establish the Kingdom of God on earth; that Kingdom in which "The Will of God shall be done as it is in Heaven"; a higher state than that of the Apostolic church; worthy even to be called the Second Coming of Christ, and the beginning of the Day of Judgment. That there was anything socialistic about it Miss Peabody specially disclaimed. In the January issue of the *Dial*, 1842, the lady went further into details.

"The plan of the community," she observes, "is in brief this: All who have property to take stock, and receive a fixed interest thereon; then to keep house or board in common, as they shall severally desire, at the cost of provisions purchased wholesale, or raised on the farm; all to labor in community and to be paid by the hour; choosing their own number of hours and kind of work. With the results of their labor and their interest they are to pay their board, and also to purchase whatever else they require at cost, at the warehouses of the community, which are to be filled by the community as such. To perfect this economy in the course of time, they must have all trades and all manner of business carried on among themselves, from the lowest mechanical trade, which contributes to the health and comfort of life, to the finest art, which adorns it with food or drapery for the mind. All labor, whether bodily or intellectual, to be paid at the same rate of wages; on the principle that, as wages become merely bodily, it is a greater sacrifice to the individual laborer to give his time to it; because time is desirable for the cultivation of the intellectuals in exact proportion to ignorance. Besides, intellectual labor involves in itself higher pleasures and is more its own reward than bodily labor."

Not so foolish as it sounds—if it could be made to work. Charles A. Dana in a hopeful moment at a Fourierite convention, held at Clinton Hall, New York, April 4, 1844, described the farm life thus: "As a member of the oldest association in the United States, I deem it my duty to make some remarks on the practical results of the system. We have an association at Brook Farm, of which I now speak from my own experience. We have there abolished domestic servitude as one of the first considerations; it gave one of the first impulses to the movement at Brook Farm. It seemed that a continuation in the relations which it established could not possibly be submitted to. It was a deadly sin—a thing to be escaped from. Accordingly, it was escaped from; and we have now for three years lived at Brook Farm and have carried on all business of life without it. At Brook Farm they are the servants of each other; no man is master. We do freely, from the love of it, with joy and thankfulness, those duties which are usually discharged by domestics. The man who performs one of these duties—he who digs a ditch or executes any other repulsive

Charles A. Dana.

work—is not at the foot of the social scale; he is at the head of it. Again, we have in association established a nature system of education; a system of education which does justice tò every one; where the children of the poor receive the integral development of all their faculties, as far as the means of the association in its present condition will permit. Here we claim we have made an advance upon civilized society.''

Dana enlarged a little upon lines which he very much forsook in after life: ''In the best society that has ever been in this world, with very small exceptions, labor has never had its just reward. Everywhere the gain is in the pocket of the employer. He makes the money. The laborer toils for him and is his servant. The interest of the laborer is not consulted in the arrangement of industry; but the whole tendency of industry is perpetually to disgrace the laborer, to guard his door and reduce his wages, and to render deceit and fraud almost necessary for him, and all for the benefit of whom? For the benefit of our excellent monopolists, our excellent companies, our excellent employers. The stream all runs into their pockets, and not one little rill is suffered to run into the pockets of those who do the work. In the association we have changed all this! We have established a true relation between labor and the people, whereby labor is done not entirely for the benefit of the capitalist as in civilized society, but for the mutual benefit of the laborer and the capitalist. We are able to distribute the results and advantages which accrue from labor in joint ratio.''

At the time Dana made these hopeful remarks,

Brook Farm had ceased to be Transcendental and had become Fourierite. Margaret Fuller had proved to be a poor cook, and Nathaniel Hawthorne could not be relied on to feed the pigs. Dana did fairly well at pitching manure—an accomplishment he never lost.

The extreme destitution caused by lack of employment that prevailed for several years after the panic of 1837, had prompted Greeley to write some serious articles for the *New Yorker*, under the heading: *What Shall be Done for the Laborer?* These caught the eye of Albert Brisbane, then of Batavia, New York, a man of means, father of the brilliant Arthur Brisbane of our day. Albert Brisbane, traveling in Europe, became enamored of Fourier's ideas, and the introduction of Fourierism into the United States was due to him, though Greeley was responsible for the stir it made. He had read the *New Yorker* articles and, afire with his scheme, in due time sought out Greeley. Temperamentally, Brisbane the elder was like his son. He had all the tastes and habits of an aristocrat, with a mind that burned over the wrongs of the proletariat. He was anxious to place his views before the world and decided to start a paper, which H. Greeley and Co., of 30 Ann Street, New York, undertook to print at Brisbane's expense. The *New Yorker* for March 6, 1841, contained the announcement that there would appear every Saturday from the Greeley press a weekly called *The Future,* edited by A. Brisbane, on behalf of "The Friends of Association and Social Progress," the paper to be "devoted to the inculcation and diffusion of Practical Philanthropy, to the faithful chronicling of all important advances in Philosophy, Science and Arts, and to the advocacy and dissemination of whatever shall seem calculated to promote the Progress of the Human Race, through Knowledge and Virtue to Universal Happiness.''

It reads like a large order, and looms larger when it appeared that the ''primary, positive and definite object'' was to show that ''Human Happiness may be promoted, Knowledge and Virtue increased, Vice, Misery, Waste and Want infinitely diminished, by a reorganization of society upon a principle of Association, or combination of effort, instead of the present system of isolated households with their discordant interests, conflicting Efforts and envious Competition. It will prove that Industry can be ennobled and rendered honorable and rendered attractive.'' All this was for the trifling sum of one dollar and fifty cents per annum—in advance.

Greeley was cognizant of the Brook Farm movement and in sympathy with its promoters. It was not, however, until the elder Brisbane had failed with *The Future* that Greeley became involved in Fourierism, to which its rivals ascribed the name socialism, with the desire of doing the *Tribune* injury. In March, 1842, this announcement topped a column: ''Association; or principles of a true organization of society. This column has been purchased by the Advocates Association, in order to lay their principles before the public. Its editorship is entirely distinct from that of the *Tribune*.''

This disavowal was soon rendered of no effect by the frank entrance of the *Tribune's* editor into the schemes advocated in the column, which from March 28, 1842, to May 28, 1843, was filled by Brisbane, in advocacy of Fourierism, or the Socialization of Communities. Neither Fourier nor Brisbane was a pioneer. Robert Owen, a wealthy Scotch manufacturer of linens at Lanark, had come to America in 1824 and taken over a cooperative enterprise founded by George Rapp, at Harmony, Clay County, in southwestern Indiana. Rapp's followers were Germans, who had built up a community of one thousand souls. They did not like the country and followed their leader back to Pennsylvania. Owen rechristened the locality "New Harmony" and proceeded to carry out his ideas. The Shakers were also well established in several centers in the East, and the Ohio community called Zoar was then flourishing. In all, some sixty-three "communities" sprang up, to say nothing of the firmly cooperating Mormons, under Joseph Smith and Brigham Young.

Brisbane pushed his propaganda with vigor in and out of the *Tribune,* where his articles appeared two or three times a week. Although he was aiming at socialism, he appealed to capitalism to give it a start.

"If a few rich men," he wrote, "could be interested in the subject, a stock company could be formed among them with a capital of four or five hundred thousand dollars, which would be sufficient. Their money would be safe; for the lands, edifices, flocks, etc., of the Association would be mortgaged to secure it. The sum which is required to build a small railroad, a steamship, to start an insurance company or a bank, would establish an association. Could not such a sum be raised?

"A practical trial of Association might be made by appropriation from a state legislature. Millions are now spent in constructing canals and railroads

that scarcely pay for repairs. Would it endanger the
Constitution, injure the cause of Democracy, or shock
the consciences of politicians, if a legislature were to
advance for an Association, half a million dollars
secured by mortgage upon the lands and personal
estate?

"The most easy plan, perhaps, for starting an
Association, would be to induce four hundred persons
to unite and take each $1,000 worth of stock, which
would form a capital of $400,000. With this sum an
Association could be established, which could be made
to guarantee to every person a comfortable room in
it and board for life, as interest upon the investment
of $1,000; so whatever reverses might happen to those
forming the Association, they would always be certain
of having the two great essentials of existence—a
dwelling and a table at which to sit.

"The stockholders would receive one quarter of
the total products or profits of the Association; or, if
they preferred, they would receive a fixed interest of
eight per cent. At the time of general division of
profits at the end of the year, the stockholders would
first receive their interest, and the balance would be
paid over to those who performed the labor. A slight
deviation would in this respect take place from the
general law of the Association, which is to give one
quarter of the profits to capital, whatever they may be;
but additional inducements of security should be held
out to those who organize the first association."

Brisbane illustrated further:

"The investment of $1,000 would yield $80 annual
interest. With this sum the Association must guarantee a person a dwelling and a living; and this could
be done. The edifice could be built for $150,000, the
interest upon which at 10 per cent. would be $15,000.
Divide the sum by 400, which is the number of persons,
and we have $37.50 per annum, for each person as

rent. Some of the apartments would consist of several rooms and rent for $100, others for $90, others for $80, and so on in a descending rating, so that above one-half of the rooms could be rented for $20 per annum. A person wishing to live at the cheapest rates would have, after paying his rent, $60 left. As the Association would raise all its fruit, grain, vegetables, cattle, etc., and as it would economize immensely in fuel, number of cooks, and everything else, it could furnish the cheapest priced board at $60 per annum, the second at $100 and the third at $150. Thus a person who invested $1,000 could be certain of a comfortable room and board for his interest, if he lived economically, and would have whatever he produced by his labor in addition. He would live, besides, in an elegant edifice surrounded by beautiful fields and gardens.

"If one-half of the persons taking stock did not wish to enter the Association at first, but to continue their business in the world, receiving the chance of so doing later, they could do so. Experienced and intelligent agriculturists and mechanics would be found to take their places; the buildings would be gradually enlarged and those who remained out, could enter later as they wished. They would receive in the meantime their interest in cash upon their capital. A family with two or three children could enter upon taking from $2,000 to $2,500 worth of stock."

The word "phalanx" was applied to the form of association, and numbers of these proceeded to organize. Greeley became an active factor in the movement to establish these settlements where, in effect, the residents were to make a living and earn dividends by supporting each other.

Brisbane established a weekly, called the *Phalanx,* edited by himself and Osborne Macdaniel, on October 5, 1843, and this kept up steam until May 28, 1845.

Numerous communities were established, with one of which Greeley was closely identified. This was Sylvania, in Pike County, Pennsylvania. Thomas W. Whitely became president and Horace Greeley treasurer. Brisbane himself headed a phalanx on thirty thousand acres of pine barrens in Monmouth County, New Jersey. The Brook Farm folk also became a phalanx, and, dropping the *Dial,* inaugurated in 1845 a weekly *Harbinger* that lived to pile up seven and one-half semi-annual volumes. Five of these were printed at the farm, the remainder in New York, under the editorship of George Ripley and Charles A. Dana.

The *Harbinger* did not flourish, and died in 1849. The two conductors fell into hard straits. Ripley was better off for employment than Dana, who appealed to Albert Brisbane for aid in getting him a job on the *Tribune.* This Brisbane undertook to do. He felt that Greeley was under some personal obligations to him. He had helped the editor a bit financially, and his paid column in the *Tribune* aided its revenues. It also increased circulation. Greeley demurred at taking Dana on, because he came from Brook Farm. ''Those Brook Farm people are all lazy,'' he told Brisbane. The latter insisted, so Greeley said Dana could come in and read exchanges at five dollars per week. In six months he was managing editor. Ripley became literary editor, and his work gave great distinction to the paper.

The *Harbinger* and the *Phalanx* had some notable contributors—Greeley and Dana themselves, Theodore Parker, William Ellery Channing, George William Curtis, Otis Clapp, James Freeman Clarke, Christopher P. Cranch, Thomas Wentworth Higginson, Henry James, the elder; Parke Godwin, son-in-law of William Cullen Bryant; James Russell Lowell, John Greenleaf Whittier, W. W. Story, the sculptor; George Ripley and Francis Gould Shaw.

Thus it will be seen that some of the best brains in the land were in favor of the Association plan, foolish and impracticable as it proved to be, which may explain why the *Tribune* survived connection with a project so opposite to our every-man-for-himself Americanism, with the devil chasing the hindmost.

The convention of April 4, 1844, at which Dana explained Brook Farm, was largely attended. Ripley presided, and Greeley was one of the vice-presidents. The "business committee" was composed of Greeley, Dana, Ripley, Brisbane, John Allen, Parke Godwin, L. W. Ryckman, Osborne Macdaniel, James Kay, William H. Channing, A. M. Watson and Solyman Brown. A special committee was appointed to edit the *Phalanx*, which included Greeley, Brisbane, Godwin and Rufus Dawes. Brisbane was appointed special representative to confer with the Associationists of Europe as to the best methods of mutual cooperation. The report of the proceedings says that Albert Brisbane pronounced an enthusiastic and hearty tribute of his gratitude, esteem and respect for Horace Greeley, for the "manly, independent, and generous support he had given the cause from its infancy. . . . He has done for us what we never could have done. He has created the cause on this continent. He has done the work of a century. Well, then, I will give a toast: 'One Continent, One Man!' "

Greeley, responding, deprecated the compliments

as the "extravagant eulogium of a partial friend," and then said this much for himself:

"When I took up this cause, I knew that I went in the teeth of many of my patrons, in the teeth of prejudices of the great mass, in the teeth of religious prejudices; for I confess I had a great many more clergymen on my list before than I have now, as I am sorry to say, for had they kept on I think I could have done them a little good. But in the face of all this, in the face of constant advices, 'Don't have anything to do with that Mr. Brisbane,' I went on. 'Oh!' said many of my friends, 'consider your position and your influence.' 'Well,' said I, 'I shall endeavor to do so, but I must try to do some good in the meantime, or what is the good of influence?' And thus I have gone on, pursuing a manly, and at the same time, a circumspect course; treading wantonly on no man's prejudice, telling, on the contrary, universal man, I will defer to your prejudices, as far as I can consistently with my duty; but when duty leads me, you must excuse my stepping on your corn, if it be in the way."

Cheers greeted his conclusion. They might well have been drowned in the groans from the owners of corns which had been stepped upon.

The Sylvania phalanx established itself, through followers from New York and Albany, in 1842-43 on 2,394 acres of miserable land in Pike County. It was too poor to raise more than scrub oak and pine, six miles from Lackawanna, up a six-mile road padded with rough stone, 1,500 feet above sea level. The Society gave $9,000 for the forlorn farm. Of this, $1,000 was paid down and the owner agreed to take $1,000 in stock. In all, $10,400 was subscribed toward the experiment. Twenty-eight married couples were on the ground in August, 1843, also twenty-four young men and six young women, plus fifty-one children. These were all packed in three shaky, two-story houses and in the upper story of a grist mill that had no stones for grinding. The children ran wild and their parents quarreled. An old saw-mill was available, but none of the timber was fit for use. Only four acres were tillable. The first comers had plowed and planted this and it gave back eleven and a half bushels of grain! Next year seventeen acres were cleared and planted, but these no more than returned the seed. The experiment lasted a year and a half and disbanded. Greeley had put in $5,000. Some of the tough soil became his property, and, strangely enough, made a good return to his estate, the timber having regrown to valuable proportions.

The other phalanxes had much the same sort of luck. The buildings at Brook Farm were destroyed by fire March 3, 1846, and the community broke up thereafter. Meanwhile Greeley's feelings had to endure considerable bruising. Henry J. Raymond, his brilliant young assistant, had parted company with him the year before to join James Watson Webb's *Courier and Enquirer,* whence he volleyed vigorously at his old master for taking up the Fourierite fad. The pair entered into a fierce debate in the columns of their respective journals, which ran from November 20, 1846, to May 20, 1847. Each wrote twelve articles, which were reprinted in pamphlet form by Harper and Brothers. Fourierism itself wound up with the debate. Greeley threw up his hands in these terms:

"A serious obstacle to the success of any socialistic experiment must always be confronted. I allude
to the kind of persons who are naturally attracted to
it. Along with many noble and lofty souls, whose
impulses are purely philanthropic, and who are willing
to labor and suffer reproach for any cause that promises to benefit mankind, there throng scores of whom
the world is quite worthy—the conceited, the crotch-
ety, the selfish, the headstrong, the pugnacious, the
unappreciated, the played-out, the idle, and the good-
for-nothing generally; who, finding themselves utterly
out of place and at a discount in the world as it is,
rashly conclude that they are exactly fitted for the
world as it ought to be. These may have failed again
and again, and been protested at every bank to which
they have been presented; yet they are sure to jump
into any new movement as if they had been born expressly to superintend and direct it, though they are
morally certain to ruin whatever they lay their hands
on. Destitute of means, of practical ability, of prudence, tact and common sense, they have such a wealth
of assurance and self-confidence, that they clutch the
responsible positions which the capable and worthy
modestly shrink from; so responsibilities that would
tax the ablest, are mistakenly devolved on the blindest
and least fit. Many an experiment is thus wrecked,
when, engineered by its best members, it might have
succeeded."

The fading hopes were well portrayed by Greeley
in an article in the *People's Journal* in July, 1847, in
which he said:

"As to the Associationists (by their adversaries
termed 'Fourierites'), with whom I am proud to be
numbered, their beginnings are yet too recent to justify me in asking for their history any considerable
space in your columns. Briefly, however, the first
that was heard in this country of Fourier and his views

(beyond a little circle of perhaps a hundred persons in two or three of our large cities, who had picked up some notion of them in France or from French writings), was in 1840, when Albert Brisbane published his first synopsis of Fourier's theory of industrial and household Association. Since then, the subject has been considerably discussed, and several attempts of some sort have been made to actualize Fourier's ideas, generally by men destitute alike of capacity, public confidence, energy and means. In only one instance that I have heard of was the land paid for on which the enterprise commenced; not one of these vaunted 'Fourier Associations' ever had the means of erecting a proper dwelling for so many as three hundred people, even if the land had been given them. Of course, the time for paying the first installment on the mortgage covering their land has generally witnessed the dissipation of their sanguine dreams. Yet there are at least three of these embryo Associations still in existence; and, as each of these is in its third or fourth year, they may be supposed to give some promise of vitality. They are the North American Phalanx, near Leedsville, New Jersey; the Trumbull Phalanx, near Braceville, Ohio; and the Wisconsin Phalanx, Ceresco, Wisconsin. Each of these has a considerable domain nearly wholly paid for, is improving the soil, increasing its annual products, and establishing some branches of manufactures. Each, though far enough from being a perfect Association, is animated with the hope of becoming one, as rapidly as experience, time and means will allow.''

Albert Brisbane's New Jersey experiment in Monmouth County lasted from September, 1843, to September, 1844,—after a fashion—and was called the North American phalanx. Its mill burned in the latter year, and Greeley offered to loan twelve thousand dollars for reconstruction, but the phalanxers disagreed on location, and the division became so irreconcilable that they voted to dissolve. In recent years Arthur Brisbane bought back Allaire, as the barrens became known, and set up a little colony of his own, with a wood-working shop and some farming that did not go very far. It was, however, an interesting touch of atavism. Greeley often visited and addressed the North Americans. They possessed a central mansion that gave fair quarters and excellent meals, with "good, cold water" as the sole beverage.

Referring to his adventures in his *Recollections of a Busy Life,* Greeley appears to have been convinced that successful socialism must have some sort of religious binding: "That there have been—nay, are—decided successes in practical socialism, is undeniable; but they all have that communistic basis which seems to be irrational and calculated to prove fatal. I can easily account for the failure of communism at New Harmony and in several other experiments. I can not so easily account for its successes. The fact stares us in the face that, while hundreds of banks and factories, and thousands of mercantile concerns managed by shrewd, strong men, have gone into bankruptcy and perished, Shaker communities, established more than sixty years ago upon a basis of little property and less worldly wisdom, are living and prosperous to-day. And their experience has been imitated by the German communities at Economy, Zoar, the Society of Ebenezer, et cetera. Theory, however plausible, must respect the facts."

It should be held in mind that Greeley's two passions were politics and economics. His interest in some sort of cooperation was raised by the doleful after-consequences of the panic of 1837, when long idleness bred so much degradation and despair among the poor, and many well-to-do persons fell into poverty. He thought there was something wrong with a social system that permitted this to happen—as there is— and groped for remedies, that proved impracticable for reasons he himself so clearly stated. Experiment interested him, and conservatives looked upon him as fanatic, but he was not too susceptible at any time.

Like many who feel deeply the experiences of family bereavement, Mrs. Greeley was moved to experiment with spiritualism. Her husband brought the celebrated Fox sisters to his house, where some notables attended a seance, among them Jenny Lind, the songstress, then in great vogue under the management of P. T. Barnum. Greeley was puzzled but not ensnared. He took some interest in the performance of "mediums," who suddenly became numerous, until, observing "what I strongly suspected to be a juggle or trick" on the part of one, he acquired a "disrelish" that took him out of further experimenting. The Greeley head was too hard to be fooled by anything except a tale of need, and sometimes it was too hard, even then.

Greeley died before the Beecher-Tilton scandal became public in 1874, or he probably would have had a hand in it. He was intimate with about everybody concerned, close to Beecher and very friendly with Tilton, and his name was mentioned in the testimony. One of the campaign slanders used against him in 1872 was that he consorted with Victoria C. Woodhull and Tennessee Claflin, the two sensational sisters who sprang the publicity. They interested him, as did all other unusual types. Here again he was reviled as associating with "free lovers."

Bessie Turner, the young girl who really started the Beecher-Tilton affair, testified before the Plymouth Church Investigating Committee that Mr. Greeley was at the Tilton house one night when Tilton took her from her bed and carried her to his own on the excuse that he was lonesome. She fled from his touch when fully awake, but did not make noise enough to arouse Mr. Greeley. She also declared that on another evening she saw Susan B. Anthony sitting on Tilton's lap, from which Miss Anthony removed herself hastily at sight of her. This seems incredible. Miss Anthony was then fifty years old, besides being tall and angular. Bessie also declared that Elizabeth Cady Stanton would sit up until two and three A. M. playing chess with Theodore, but she cast no doubts on the character of the game.

CHAPTER VII

HORACE GREELEY approached the great cause of which he was to become the chief evangel by very gradual processes. He had caught his first glimpse of slavery while an apprentice at East Poultney and received a lasting impression. The state of New York had decreed slavery's gradual elimination, but it kept those born in bondage under ownership until they reached the age of twenty-eight. One of the bondmen escaped to Vermont and found work in the village. He was located by his owner, who came to reclaim him. The village rose, and, as the apprentice said, "The result was a speedy disappearance of the chattel, and the return of the master, disconsolate and niggerless, to the place whence he came. Our people hated injustice and oppression, and acted as if they couldn't help it."

The files of the *New Yorker* fail to disclose any decided stand against the institution of slavery per se, but incidents growing out of it were given full space and sometimes severe comment.

The Reverend E. P. Lovejoy, who had removed, under threats, his anti-slavery plant from St. Louis to Alton, Illinois, was murdered by a mob that disapproved of his teachings, and that was reputed to have followed him from Missouri. This stirred Greeley deeply. The tragedy occurred on November 7, 1837. "Mr. Lovejoy's errors," Greeley wrote in the *New Yorker* of November twenty-fifth, "or those of abolitionists generally, have nothing to do in any shape with the turpitude of this outrage. But for the act of inflexibly maintaining the common rights of every citizen, in defiance of the audacious tyranny of the multitude, he may well be deemed a martyr to public liberty. To talk of resisting what is called public opinion as a crime, is to make Socrates an anarchist and Jesus Christ a felon. . . . We loathe and abhor the miserable cast of those that talk of Mr. Lovejoy as guilty of resisting public opinion. Public opinion, forsooth! What right have five hundred or five thousand to interfere with the lawful expression of a freeman's sentiments, because they happen to number more than those who think with him? We spurn the base tyranny—this utter denial of all rights, save as the tender mercies of a mob may vouchsafe them. . . . We ask the South to come forward promptly and put the seal of its emphatic condemnation on this horrible outrage. Let the press speak out and public meetings be called to express the sentiments of the people. This tragedy, if its effect be not thus counteracted, is calculated to give fearful impetus to the cause of abolition. It will immediately add thousands to the unwelcome petitions with which the halls of Congress are now crowded. We ask the South, then, to come forward, to declare that she asks nobody in other states to enter upon an unsolicited defense of her peculiar institutions by means of burglary, robbery, arson and murder. Is there never to be an end to the infernal domination of lynch law and mobocracy in this country? If not, the lover of peace and security from wrong may almost sigh for the soldiers of Louis Philippe, or the sterner despotism of Russia.''

Alas, the South did not ''come forward,'' but the abolitionists did. (It has been estimated that in the preceding year, 1836, there were something like two thousand anti-slavery organizations in the North, numbering nearly two hundred thousand members.)   The number of petitions grew as Greeley had prophesied, and on Wednesday, December 20, a fury broke out in Congress when William Slade, of Vermont, presented a memorial from his state, in line with many memorials in kind, praying that slavery be abolished in the District of Columbia. The *New Yorker* reports Slade as frequently interrupted by Henry A. Wise and John Robertson, of Virginia; Hugh S. Legaré, Robert B. Rhett and John K. Griffen, of South Carolina; James J. McKay, of North Carolina, and David Petriken, of Pennsylvania. Clamorous motions to adjourn were made, with other parliamentary efforts to stop the proceedings of the resolute Vermonter. The Speaker held that Slade had the floor. After more turmoil the House adjourned, the southern delegates gathering in great excitement to decide upon their next step.

In printing the report of all this, Greeley said: ''We learn that the event that we have long anticipated—a disruption of the ties which bind us together as a nation, through the influence of the abolition question—seems on the brink of occurrence.'' This fear proved groundless. The day after the affair John M. Patton, of Virginia, who had presided over the meeting of the southern congressmen, presented this resolution, choking off the right of petition which is especially observed in the Constitution:

"Resolved, that all petitions, memorials and papers touching the abolition of slavery, or the buying, selling or transferring of slaves, in any state, district or territory of the United States, be laid on the table without being debated, printed, read or referred, and that no further action whatever shall be had thereon."

John Quincy Adams alone lifted up his voice in protest. It was drowned in calls of "question" and the resolution was jammed through by a vote of one hundred and twenty-nine to sixty-three. Neither Adams nor Wise voted, Adams because he deemed it unconstitutional, and Wise because he thought it inadequate. Both were right.

Greeley printed, without comment, on May 26, 1838, a full account of the riots in Philadelphia on the sixteenth and seventeenth, produced by resentment against abolitionists following lectures in Pennsylvania Hall, given by William Lloyd Garrison and such fine characters as Lucretia Mott and Mrs. Marie W. Chapman. The first night was simply one of disorder in and about the hall. The next night the mob wrecked and burned it. Another affray followed at Paterson, New Jersey, from the same resentment—an audience being driven from a church, the windows of which were broken by stones. Other wrongs did not get by so easily; for example: "Poor old Abner Kneeland, the apostle clergyman, who turned atheist some ten years ago, has been sentenced to sixty days' imprisonment in the jail in Boston for blasphemy. This is miserable business—we hope the like will never occur again, though we can not see that anybody is blamable but the laws. Let us have done with this contrivance for making this blasphemy popular."

Greeley began in his early writings in the *New Yorker* to discuss the evil of slavery, not at first from the humane but from the economic side. He did not then believe that two such races as white and black could live together in a state of political and social equality, and ventured the assertion that if the people of the South could have "the objections to slavery, drawn from a correct and enlightened political economy, laid before them, they would need no other inducements to impel them to enter upon an immediate and effective course of legislation with a view to the utter extinction of the evil."

Anti-slavery took its aggressive form under the leadership of James G. Birney, a southern man who came north and there fought valiantly for his cause, both against the Garrison non-resistants and the two major parties. Birney ran for president in 1840 as candidate for the Liberty party and received seven thousand one hundred votes. By 1844 his cause had grown measurably, but without support from Garrison, and with no help from Greeley.

On January 23, 1841, the attempt of Thomas Morris, an Ohio Senator, to speak for anti-slavery in Dayton was arrested by a mob, and one man was killed and a number wounded in the affray, which centered about the colored quarter. The Dayton *Transcript* reported that after the event "our streets are promenaded by men in whose countenance are depicted sorrow, consternation, horror and vengeance." Greeley thought the streets in such a case should be "promenaded by men of quite another stamp—in whose countenance might be depicted a determination to hold the protective shield of the law and the Constitution over the citizens of this republic."

Though a believer in the liberty of the slave, Greeley was not attracted to the Liberty party. Nor did he advocate the softer creed of William Lloyd Garrison and Wendell Phillips. These gentlemen, while non-resistants, were secessionists, their followers going squarely on record at the New England convention held at Boston on May 8, 1844, when by a vote of two hundred fifty to forty-four they resolved against further union with slave holders. The Garrisonians all over the country held to the same principle, which then fastened on the Liberty party. General William Birney, in his life of James G. Birney, lays the pinning on of the label to Greeley. He says: "This was in May, 1844. The Whig newspapers from one end of the North to the other immediately charged secession and disunion upon the Liberty party as its logical results, if not its avowed doctrine, and the charge was reiterated by the numerous speakers of that party. The members of the Liberty party defended by denial and by counter-charge that the passage of the secession resolution in the American Anti-Slavery Society was an electioneering trick concocted between Garrison, a former Whig and ardent friend of Henry Clay, and Horace Greeley, the Whig manager, to whom had been assigned the task of defeating the Liberty party and swinging the anti-slavery vote for Clay. They pointed also to the fact that David Lee Child, an intimate friend of Garrison, and editor of the latter's anti-slave organ at New York, had abandoned his post in order to devote his whole time to promoting the success of Henry Clay; and to the further fact that the negroes of Boston and the non-residents generally were ranging themselves in the Whig cohorts. In after years they regarded Greeley's frequent praise of Garrison and the appointments on the *Tribune* staff of several sub-editors of the *Liberator* as so many manifestations by Greeley of his secret obligations to Garrison. Von Holst intimates obscurely his belief in such a bargain when he says of the Garrison heresies: 'These differences and heresies were, so to speak, treated in open market from the very beginning.' "

The victory of James K. Polk for president, carrying seven free and eight slave states, was by a popular majority of only 39,000. Clay was victor in five free and six slave states. Birney had 62,300 votes counted for him, but thought he received many more. In his inquest on the result, Greeley laid Clay's defeat to the abolitionists, who could have swung the slender majority the other way, intimating that they might have saved a friend and so prevented the extension of slavery to Texas. Greeley owned up in due season that the anti-slavery voters were not to blame, and that Clay had failed to win because he had interposed to "derange our order of battle and prevent our fighting it on the anti-slavery ground we had chosen." Yet despite his pro-slavery Greeley clung to Clay.

Greeley's objection to any extension of slavery was the real basis of his support for its abolition. When extension became an acute question, through the pressing of the "proviso" by Congressman David Wilmot, of Pennsylvania, which forbade the introduction of involuntary servitude in any of the possessions acquired from Mexico as the result of the war, Greeley took no sides. "The southern Whigs," he declared, wanted the question "settled in such a manner as shall not humble and exasperate the South; the southern Locofocos [extreme pro-slavery Democrats] wish it so settled as to conduce to the extension of the power and influence of slavery."

The "proviso" did not prevail, but its purpose did. As a Whig, Greeley tried to follow the policy of his party, which in New York, according to the *Tribune,* held "the restriction of slavery within its present limits as one of the cardinal principles of our political faith." This utterance came in 1849. The previous year saw the birth of the Free Soil party, which ran a presidential ticket with no less a person than the Jacksonian Martin Van Buren at its head. Slavery per se was not made an issue by any party, save the despised abolitionists, whose following was much less than the noise they made would indicate.

The election of 1848 resulted in a victory for the Whigs which was again to be circumvented by death. Lewis Cass, Democratic candidate, was defeated by Zachary Taylor by a vote of 1,360,099 to 1,220,544, a plurality of 139,555. Van Buren, on the Free Soil ticket, polled 291,263, and Gerrit Smith, for the Liberty party, about 10,000. Taylor was a sound Unionist who gave no ear to the secession clamor, but unhappily his days were numbered. And Clay came back to meddle fatally in the situation with his policy of compromise and conciliation.

President Zachary Taylor, though born in Virginia and hailing from Louisiana, was firmly against extension. In a speech at Mercer, Pennsylvania, he went on record, saying: "The people of the North need have no apprehension of the further extension of slavery; the necessity of a third party organization on this score would soon be obviated." The Whigs lost some ground in Tennessee and Kentucky in the 1849 elections, because credited with anti-slavery leanings. The problem was fast becoming political and perilous.

California, the new Golconda, organized as a state and adopted a constitution forbidding slavery. This sent the first real thrill of alarm through the oligarchy in control of the South. President Taylor foresaw the storm and sent a soothing message to Congress, requesting it not to borrow trouble, and to "abstain from the introduction of those exciting topics of sectional character which have hitherto produced painful apprehensions in the public mind." The President now lost the support of Henry Clay, and the "exciting" topics intruded forcefully. Clay introduced a series of compromises dealing with the question, which included the admission of California as a free state. The resulting dissatisfaction was in the North. Samuel Bowles asserted in the Springfield *Republican*: "Rather than consent voluntarily to the extension of the slave institution to one foot of free territory—rather than surrender their principles—they would submit to have the Union severed. This, we believe, is the true feeling of the North."

It certainly became that of Horace Greeley and many others. On February 20, 1850, the *Tribune* said to the South: "Let the Union be a thousand times shivered rather than we should aid you to plant slavery on free soil." Daniel Webster, having supported the Clay compromises, was cast aside by the *Tribune,* with a belief that he could not command the Whig vote in a single northern state. Sectionalism thus took solid form.

Of the election of Taylor, Greeley wrote: "I was never introduced and never wrote to him; and, while I ultimately supported and voted for him, I did not hurry myself to secure his election. In fact, that of 1848 was my easiest and least anxious presidential canvass since 1824. When a resolve opposing the Wilmot Proviso was laid on the table that nominated him, I felt that my zeal, my enthusiasm for the Whig cause was also laid there."

Greeley, as a frank worshiper of Henry Clay, could not admit to his affections the inferior men who crowded him out of the presidency. He regarded the election of Taylor as a triumph of personality and not of party principles, though he had no reason to find fault with the President's course during his short tenure of office.

To the misfortune of the country, President Taylor, taken ill on July 4, 1850, died on the ninth. Millard Fillmore became president. Seward had wielded a guiding influence with Taylor; he had none with Fillmore. Precisely as John Tyler restored the régime of Jackson when William Henry Harrison died, so Millard Fillmore disappointed the progressive element in his party by his course toward slavery, signing, as he did, the Compromise of 1850, and its rider, the Fugitive Slave Law.

Seward's dictum, "There is a higher law than the Constitution," became almost a watchword in the North. He then, March 11, 1850, though a Whig

senator, definitely parted company with Webster and
Clay, the latter declaring he, Seward, had lost the respect of almost all men.

The new legislation went into effect in September,
1850. At the moment it unquestionably brought a distinct sense of relief. Franklin Pierce, who was yet to
become president, C. L. Vallandigham, Rufus Choate
and Benjamin R. Curtis endorsed it. A meeting held
in Faneuil Hall, Boston, declared that it "ought to be
carried out in good faith," something that was never
done. In New York ten thousand names were secured
to a call for its endorsement at a public meeting, which
moved Greeley to express in the *Tribune* his wonder
that "considering the threats held out of publishing
the names of all traders who refused to sign, as men
to be avoided by southern purchasers in our market,
it is rather surprising that they were not able to sweep
clean the mercantile streets."

Clay and Webster were both tottering toward their
graves. New men stood up in the Senate opposed to
slavery, sent there by Whig votes in the North—William H. Seward, of New York; Charles Sumner, of
Massachusetts; Salmon P. Chase and Benjamin F.
Wade, of Ohio, and John P. Hale, of New Hampshire.
The one Democrat who for years had stood alone
against extension, Thomas H. Benton, of Missouri, had
been shut out of the Senate, after thirty years of noble
service, because of his anti-slavery stand. The new-
comers were all in the prime of life and made great
names for themselves.

The Whigs did not name Fillmore in 1852. Seward
controlled the convention, which gave the nomination
to Major-General Winfield Scott, Commander-in-Chief

of the Army and conqueror of Mexico. The Democrats
named Franklin Pierce, of New Hampshire, and won.
It looked as though the country would quiet down and
remain whole under Democratic auspices. Clay died
June 29, 1852, and Webster's death followed on October twenty-fourth. Thus neither lived to see the finish
of their party on election day.

In New York state Gerrit Smith, with whom Greeley was afterward so closely associated, was elected to
Congress from the Rochester district as an Independent.

Of Smith, Greeley wrote: "We are heartily glad
that Mr. Smith is going to Washington. He is an
honest, brave, kind-hearted Christian philanthropist,
whose religion is not put aside with his Sunday cloak,
but lasts him clear through the week. We think him
very wrong in some of his notions of political economy,
and quite mistaken in his ideas that the Constitution
is inimical to slavery, and that injustice can not be
legalized; but we heartily wish more such great, pure,
loving souls could find their way into Congress. He
will find his seat anything but comfortable, but his
presence there will do good and the country will know
him better and esteem him more highly than it has yet
done."

Excitement spread and intensified with respect to
the Fugitive Slave Law. One of its curious phases
was that the strongest supporters of slavery were opposed to the use of United States forces to enforce the
act. President Fillmore made the announcement that
he proposed to use the marines to protect the process
of rendering the escaped chattel to his owners. The
need of this action was explained by Senator John

Davis, of Massachusetts, as due to the fact that the sentiment of the state was solidly against enforcement, and the local authorities would give the law no support. "If that be so," said Senator Jefferson Davis, of Mississippi, "the law is dead in that state. Wherever mobs can rule, and law is silenced beneath tumult, this is a wholly impracticable government. It was not organized as one of force. Its strength is moral, and moral only. I for one will never give my vote to extend a single arm of the Federal power for the coercion of Massachusetts."

Ominous as was the resistance to the Fugitive Slave Law in the North, the real trouble that was to precede disunion did not develop until Stephen A. Douglas, Senator from Illinois, secured the repeal of the Compromise of 1850 and the passage of the Kansas-Nebraska Bill, leaving the voters of the new states to decide whether or not they would be slave or free. Into this fight Horace Greeley threw himself with fervor, and from it dates his real adoption of the cause of freedom against that of bondage. His pen breathed fire and he became the center of hostile opinion in the South. Men like Henry A. Wise, of Virginia, read him out of all forms of society, and the pro-slavery North manifested a like opinion. Yet the cause grew. Both sides took to bloodshed in Kansas to determine which set of "squatters" should be sovereign under the Douglas law, Greeley, of course, backing the swarm sent from New England, though he was of the opinion that any collision in Kansas that resulted in bloodshed could "hardly fail to shake the Union to the center." It came quickly enough; and the Sharp's rifles used by the Free Soilers were sent by Greeley and his militant friends—Gerrit Smith, Frederick Law Olmstead, Eli Thayer and Henry Ward Beecher. They came via Topeka in shoe boxes, and under that label. "Beecher Bibles" they were grimly named. Not much blood was spilled, but John Brown tasted it and liked the flavor. He was to be well refreshed with it. Plus the rifles, Greeley, Charles King, David Dudley Field and other sympathizing New Yorkers contributed a six-pound cannon to the cause.

Greeley was not hopeful in the early days of the Kansas controversy. "We believe," he said in the *Tribune* of December 7, 1854, "that there are at this hour four chances that Kansas will be a slave state to one that she will be free."

The Free Soil platform of 1855 excepted free negroes from citizenship. "Why free blacks should be excluded," observed Greeley, "is difficult to understand; but if slavery can be kept out by a compromise of that sort, we shall not complain. An error of this character may be corrected; but let slavery obtain a foothold, then it is not so easily removed."

He was harsh toward the Missourians who raided Lawrence in 1856. They were "discomfited and lop-eared invaders." Indeed, his language was never tender. Writing from Washington to the *Tribune* under date of March 6, 1856, he observed: "The free state men from Kansas now in this city have letters from various points in that embryo state down to the eighteenth and nineteenth ult. Their general tone implies apprehension that a bloody collision is imminent. The Border Ruffians have been raised entirely off their feet by Pierce's extraordinary messages, which they regard as a complete enforcement of all their diabolical work. It is believed by our friends that the organization will be made the pretext for a raid, and a possible butchery at the hands of the slavery party."

The *Tribune* was really more violent on the Kansas question than Greeley, who thus instructed Charles A. Dana to temper the zeal of the shop: "Do not let your folks write more savagely on the Kansas question than I do. I am fiery enough."

The thunder-clap that was to precede the storm came on October 17, 1859, when John Brown and his men raided Harper's Ferry, tragically, with the object of raising an insurrection among the slaves of the South. The result was a harsh reaction against Greeley, whose militant support of that zealot in the Kansas affair now counted doubly against him. *Harper's Weekly*, owned by three sterling Methodists, John, James and Wesley Harper, lent itself to the clamor. The *Weekly* published a cartoon of Greeley, cringing before a hangman, and pleading against the use of the rope, although cringing was not in his line. The *Weekly* also remarked: "It is urged that, after all, John Brown only carried into practical effect the teachings of the New York *Tribune* and other abolitionist organs," intimating there was no sense in hanging Brown if Greeley, et al., escaped!

Strenuous efforts were made to link Greeley with the enterprise. It would have gone ill with him to have ventured below Mason and Dixon's line. The effects of the raiders were diligently searched for evidence that would link up with Brown men like Charles Sumner, Henry Wilson, Henry Ward Beecher and Greeley. Gerrit Smith furnished evidence of prac-

THE MODERN ÆSOP.

TRUMPETER GRE-L-Y. "What! hang me? I protest that I neither have killed, nor can kill any man, as I bear no arms but my trumpet, which I sound as occasion serves."

VIRGINIAN. "For that reason are we determined not to spare you; for though you never fight yourself, yet, with that wicked instrument of yours, you stir up animosity between other people, and so are the occasion of much bloodshed   [See Æsop, Fable 158.

(*From Harper's Weekly, Dec. 3, 1859*)

tical support in a note forwarding a check for two hundred dollars, which had gone toward outfitting and sustaining the expedition. It was also revealed that Horace Greeley & Co. had sent a check to John Henry Kagi for work as a correspondent. Kagi was born Kagy, and members of his family survive in Virginia and Ohio. Other men close to Brown and having a hand in the affair were James Redpath and Richard J. Hinton, both of whom were contributors to the *Tribune* and followers of Brown in Kansas. Hinton told once of being a member of the party that went out from Topeka to receive the first shipment of "Beecher Bibles," toward the purchase of which Greeley had contributed. The South fervently believed that Greeley backed Brown in his raid. To the contrary, he knew nothing about it, though quite cognizant of the fact that Brown was plotting against the slave powers. No man was responsible. The hour had struck.

Hinton, who with Redpath had been with Brown at the farm-house where the party rendezvoused, was sent off on an errand that kept him out of the fight. He thought he would like to report the trial for the *Tribune* and made a personal appeal to the editor for the assignment.

"You d—d fool!" was the response. "Do you want to get yourself hanged?" So Henry S. Olcott, afterward the Hierophant of Theosophy, succeeding Madame Blavatsky, covered the case.

In the *Tribune* of October 24, 1859, Greeley stated that he and others had given seven hundred dollars to John Brown's cause, through an adventurer named Hugh Forbes who seems to have kept the money.

Of the Harper's Ferry raid Greeley remarked that

it was "the work of madness," adding, "but John Brown has so often looked death in the face that what seems madness to others doubtless wore a different aspect to him."

Of the effect of the raid he judged accurately. "It will drive the slave power to new outrages," he wrote Schuyler Colfax, overlooking the somewhat substantial provocation. "It passes on the 'irrepressible conflict,' and I think the end of slavery in Virginia, and the Union, is ten years nearer than it seemed a few weeks ago." He was half a decade slow in his prophecy.

It must be said in common justice that William H. Seward has never received the full meed of credit for his great services in the cause of freedom. He has been overshadowed by Greeley and Abraham Lincoln. Yet while both these worthies were feeling their way in journalism and politics toward the stand each finally took (Lincoln last of all), Mr. Seward had planted his feet firmly in favor of a cause which he never forsook, and in the interest of which he never wavered. Seward first comes into bold relief while governor of New York in July, 1839, when Peter Johnson, Edward Smith and Isaac Gansey of the schooner *Robert Centre* were accused of carrying away one Isaac, a slave owned by John G. Colley, from Norfolk, Virginia, to freedom in New York. Seward declined to deliver the men under a requisition from Virginia which charged them with "feloniously stealing" Isaac. David Campbell, Governor of Virginia, concluded his request: "And I understand stealing to be recognized as a crime by all laws, human and divine."

To which Seward replied: "It is freely to be admitted that the argument would be at an end if it were as clear that one human being may be the property of another, as it is that stealing is a crime."

Greeley left "the judgment in the premises to be pronounced by others," though rather sustaining the belief that a state that did not tolerate slavery could hardly be expected to accept the demands of one that did. Nor could he find any precedent by which he would consider the Governor "bound" in "a question so vitally affecting the rights and liberties, perhaps even the lives entrusted to his guardianship and protection." This opinion was published February 6, 1840.

There was no supposing about Seward's stand on slavery. Here are his words in discussing the bloody clashes in Kansas: "Shall I tell you what this collision means? They who think it accidental, unnecessary, the work of interested or fanatical agitators, and therefore ephemeral, mistake the case altogether. It is an irrepressible conflict between opposing and enduring forces; and it means that the United States must and will, sooner or later, become either entirely a slaveholding nation or a free nation. It is the failure to apprehend this great truth that induces so many unsuccessful attempts at final compromise between the slave and the free states; and it is the existence of this great fact that renders all such pretended compromises when made, vain and ephemeral."

For this Seward became at once the target of unseemly attacks, north and south. Yet he had told the truth as it never had been expressed before.

Now while Seward was squarely against slavery, and had made its existence an issue, Lincoln was not and had not been. The celebrated Cooper Union speech of February 17, 1860, did not attack slavery. It merely defended the right of the territories to be free as the compromises of both 1820 and 1850 had provided: "Let all who believe that our fathers who framed the government under which we live, understood the question just as well, and even better, than we do now, speak as they spoke and act as they acted upon it." It also averred that no Republican "designedly" aided or encouraged John Brown's raid on Harper's Ferry—which rather begged the question. The whole tone of the address was more than remote from Seward's bold assertion that slavery was "an irrepressible conflict between opposing and enduring forces."

Abraham Lincoln became the candidate of the Republican party, which earned the fame of freeing the slaves, without having had the slightest intention of doing so at the start. The force that did it was the one headed by Horace Greeley who so irritated the South that it threw itself upon the sword. The North, per se, would never have done anything.

Greeley's opinion of the Cooper Union speech was that "simply as an effort to convince the largest possible number of people that they ought to be on the speaker's side it was unsurpassed."

CHAPTER VIII

HORACE GREELEY did not bring the Republican party into being, but the things he so ardently advocated did. He was, or thought he was, a firm Whig, and believed the party safe, though it had met no issues and had been deeply honeycombed by Free Soilers, Know-Nothings and anti-slavery agitators. Webster and Clay had taken it with them to the tomb, though Greeley seems, with all his political prescience, to have been unaware of the fact. Neither abolitionists, Know-Nothings nor Free Soilers rallied many votes. Greeley believed the party could be pulled together, though all the while doing his best to pull it apart. As a party it refused to take up the burning issue as its own, and so made way for a successor.

Major-General Winfield Scott, Commander-in-Chief of the Army and conqueror of Mexico, had been nominated for president in 1852 on the theory that a "hero" could win as Zachary Taylor did. This "hero" wrote some silly letters and said some silly things, and besides this, the Whigs endorsed the Fugitive Slave Law. The result was the election of Franklin Pierce, and the passing of Whig potency.

The Kansas-Nebraska Bill came into being and the question of slavery extension turned acute. Feeling the need of a new party, Alvan E. Bovay, born in

155

Adams, Jefferson County, New York, who had become
a lawyer in Ripon, Wisconsin, called a meeting in the
Congregational Church in that place on February 28,
1854, at which it was resolved that, if the Senate
passed the pending Kansas-Nebraska Bill, those present, about fifty in number, would abandon the old
parties and set up a new one, to be called the Republican. The bill was passed on March third. Bovay
brought his idea to New York and laid it before
Greeley, who was not receptive. He refused to believe
the Whigs could be discarded. When Greeley idly
asked Bovay what he would call his new party he
replied: "Republican." This was as far as the suggestion went for the moment.

Greeley wrote Bovay, March 7, 1854: "I faintly
hope the time has come which Daniel Webster predicted when he said, 'I think there will be a North!'
But I am a beaten, broken-down, used-up politician,
and have the soreness of many defeats in my bones.
However, I am ready to follow any lead that promises
to hasten the day of northern emancipation. Your
plan is all right if the people are ripe for it. I fear
they, too, generally wish (with John Mitchell) that
they had a good plantation and negroes in Alabama—
or even Kansas. However, we will try and do what
we can. But remember that editors can only follow
where the people's heart is already prepared to go
with them. They can direct and animate a healthy
public indignation, but not create a soul beneath the
ribs of death." There was not much enthusiasm in
this.

"I was an intimate friend of Horace Greeley,"
said Bovay in after years, "and he would always

listen to me on political matters. He did not always assent to my propositions, but in the end he did to most of them, and he did to this one after a good deal of nagging. It was not one letter that I wrote him, but many, before he displayed the Republican flag in the *Tribune's* columns. I was more solicitous about the name than about the organization. My friend Greeley valued names too lightly. I wanted the name to appear early editorially in the *Tribune* and it did.''

Bovay is entitled to the name and initiative, but the party first took form at the instance of A. N. Cole, of Wellsville, in Allegany County, New York, editor of the Genesee Valley *Free Press,* with the aid of a free-soil Democrat, General James S. Wadsworth, afterward killed at the battle of the Wilderness. The paper was strong for the non-extension and repression of slavery. Cole had become intimate with Greeley, Charles Sumner, William H. Seward, Salmon P. Chase, Gerrit Smith and like leaders of the cause, who found themselves out of consonance with both Whig and Democratic parties. Cole called a ''convention,'' as he termed it, for May 18, 1854, at Friendship, New York, a center of liberal feeling. His plan was to construct there the foundation of a national party, having which in mind he wrote to Greeley and asked him for a name. ''Call it Republican,'' was the prompt response, ''no prefix, no suffix, but plain Republican.'' June 24, 1854, Greeley blazoned ''Republican'' for the first time in an editorial, ''Party Names and Public Duty,'' in the *Tribune.*

Few came to the convention, so few that Cole was turning away from the unlit hall when he fell in with a handful of sympathizers. They formally organized, adopted the name Republican, and named a committee to call a state convention. This was set for October 15, 1584, at Angelica, where a county ticket was named that won.

It should be here interpolated that the Know-Nothing party, as it was termed, or the "American," as it called itself, had considerable strength in 1854. It was a secret organization on the lines of the several modern Ku Klux Klans, with a code of grips, signs and passwords, and was fully one hundred per cent. American, seeking to shut out foreigners from the franchise, with special hostility to the Catholic Church. It was lying around loose, politically speaking. So were the Free-Soilers, abolitionists, and a lively lot of prohibitionists. The latter were especially active in New York, where Myron H. Clark, a State Senator from Canandaigua, had become leader. He was an anti-slavery man, also.

These elements variously convened, and four kinds of "parties" agreed upon Clark as their candidate for governor. An anti-Nebraska convention was held at Saratoga in mid-August, and after much resolving, Greeley being among those present, adjourned until September twenty-sixth, when it joined the Clark procession. Greeley was a member of the Saratoga Committee on Resolutions, along with his former associate, Henry J. Raymond, editor of the rival New York *Times*. Previous to the convention, according to Thurlow Weed: "Mr. Greeley called upon me at the Astor House and asked if I did not think that the time and the circumstances were favorable to his nomination for governor. I replied that I did not think the time and circumstances were favorable to his election, if nominated, but that my friends had lost control of the [Whig] state convention. This answer perplexed him, but a few words made it clear. Admitting that he had brought the people up to the point of accepting a temperance candidate for governor, I remarked that another aspirant had 'stolen his thunder.' In other words, while he had shaken the temperance branch, Myron H. Clark would catch the bird. . . . I informed Mr. Greeley that Know-Nothing or 'Choctaw' Lodges had been secretly organized throughout the state, by means of which many delegates for Mr. Clark had been secured. Mr. Greeley saw that the 'slate' had been broken, and cheerfully relinquished the idea of being nominated. But a few days afterward Mr. Greeley came to Albany and said in an abrupt, but not unfriendly way, 'Is there any objection to my running for lieutenant-governor?' . . . After a little more conversation Mr. Greeley became satisfied that a nomination for lieutenant-governor was not desirable and left in good spirits.''

Weed was a shrewd and able man, who filled his pockets by the sale of law and the influence of his Albany *Evening Journal*. Whatever his motive, honest or corrupt, for keeping Greeley off the ticket, politically it was sound. Public office was no place for a man who would not submit to control, either by himself or a boss. Weed may have killed off Greeley's ambitions in all kindness, and the chances are that he did. He knew a great editor would descend a long way when he assumed so small a place as that of lieutenant-governor. He was correct, too, about the way Clark had acquired delegates.

So, instead of Greeley, his young former assistant,
Henry J. Raymond, was placed on the tail of the ticket.
That Greeley felt he had been lightly set aside by
Weed and Seward was soon to become apparent.
Clark and Raymond were elected and the Republican
party came into being. So did prohibition—for a six
months' trial in New York state.

On Saturday, November 11, 1854, super-smarting
under a sense that he had long been used without return by his associates, Greeley dissolved the famous
"firm" of Seward, Weed and Greeley in a letter
which reached the senior partner the next day. It
read:

"New York, Saturday eve. November 11, 1854.
"The Election is over, and its results sufficiently
ascertained. It seems to me a fitting time to announce
to you the dissolution of the political firm of Seward,
Weed and Greeley, by the withdrawal of the junior
partner—said withdrawal to take effect on the morning after the first Tuesday in February next. And,
as it may seem a great presumption in me to assume
that any such firm exists, especially since the public
was advised, rather more than a year ago, by an editorial rescript in the *Evening Journal,* formally reading me out of the Whig party, that I was esteemed no
longer either useful or ornamental in the concern, you
will, I am sure, indulge me in some reminiscences
which seem to befit the occasion.

"I was a poor young printer, and editor of a Literary Journal—a very active and bitter Whig in a small
way, but not seeking to be known out of my own Ward
Committee—when, after the great political revulsion
of 1837, I was one day called to the City Hotel, where
two strangers introduced themselves as Thurlow
Weed and Lewis Benedict, of Albany. They told me
that a cheap campaign paper of a peculiar stamp at

Albany had been resolved on, and that I had been selected to edit it. The announcement might well be
deemed flattering by one who had never even sought
the notice of the great, and who was not known as a
partisan writer, and I eagerly embraced their propo-
sals. They asked me to fix my salary for the year; I
named one thousand dollars, which they agreed to; and
I did the work required to the best of my ability. It
was work that made no figure and created no sensation; but I loved it and did it well. When it was done,
you were governor, dispensing offices worth three
thousand dollars to twenty thousand dollars per year
to your friends and compatriots, and I returned to my
garret and my crust, and my desperate battle with
pecuniary obligations heaped upon me by bad partners
in business and the disastrous events of 1837. I believe it did not then occur to me that some of these
abundant places might have been offered to me without injustice; I now think it should have occurred to
you. If it did occur to me, I was not the man to ask
you for it; I think that should not have been necessary.
I only remember that no friend at Albany inquired as
to my pecuniary circumstances; that your friend (but
not mine), Robert C. Wetmore, was one of the chief
dispensers of your patronage here; and that such devoted compatriots as A. H. Wells and John Hooks
were lifted by you out of pauperism into independence,
as I am glad I was not; and yet an inquiry from you
as to my needs and means at that time would have
been timely, and held ever in grateful remembrance.

"In the Harrison campaign of 1840, I was again
designated to edit a campaign paper. I published it
as well, and ought to have made something by it, in
spite of its extremely low price; my extreme poverty
was the main reason why I did not. It compelled me
to hire press-work, mailing, etc., done by the job, and
high charges for extra work nearly ate me up. At
the close, I was still without property and in debt, but
this paper had rather improved my position.

"Now came the great scramble of the swell mob of coon minstrels and cider-suckers at Washington—I not being counted in. Several regiments of them went on from this city; but no one of the whole crowd—though I say it who should not—had done so much toward General Harrison's nomination and election as yours respectfully. I asked nothing, expected nothing; but you, Governor Seward, ought to have asked that I be postmaster of New York. Your asking would have been in vain; but it would have been an act of grace neither wasted nor undeserved.

"I soon after started the *Tribune,* because I was urged to do so by certain of your friends, and because such a paper was needed here. I was promised certain pecuniary aid in so doing; it might have been given me without cost or risk to any one. All I ever had was a loan by piecemeal of one thousand dollars, from James Coggeshall. God bless his honored memory! I did not ask for this, and I think it is the one sole case in which I ever received a pecuniary favor from a political associate. I am very thankful that he did not die till it was fully repaid.

"And let me here honor one grateful recollection. When the Whig party under your rule had offices to give, my name was never thought of; but when, in 1842-43, we were hopelessly out of power, I was honored with the nomination for state printer. When we came again to have a state printer to elect as well as nominate, the place went to Weed, as it ought. Yet it was worth something to know that there was once a time when it was not deemed too great a sacrifice to recognize me as belonging to your household. If a new office had not since been erected on purpose to give its valuable patronage to H. J. Raymond, and enable St. John to show forth his *Times,* as the organ of the Whig State Administration, I should have been still more grateful.

"In 1848 your star again rose, and my warmest hopes were realized in your election to the Senate.

I was no longer needy, and had no more claim than desire to be recognized by General Taylor. I think I had some claim to forbearance from you. What I received thereupon was a most humiliating lecture in the shape of a decision in the libel case of Redfield and Pringle, and an obligation to publish it in my own and the other journal of our supposed firm. I thought, and still think, this lecture needlessly cruel and mortifying. The plaintiffs, after using my columns to the extent of their needs or desires, stopped writing and called on me for the name of their assailant. I proffered it to them—a thoroughly responsible name. They refused to accept it, unless it should prove to be one of the four or five first men in Batavia!—when they had known from the first who it was, and that it was neither of them. They would not accept that which they had demanded; they sued me instead for money, and money you were at liberty to give to them to their heart's content. I do not think you were at liberty to humiliate me in the eyes of my own and your public as you did. I think you exalted your own judicial sternness and fearlessness unduly at my expense. I think you had a better occasion for the display of these qualities when Webb threw himself entirely upon you for a pardon which he had done all a man could do to demerit. (His paper is paying you for it now.)

"I have publicly set forth my view of your and our duty with respect to Fusion, Nebraska, and party designations. I will not repeat any of that. I have referred also to Weed's reading me out of the Whig party—my crime being, in this as in some other things, that of doing to-day what more politic persons will not be ready to do till to-morrow.

"Let me speak of the late canvass. I was once sent to Congress for ninety days, merely to enable Jim Brooks to secure a seat therein for four years. I think I never hinted to any human being that I would have liked to be put forward for any place. But James

W. White (you hardly know how true and good a man
he is) started my name for Congress, and Brooks'
packed delegation thought I could help him through;
so I was put on behind him. But this last spring, after
the Nebraska question had created a new state of
things at the North, one or two personal friends, of
no political consideration, suggested my name as a
candidate for governor, and I did not discourage them.
Soon, the persons who were afterward mainly instru-
mental in nominating Clark came about me, and asked
if I could secure the Know-Nothing vote. I told them
I neither could nor would touch it; on the contrary,
I loathed and repelled it. Thereupon they turned
upon Clark.

"I said nothing, did nothing. A hundred people
asked me who should be run for governor. I sometimes indicated Patterson; I never hinted at my own
name. But by-and-by Weed came down, and called
me to him, to tell me why he could not support me for
governor. (I had never asked nor counted on his
support.)

"I am sure Weed did not mean to humiliate me;
but he did it. The upshot of his discourse (very cau-
tiously stated) was this. If I were a candidate for governor, I should beat not myself only, but you. Perhaps
that was true. But as I had in no manner solicited
his or your support, I thought this might have been
said to my friends rather than to me. I suspect
it is true that I could not have been elected governor
as a Whig. But had he and you been favorable, there
would have been a party in the state ere this which
could and would have elected me to any post, without
injuring itself or endangering your reelection.

"It was in vain that I urged that I had in no manner
asked a nomination. At length I was nettled by his
language—well intended, but very cutting as addressed by him to me—to say, in substance, 'Well,
then, make Patterson governor, and try my name for
lieutenant. To lose this place is a matter of no im-

portance; and we can see whether I am really so odious.'

"I should have hated to serve as lieutenant-governor, but I should have gloried in running for the post. I want to have my enemies all upon me at once; I am tired of fighting them piecemeal. And, though I should have been beaten in the canvass, I know that my running would have helped the ticket, and helped my paper.

"It was thought best to let the matter take another course. No other name could have been put on the ticket so bitterly humbling to me as that which was selected. The nomination was given to Raymond; the fight left to me. And, Governor Seward, I have made it, though it be conceited in me to say so. What little fight there has been, I have stirred up. Even Weed has not been (I speak of his paper) hearty in this contest, while the journal of the Whig Lieutenant-Governor has taken care of its own interests, and let the canvass take care of itself, as it early declared it would do. That journal has (because of its milk-and-water course) some twenty thousand subscribers in this city and its suburbs, and of these twenty thousand, I venture to say more voted for Ullmann and Scroggs, than for Clark and Raymond; the *Tribune* (also because of its character) has but eight thousand subscribers within the same radius, and I venture to say that of its habitual readers, nine-tenths voted for Clark and Raymond—very few for Ullmann and Scroggs. I had to bear the brunt of the contest, and take a terrible responsibility in order to prevent the Whigs uniting upon James W. Barker, to defeat Fernando Wood. Had Barker been elected here, neither you nor I could walk these streets without being hooted, and Know-Nothingism would have swept like a prairie fire. I stopped Barker's election at the cost of incurring the deadliest enmity of the defeated gang; and I have been rebuked for it by the Lieutenant-Governor's paper. At the critical moment, he came out against

John Wheeler, in favor of Charles H. Marshall (who would have been your deadliest enemy in the House), and even your Colonel-General's paper, which was even with me insisting that Wheeler should be returned, wheeled about, at the last moment, and went in for Marshall—the *Tribune* alone clinging to Wheeler to the last. I rejoice that they who turned so suddenly were not able to turn all their readers.

"Governor Seward, I know that some of your most cherished friends think me a great obstacle to your advancement—that John Schoolcraft, for one, insists that you and Weed should not be identified with me. I trust, after a time, you will not be. I trust I shall never be found in opposition to you; I have no further wish than to glide out of the newspaper world as quietly and as speedily as possible, join my family in Europe, and if possible stay there quite a time—long enough to cool my fevered brain and renovate my overtasked energies. All I ask is that we shall be counted even on the morning after the first Tuesday in February, as aforesaid, and that I may thereafter take such course as seems best, without reference to the past.

"You have done me acts of kindness in the line of your profession; let me close with the assurance that these will ever be gratefully remembered by

"Yours,

"HORACE GREELEY.

Honorable W. H. Seward—Present."

Although this letter echoed the cry of a seared soul, its recipient seemed to think all the writer needed was a little soothing. Seward kept the text of the note to himself, but wrote to Weed, on November twelfth, from Auburn: "To-day I have a long letter from him [Greeley], full of sharp pricking thorns. I judge, as we might indeed well know, from his, at the bottom, nobleness of disposition, that he has no idea

William H Seward

of saying or doing anything wrong or unkind; but it is bad to see him so unhappy. Will there be a vacancy in the Board of Regents this winter? Could one be made at the close of the session? Could he have it? Raymond's nomination and election are hard for him to bear.''

The two discarded partners decided not to take the separation seriously. The following Saturday they took boat from Albany, and arriving in New York, agreed to try to catch Greeley at church. They accordingly went to the Universalist edifice, on Broadway, near Spring Street, where Doctor Chapin preached, and were ushered into Greeley's pew. He did not attend service that day, and after being refreshed by a good sermon, the pair went down to the *Tribune* office. They were passed into the editor's room through another, where two young assistants, Matt Taylor and William Herries, were at work. Pausing at the door they asked if Mr. Greeley was in. Taylor knew them and informed Greeley of their presence. ''Show them in,'' he squeaked.

The pair disappeared within the sanctum and made a long stay. Now and then Greeley's high-pitched voice would pierce the keyhole, accompanied by deprecating murmurs from his visitors. Finally they came out looking much discomfited, went down-stairs and out. Presently Greeley appeared, looking unusually placid and amiable.

''Mr. Seward and Mr. Weed did not look very comfortable,'' ventured Taylor. ''You must have had a rather warm time.''

''Yes,'' said Greeley; ''we were discussing future rewards and punishments.''

From that time on he traveled for the most part alone, and never again made a hard and fast alliance. The letter did not get into print until 1860, under circumstances which will appear in due order. If Weed and Seward failed in this mission, they were at least refreshed by Doctor Chapin's sermon. "No preacher ever so impressed me," was Seward's verdict.

Greeley long after, but during Weed's lifetime, summed him up in these terms:

"Mr. Thurlow Weed was of coarser mold and fiber—tall, robust, dark-featured, shrewd, resolute, and not over-scrupulous—keen-sighted, though not far-seeing. Writing slowly and with difficulty, he was for twenty years the most sententious and pungent writer of editorial paragraphs on the American press.

"In pecuniary matters, he was generous to a fault while poor; he is said to be less so since he became rich; but I am no longer in a position to know. I can not doubt, however, that if he had never seen Wall Street or Washington, had never heard of the Stock Board, or had lived in some yet undiscovered country, where legislation is never bought and sold, his life would have been more blameless, useful and happy."

Weed resented Greeley's frequent references to his use of money in politics, remarking on one occasion that for forty years he had been the collector of campaign funds by methods with which Mr. Greeley was quite familiar, and with which he never found fault while they were in partnership.

On November 9, 1854, two days before sending the letter to Seward, Greeley had written, apropos of the foolish naming of the successful Clark, who held no future: "The man who should have impelled and guided the general uprising of the free states is W. H. Seward,'' but it is not clear whether he meant this as a compliment or a reproach.

Although Seward continued in public life ten years longer, Greeley's last meeting with him was in 1859, ''when he came one evening to my seat in Doctor Chapin's church—as he had repeatedly done during former visits to our city.'' Seward had just returned from a trip to Europe and the Holy Land concerning which Greeley quoted J. Ross Browne's remark that he had found but one man doing anything in Syria, and he was falling off a house.

By one of those amazing tipovers common in American politics, the Democrats lost control of the House of Representatives in the election of 1854. When the Thirty-fourth Congress got together it hardly knew what it was, though one thing was plain. There were not enough Democrats among those present to organize it when it met on December 3, 1855. The hold-over Senate held forty-three members of the party, against seventeen of other brands, who decided to call themselves Republicans. In the House there were eighty-three Democrats only, to whom were opposed one hundred and eight who elected to take on the title of Republican, and forty-three classed as third party. Most of the members calling themselves Republican and some anti-Nebraskans settled on Nathaniel P. Banks, of Massachusetts, as their candidate for speaker, when a deadlock set in that lasted until February 2, 1856.

To get Greeley out of the *Tribune* office Dana and McElrath urged him to go to Washington and report in person the political phenomena there developing. This he rather reluctantly did, with evil consequences to his person. The early vote on the speakership had given Banks one hundred and seven, the highest cast, but not a majority. The other mixed votes were divided between Lewis D. Campbell, of Ohio, and William Pennington, of New Jersey, who came to consider himself a Republican. Banks' vote stood at one hundred and seven until January thirty-first, when Albert C. Rust, of Arkansas, a Democrat, moved that the three candidates named and James D. Richardson, of Tennessee, the Democratic nominee for speaker, withdraw in the interest of perfecting the organization of the House and getting down to business. Neither Banks nor Richardson would comply, and after being discussed for a couple of days, the resolution was tabled. Under his initials, Greeley had written some very caustic comments on what would appear to have been a very sane suggestion, calling it a "discreditable and humiliating proposition" designed to ensnare Banks and take him out of the race.

When the *Tribune,* containing strictures, reached Washington, Rust was very angry and waylaying Greeley on the street, demanded.

"Is your name Greeley?"

"It is," was the reply.

"Are you a non-combatant?" was the next query.

"That is according to circumstances," responded the editor, all unaware as to the identity or purpose of his accoster, a very powerful and passionate man six feet tall and weighing upward of two hundred pounds.

Greeley carried his hands in his deep overcoat pockets and had no thought of what was to follow. Rust struck him several heavy blows on the head, which he was unable to fend off. Dazed, he fell against a fence, and on recovering asked the bystanders: "Who is this man?"

The big Congressman turned away with an oath. "You'll know me soon enough," he said as he walked on.

Two friends of Greeley now came up and escorted the bewildered man toward his hotel, the National, near which they again encountered Rust, surrounded by a curious and admiring crowd.

He greeted Greeley with, "You know me now."

"Yes," replied the editor quietly, "you are Rust, of Arkansas."

The Congressman then observed contemptuously that if Greeley were a combatant he would show him more of his capabilities in resenting insults. Greeley retorted with some spirit that this need not deter him, when Rust raised a heavy cane and aimed a blow at Greeley's head. This he warded off by raising his arm. The stroke was so heavy that the cane broke in two. That the arm was not shattered is surprising. Rust raised the remains of the stick to repeat the blow, and Greeley endeavored to close with him, but was pulled off, while Rust was hurried away by his friends. The assault was not renewed. It sent Greeley to bed for a couple of days, but he kept on writing and even reported the assault.

"I did not strike him at all, or lay a finger upon him," he wrote in the *Tribune;* "but it certainly would have been a pleasure to me to have performed the public duty of knocking him down." Commenting further, he remarked: "I came here with a clear understanding that it was about an even chance whether I should or should not be allowed to go home alive. . . . But I shall stay here just as long as I think proper, using great plainness of speech, but endeavoring to treat all men justly and faithfully. . . . I shall carry no weapons and engage in no brawls; but if ruffians waylay and assail me, I certainly shall not run, and so far as able, shall defend myself. . . . If Rust's assaults were intended to convince me that his position was fair and manly, they certainly failed to subserve their purpose." He took no legal action, which he might have quite justly done, feeling that he had left Rust in a rather shameful light.

The congressional deadlock was ended on February 2, 1856, by the viva voce passage of a resolution offered by Samuel A. Smith, of Tennessee, providing that the member receiving the highest number of votes was to be considered elected speaker. Banks thus secured the coveted place by one hundred and three votes, to one hundred for William Aiken, of South Carolina. There were eleven recorded as scattering. The South had lost from that day to this the control of Congress.

"It was," wrote Greeley, "memorable as the very first instance in our national history wherein northern resistance to slavery extension ever won in a fair, standup contest (there had been one hundred and three ballots), without compromise or equivocation." Though there were not seventy-five Simon-pure "Republican" votes in the House out of its two hundred and thirty-four members, the Republican party forthwith crystallized and grew national.

The *Tribune* printed its own version of the Rust assault and drew this remonstrance from Greeley to Dana:

"I do wish you would consider my position. In yesterday's paper I see you talk of Rust as drunk when he assaulted me. Now, I don't know this and have never asserted it. Of course, the barbarian will regard this as a fresh attack upon and defiance of him by me, and I can do nothing to undeceive him. I wish you had said nothing of the sort. I doubt that it is just; I am sure it will tend to harm. Let others denounce or revile Rust; I mean never to speak of him unless obliged to. He is very likely to have trouble here before the session closes, and I must not even be suspected of it."

A few days later he was willing to take his chances at being pistoled or horsewhipped "if you will keep me clear of being knocked down by the *Tribune*." A burning personal note was written under date of March 8, 1856:

"As to salary I am indifferent, and as to the *Tribune,* discouraged. The infernal picayune spirit in which it is published has broken my heart. . . . I know you do your best, but you have never seconded me as you ought in defense of the great principle that a daily newspaper should print everything as fast as it is ready, though this should oblige it to issue two supplements a day. If you can't do this, better give up the ghost at once. We ought to have published ten supplements during the past year—and should have been the richer for it. We ought to get back to our noble size soon and print a supplement at least every Saturday. No Jew ever managed a pawnbroker's shop in a baser, narrower, more short-sighted spirit than the *Tribune* is managed, and I am heartsick. I would stay here forever and work like a slave if I could get my letters printed as I send them, but the Tribune is doomed to be a second-rate paper, and I am tired."

He got his supplements and felt better. Some golden maxims followed: "Now, about ferocity. I am in favor of it judiciously applied." Referring to a leave of absence for Dana, and who was to watch the paper: "I mean to be extra good this year and rather doubtful about the next."

Rust became, in season, a Confederate brigadier. The episode does not seem to have excited much sympathy for Greeley. Statesmen and politicians had a poor opinion of editors; the public was badly informed, and perhaps not much interested. The greater Greeley following had yet to be created, and was a scattered one at the time. Something more serious occurred on May 22, 1856, when Charles Sumner, sitting at his seat in the Senate, received injuries at the hands of Preston S. Brooks, a Congressman from South Carolina, from which he never completely recovered, involving, as they did, spinal complications. Brooks resented an incautious and insulting speech Sumner had made two days before in answer to Brooks' uncle, Senator Andrew Pickens Butler, of South Carolina. The speech was scarcely parliamentary and without excuse as a matter of taste, but Sumner felt respectable enough to say anything. The North roused as never before, however, in consequence, and Massachusetts was taken into the new Republican camp. The House voted to expel Brooks, one hundred and twenty-one to ninety-five, but it needed a two-thirds vote to be effective. Brooks resigned, and was then sent back from his district by all but six of the votes cast. He was not, however, proud of either this or the praise accorded him as a hero. In the following January Brooks died. Butler lived but two days more than a year after the attack, the result of which signalized the existence of the Republican party.

The Know-Nothings were a factor in the Banks speakership contest. Greeley advised Dana from Washington: "The majority of the Banks men are now members of Know-Nothing councils, and some twenty or thirty of these actually believe in the swindle. Half of the Massachusetts delegation, two-thirds of that of Ohio, and nearly all of that of Pennsylvania are Know-Nothings this day. We shall get them gradually detached." One of the outcomes of his share in the contest was that he "began to see the utility of rascals," as he wrote Dana, "in the general economy of things." One of the breed from New York had made Banks' election possible, and Greeley was grateful.

The Republican party took national form at Pittsburgh on February 22, 1856. All the free states were in evidence, and delegates came also from Maryland, Virginia, South Carolina, Kentucky and Missouri. A great crowd rallied in response to a call issued in Washington on January seventeenth, signed by the chairmen of the state committees of Ohio, Maine, Michigan, Indiana, New York, Vermont, Massachusetts, Pennsylvania and Wisconsin. Frank P. Blair was chosen permanent chairman. Greeley attended and sent this report of the first day's proceedings to the *Tribune:*

"The Republican Convention has completed its first day's session, and has accomplished much to cement former political differences and distinctions and here to mark the inauguration of a national party, based upon the principle of Freedom. The gathering is very large and the enthusiasm unbounded. Men are acting in the most perfect harmony and with a unity of feeling seldom known to political assemblages of this magnitude. The body is eminently Republican in principle and tendency. It combines much of character and talent, with integrity of purpose and devotion to the great principles which underlie our government. Its moral and political effect upon the country will be felt for the next quarter of a century. In its deliberations everything has been conducted with marked propriety and dignity. The appointment of the Honorable F. P. Blair as president was hailed with unbounded enthusiasm.

"The scene which followed was exciting beyond description. Cheers went forth and handkerchiefs were waved for some minutes after he took his seat as presiding officer. The great hall has been crowded throughout the day and during the evening. Hundreds went away because it was not possible to gain admittance. The day has been principally occupied by the committee in preparing their reports and by the delegates in Committee of the Whole in listening to speeches from eminent gentlemen who represent the several states. Among the most effective speeches of the occasion was one by Mr. Remeline, of Cincinnati. It was pointed and eloquent and was received with much applause. The speaker has until recently been a supporter of the administration. He is now thoroughly Republican. The Committee on Address will not report until to-morrow morning. The business of perfecting a national organization will come up to-morrow forenoon. Adjourned.   H. G."

Petulantly Greeley wrote Dana from Pittsburgh anent the "address" written for the occasion by Henry J. Raymond: "Have we got to surrender a page of the next weekly to Raymond's bore of an address? The man who could inflict six columns on a long-suffering public, on such an occasion, can not possibly know enough to write an address."

He wanted the new party to soft-pedal a bit. "Not only our acts, but our words should indicate an absence of ill-will toward the South," he urged, and "the American question be treated with prudence and forbearance. There are hundreds of whole-hearted Republicans in the American ranks, but the American organization as a national organization is not friendly to us."

Resolutions were passed demanding the repeal of the law permitting slavery in territories once free; indorsing the armed resistance of the Kansas Free Staters; and urging upon the Republican organization the duty of overthrowing a Democratic administration as identified with the progress of the slave power toward national supremacy. The next evening, February twenty-third, the conference turned into a mass meeting to encourage the migration of Free Soil sympathizers to Kansas. Greeley was one of the most fervent speakers.

The Executive Committee, to whom the duty had been delegated, met in Washington on March twenty-seventh and issued a call for a national convention to be held in Philadelphia on June seventeenth for the purpose of naming nominees for president and vice-president. To this five hundred and sixty-five delegates came with credentials. Every free state was represented, as well as Virginia, Delaware, Kentucky and Maryland. No man dared or cared to come from the others. Three men, conspicuous later as Democrats, were in the New York delegation—Philip Dor-

sheimer, A. Oakey Hall and John Bigelow. James G.
Blaine was among those from Maine. Gideon Welles,
who had been a free-soil Democrat, was a Connecticut
delegate. David Wilmot, author of the famous proviso, was there from Pennsylvania. John M. Palmer, who was to be a "gold" Democratic candidate for
president forty years later, was present from Illinois.

The platform called for the immediate admission
of Kansas as a free state, while the backbone of the
document lodged in its second and third paragraphs:

"*Resolved,* That the maintenance of the principles
promulgated in the Declaration of Independence and
embodied in the federal Constitution is essential to
the preservation of our Republican institutions, and
that the federal Constitution, the rights of the states,
and the union of the states, shall be preserved.

"*Resolved,* That with our republican fathers we
hold it to be a self-evident truth, that all men are en-
dowed with the unalienable rights to life, liberty, and
the pursuit of happiness, and that the primary object
and ulterior designs of our federal government were
to secure these rights to all persons within its exclusive jurisdiction; that, as our republican fathers,
when they had abolished slavery in all our national
territory, ordained that no person should be deprived
of life, liberty, or property without due process of
law, it becomes our duty to maintain this provision of
the Constitution against all attempts to violate it for
the purpose of establishing slavery in any territory of
the United States, by positive legislation prohibiting
its existence or extension therein; that we deny the
authority of Congress, of a territorial legislature, of
any individual or association of individuals, to give
legal existence to slavery in any territory of the
United States, while the present Constitution shall be
maintained."

Salmon P. Chase, of Ohio, had been a favorite for the nomination. He sent a letter withdrawing his name. On an informal ballot Colonel John C. Fremont, of California, famous as the "Pathfinder," had three hundred and fifty-nine votes to one hundred and ninety for John McLean, of Ohio. On a formal vote he was nominated by five hundred and twenty votes to thirty-seven for McLean. In the balloting for vice-president, Abraham Lincoln, of Illinois, received one hundred and ten votes. William L. Dayton of New Jersey had two hundred and fifty-eight. Lincoln's name was then withdrawn by John M. Palmer, and Dayton received the nomination. Against the ticket thus chosen the Democrats on June second met at Cincinnati, naming James Buchanan, of Pennsylvania, and James C. Breckinridge, of Kentucky. The Whigs held a convention at Baltimore on September seventeenth, nominating ex-President Millard Fillmore of New York and Andrew Jackson Donelson, of Tennessee.

Fremont had been cashiered by an army court-martial, and although reinstated by the President had declined to reenter the service. He drew the short term in the Senate when California came into the Union as a free state in 1850. He had many graces but little wisdom, and made a poor candidate.

Fremont's campaign chest was lean. In one of Greeley's letters, written to James S. Pike, he says: "We Fremonters of this town [New York] have not one dollar where the Fillmoreans and Buchananians have ten each, and we have Pennsylvania and New York both on our shoulders. Each state is utterly miserable, so far as money is concerned; we must supply them with documents, canvass them with our best speakers, and pay for their rooms to speak in and our bills to invite them.''

Buchanan and Breckinridge won, to the relief of the conservative parts of the country. Each received 174 electoral votes. Their popular vote was 1,838,169 or 45.4 per cent. of the total. Fremont and Dayton had 122 votes in the electoral college, and 1,335,264 from the people. The Whigs cast 874,534 ballots, but carried Maryland only, with eight electoral votes. No Republican ballots were cast in Alabama, Arkansas, Florida, Georgia, Louisiana, Mississippi, Missouri, North Carolina, Tennessee or Texas, where the Whigs afforded the sole opposition. In South Carolina there was no popular vote, the electors being chosen by the legislature. Though defeated, the showing of the party was formidable. It was demonstrated that it possessed the strength to stay. The feeble Whigs, having failed to take up even part of the issues before the country, gave way to the Republicans with their stand against slavery extension.

Events now moved fast and badly. The hope that Buchanan's election would smooth out the situation proved vain. On the second day after his accession to office, the United States Supreme Court handed down the famous, or infamous, Dred Scott decision, with Chief Justice Roger Brooke Taney's obiter dictum that no negro had any rights a white man was bound to respect. Soon the country was aflame. Congress was anti-Democratic, but it was not of one mind. The Kansas troubles broke out afresh, and Hinton Rowan Helper's *Impending Crisis in the South* vied with *Uncle Tom's Cabin* as a best seller.

When the party convention came together next time at Chicago, on May 16, 1860, Senator Seward, despite the opposition of Greeley, seemed certain of the nomination. With the shrewd Thurlow Weed as his manager, he had picked up a substantial support. Greeley had been excluded from the New York delegation, but secured a seat from Oregon. He exerted himself to beat Seward by advocating the selection of Edward Bates of Missouri, a rather absurd choice, as he was a holder of slaves. In this Greeley had the important backing of Frank P. and Montgomery Blair, of Missouri.

Greeley's predilection for Bates, he later explained, was because Bates was "thoroughly conservative," a quality which he certainly did not possess himself. Bates also "held fast to the doctrine of our revolutionary sages, that slavery was an evil to be restricted, not a good to be diffused." This conviction, Greeley thought, "made him essentially a Republican; while I believed that he could poll votes in every slave state and from the Whig party therein to resist secession and rebellion." He had first met and admired Bates at a River and Harbor Convention held at Chicago, July 4, 1847, when Greeley was visiting the West as stockholder in a Lake Superior iron company, in which he lost some money.

Bates rallied but forty-eight votes at the most, and Greeley feared there might be a break to Seward. He made the rounds of the delegations where he had influence—Vermont, Ohio, New Hampshire, Indiana and Massachusetts—to oppose Seward. Finally, on the night before the balloting, having become certain that the contest lay between Lincoln and Seward, he advised the support of Lincoln. It comes from one who was present that Greeley came before the Massachusetts delegation, and being called upon for a speech, responded: "Gentlemen of Massachusetts—I have but one thing to say to you. To-morrow vote for Abraham Lincoln, of Illinois."

At midnight he sent a telegram to the *Tribune*, however, expressing the belief that Seward would win. This was the outcome of attending a session of the delegates from the doubtful states and becoming convinced that they could not agree. He also wrote James S. Pike that Weed had plenty of money and was using it. The first roll call gave Seward one hundred and seventy-three and one-half votes, Lincoln one hundred and two, Bates forty-eight, Chase forty-nine and Simon Cameron fifty and one-half. The rest scattered. On the second ballot Seward reached one hundred and eighty-four and one-half, Lincoln one hundred and eighty-one; on the third, Seward dropped to one hundred and eighty, and Lincoln rose to two hundred and thirty-one and one-half. Before the call was completed, numerous states changed their votes, Lincoln getting three hundred and fifty out of the four hundred and sixty-five total. The choice was made unanimous, and the dreadful die was cast.

The manner of "carefully weighing chances," which led the majority to settle on Lincoln as the man who would poll the most votes, was not, to Greeley's mind, "our noblest test of statesmanship, but it was at least intelligible."

G. H. Stewart, of Colorado, writing in the *Century Magazine* for November, 1890, says that Greeley passed the word suggesting Hannibal Hamlin, of

Maine, for the vice-presidency, and he was nominated, as a sop to the Seward support. He was certainly not Lincoln's choice, as after events proved.

The New York delegation came home sore at Greeley. Henry J. Raymond paused at Auburn to talk the defeat over with Seward. From that point he sent a snapping letter to the New York *Times* assailing the *Tribune's* editor, and now for the first time the "partnership" letter received public mention, as the dark reason for the hostility exhibited at Chicago.

"The main work of the Chicago Convention," wrote Raymond, "was the defeat of Governor Seward, . . . and in that endeavor Mr. Greeley labored harder and did tenfold more than the whole family of Blairs, together with all the gubernatorial candidates to whom he modestly hands over the honors of the effective campaign. He had special qualification as well as special love for the task, to which none of the others could lay any claim. . . . Mr. Greeley was in Chicago several days before the meeting of the Convention, and he devoted every hour of the interval to the most steady and relentless prosecutions of the business that took him hither—the defeat of Governor Seward. He labored personally with the delegates as they arrived, commending himself always to their confidence by professions of regard and the most zealous friendship for Governor Seward, but presenting defeat even in New York as the inevitable result of his nomination. . . . While the contents of Greeley's letter of November 11, 1854, to Seward were known to some of Seward's supporters who were working at Chicago, no use was made of this knowledge in quarters where it would have disarmed the deadly effect of his pretended friendship for the man upon whom he

was thus deliberately wreaking the long hoarded revenge of a disappointed officeseeker.''

This hot charge brought out a demand from
Greeley for the publication of the letter, which Seward
then gave to the press.

Weed expressed "sincere regret" that the letter
"had been called out," saying further: "Having remained for six years in 'blissful ignorance' of its contents, we should much prefer to have ever remained
so. It jars harshly upon cherished memories. It destroys ideals of disinterestedness and generosity
which relieve political life from so much that is selfish,
sordid and rapacious."

This sounded particularly good coming from a professional seller of legislation and privileges for party
and personal gain. Greeley retorted: "The most
careful scavenger of private letters, or the most sneak-
ing eavesdropper that ever listened to private conversation, can not allege a single reason for personal
hostility on my part against Mr. Seward. I have never
received from him anything but exceeding kindness
and courtesy. He has done me favors (not of a political nature) in a manner which made them still more
obliging; and I should regard the loss of his friendship as a very serious loss. Notwithstanding this, I
could not support him for president. I like Mr. Seward
personally, but I love the party and its principles
more."

This very much begs the question when read in
the light of his letter. Moreover, as Raymond pointed
out, Seward had stood far more firmly for what

Greeley professed to advocate in the matter of slavery than Lincoln had ever done.

Lincoln and Hamlin had 180 votes in the electoral college. Their popular total was 1,866,352. Douglas and Johnson totaled 1,375,157 ballots, but gained only 12 seats in the electoral college, where Bell and Everett were represented by 39, furnished by a popular vote of 587,830. Breckinridge and Lane did much better; their popular vote was 847,514; their representation in the college was 72. So the country was badly split and the elected President nearly a million behind a majority on the popular vote. No Republican ballots were cast in Alabama, Arkansas, Florida, Georgia, Louisiana, Mississippi, North Carolina, Tennessee and Texas. In South Carolina the legislature again selected the electors, giving her eight votes to Breckinridge and Lane. Lincoln had a majority in fifteen states, a plurality in three. He carried every free state, except New Hampshire and New Jersey and in the latter he captured four electors, three going to Douglas, who received the nine from New Hampshire, making his pitiful twelve. The Whig states were Kentucky, Tennessee and Virginia, with twelve, twelve and fifteen electors respectively.

Granting that Greeley was a factor in the defeat of Seward at Chicago, Weed and Seward soon repaid in revenge. The United States senatorship from New York was due for filling in 1861. Seward's term in the Senate expired and Lincoln had selected him for his secretary of state. Greeley became a candidate for his shoes, with William M. Evarts, a native of Vermont, for chief opponent. Edwin D. Morgan, a rich New York merchant, was governor, and closely allied to both Seward and Weed. Weed camped in the executive chamber and there, with his practised hand, pulled wires against the editor, who was confident of winning. A deadlock ensued which lasted until February fifth, when Weed pulled enough votes away from Evarts to give sixty, and the election, to Ira Harris. Greeley's highest vote was forty. Weed blandly laid the defeat to Greeley's willingness to let the South secede. Greeley knew it was a neat return for his war on Seward. His attempt to play politics without the aid of politicians failed and did not improve his temper. Greeley was never very kind to Evarts after that, while the *Tribune* jabbed him whenever it got a chance. Evarts' sentences, as well as his addresses, were apt to be lengthy and to afford ample opportunity for "cracks."

Credited with overweening ambition in seeking the senatorship, and with bitter disappointment at his failure, Greeley was not so upset as might be imagined. Beman Brockway went to Albany on his behalf and quotes him as having had this to say on the subject beforehand:

"As to myself, I would like to go to the Senate, and would not like to go into the Cabinet. I think my name in that connection would exasperate the Fire-Eaters, who have been taught to believe me a decidedly vicious and dangerous Negro—a kind of Dismal Swamp 'Dred.' I don't like official routine, with great, dull dinners; I do like my little farm, if I can only get time to visit it, and stay there a little. Besides, I belong to the *Tribune,* and as a senator could continue to work for it, while as a Cabinet man I could not. But I don't want to be paraded in the newspapers as declining places never offered me."

The following week he further advised Brockway:

"I am sure I can do nothing to make myself United States senator, and I am not even sure that I would try very hard if sure of success. But I guess Seward will take it rather than have me go there; and so I guess we may as well let it go. At all events, I can do nothing for myself."

When it was all over Brockway sent Greeley a full account of what had happened and the manner of it. Greeley replied:

"I thank you for your account of the doings at Albany. I ought not to have allowed my name to go before the caucus, seeing that success was hopeless from the start, and I can not avoid the imputation of having sought the office and of quarreling with Weed and Seward because I did not get it; when, in fact, they have done nothing for a year that I so thoroughly justify and approve as I do their opposition to me. I like Seward far better than I could have done had he supported me, and wish he had always shown a corresponding spirit. My vote was so large that I do not feel at all mortified by the result; I only regret the obligation it has imposed on me of coming here to engage in a hopeless struggle to repay some friends for the efforts they have made for me."

George William Curtis, who always opposed Greeley, said to Brockway: "Do you know, I am very glad you have failed. Men are born for spheres. Mr. Greeley's sphere is to edit the *Tribune*. It would be a terrible mistake to transfer him from that position to the United States Senate."

Once more Greeley was a candidate for the Senate, this time in 1863, when the term of Preston King expired. Again the astute Weed blocked his ambition,

"Greeley, Field, Noyes and Opdyke expected to the last hour to be senator," wrote Weed to John Bigelow. "We offered to reelect King, if they would consent." They would not and the prize went to E. D. Morgan. King committed suicide two years later by jumping off a North River ferryboat.

Several other political adventures befell Greeley before he left the Republican party. He was a member of the New York State Constitutional Convention of 1867, and the next year the Republicans ran him for Congress in the hopelessly Democratic Cherry Hill district, in which the *Tribune* Building stood, and he was, of course, buried in the voting. He was put on the state ticket for comptroller in the Democratic year of 1869, when three Republicans had declined to run, and was badly beaten by William F. Allen, of Oswego, John T. Hoffman being elected governor. When named by the state committee for the slaughter Greeley was out West on a lecture trip, but he let the nomination stand. In 1870 he was given the Republican nomination for representative in Congress against S. S. ("Sunset") Cox, Democrat, and newly imported from Ohio, who had served one term from the Sixth District. Greeley was ill and could take no part in the canvass. He was beaten, although by only 1,025 majority. Thus the official compliments received by Greeley from his party were empty, first and last.

When a member of the State Constitutional Convention Greeley became tired of the dull muddlings, and after several months of fairly close attendance, departed, leaving his six-dollars-a-day colleagues to finish polishing up the document. Coming back a month later, he heard the same man talking who had been on the floor when he went away. "Great God!" he ejaculated. "Hasn't that damned fool finished his speech yet?" and fled the scene.

Another episode affected his taste for constitution making. Susan B. Anthony and Elizabeth Cady Stanton were active in urging a suffrage amendment. To this Greeley was strongly opposed, though personally friendly to both ladies and some of their supporters. These used George William Curtis, who was a member of the convention, as the medium for presenting their petitions. One day a long roll came in from Westchester County, headed with the name of Mary Y. Greeley. Mrs. Stanton noted this and mischievously planned to turn it to account against the opposing H. G. She therefore persuaded Mr. Curtis to present it as the petition of Mrs. Horace Greeley rather than of Mary Greeley, who might have passed unknown.

Mr. Curtis so announced, to the great wrath of his fellow member. Meeting Mrs. Stanton soon after at the Cary sisters', he took her to task. "You fox!" he exclaimed, "you fox! You were at the bottom of that affair! Hereafter you will be called Mrs. Henry B. Stanton in the *Tribune!*" And she was. Incidentally, her husband saw much service on the *Tribune,* and was later one of the leading members of Dana's staff on the *Sun.*

CHAPTER IX

IT IS needless to detail the steps by which the Confederacy established itself, after the election of Abraham Lincoln caused the South to separate from the North. The movement began as soon as the results were made known, and resisted all efforts at assuagement.

Greeley, in the *Tribune* of November 9, 1860, treated the threatenings rather lightly:

"We sympathize with the afflicted; but we can not recommend them to do anything desperate. What is the use? They are beaten now; they may triumph next time; in fact, they have generally had their own way; had they been subjected to the discipline of adversity so often as we have, they would probably bear it with more philosophy, and deport themselves more befittingly. We live to learn; and one of the most difficult acquirements is that of meeting reverses with graceful fortitude.

"The telegraph informs us that most of the cotton states are meditating a withdrawal from the Union, because of Lincoln's election. Very well; they have a right to meditate, and meditation is a profitable employment of leisure. We have a chronic, invincible disbelief in disunion as a remedy for either northern or southern grievances. We can not see any necessary connection between the alleged disease and this ultra-

190

heroic remedy; still, we say, if any one sees fit to meditate disunion, let him do so unmolested. That was a base and hypocritic row that was once raised, at southern dictation, about the ears of John Quincy Adams, because he presented a petition for the dissolution of the Union. The petitioner had a right to make the request; it was the member's duty to present it. And now, if the cotton states consider the value of the Union debatable, we maintain their perfect right to discuss it. Nay: we hold, with Jefferson, to the inalienable right of communities to alter or abolish forms of government that have become oppressive or injurious; and if the cotton states shall decide that they can do better out of the Union than in it, we insist on letting them go in peace. The right to secede may be a revolutionary one, but it exists nevertheless; and we do not see how one party can have a right to do what another party has a right to prevent. We must ever resist the asserted right of any state to remain in the Union and nullify or defy the laws thereof; to withdraw from the Union is quite another matter. And whenever a considerable section of our Union shall deliberately resolve to go out, we shall resist all coercive measures designed to keep it in. We hope never to live in a republic whereof one section is pinned to the residue by bayonets.

"But, while we thus uphold the practical liberty, if not the abstract right, of secession, we must insist that the step be taken, if it ever shall be, with the deliberation and gravity befitting so momentous an issue. Let ample time be given for reflection; let the subject be fully canvassed before the people; and let a popular vote be taken in every case, before secession is decreed. Let the people be told just why they are asked to break up the confederation; let them have both sides of the question fully presented; let them reflect, deliberate, then vote; and let the act of secession be the echo of an unmistakable popular fiat. A judgment thus rendered, a demand for separation so backed, would either be acquiesced in without the effusion of blood, or those who rushed upon carnage to defy and defeat it would place themselves clearly in the wrong.

"The measures now being inaugurated in the cotton states, with a view (apparently) to secession, seem to us destitute of gravity and legitimate force. They bear the unmistakable impress of haste—of passion—of distrust of the popular judgment. They seem clearly intended to precipitate the South into rebellion before the baselessness of the clamors which have misled and excited her, can be ascertained by the great body of her people. We trust that they will be confronted with calmness, with dignity, and with unwavering trust in the inherent strength of the Union, and the loyalty of the American people."

There was a rather general appeal for calmness and consideration, not a word of which was heeded. President Buchanan pointed out to the fire-eaters that Lincoln was a plurality president and temporary in his tenure, while no Congress ever had or was likely to act aggressively against their "institution." The North, as a whole, seemed unable to take the situation seriously, even though state after state joined the new Confederacy, uniting under a constitution, and setting up a congress, complete government and armed forces. To all these movements the North was blind. Government forts and property were taken over or besieged, and yet the North took no real alarm. There mainly prevailed a stupefying sense of getting rid of bad rubbish. For half a century the North had been threatening in one way or other to leave the South. That the South now proposed to do the quitting aroused few resisting thoughts that appear on the surface. An unavailing "peace conference" was called in Washington, the outcome of which was another compromise, put into legislative form by Senator J. J. Crittenden, of Kentucky, that died amid the confusions. Greeley, who ranked as the chief disturber, was for letting the slave states go, as a simple and cheap way out of it. He knew there was no legal chance for the present abolition of slavery, and preferred to live in a land of which it should have no part. That war would first intervene appeared at the moment to have no part in his thoughts.

In the *Tribune* of December 8, 1860, he went on record after this fashion:

"We again avow our deliberate conviction that whenever six or eight contiguous states shall have formally seceded from the Union and avowed the pretty unanimous and earnest resolve of the people to stay out, it will not be found practicable to coerce them into subjection; and we doubt that any Congress can be found to direct and provide for such coercion. One or two states may be coerced; but not an entire section or quarter of a Union. If you do not believe this, wait and see."

This was undoubtedly correct as to a secession without an attack upon the people or property of the United States. It would have been difficult, probably impossible, to have secured support for a federal move against the seceders as long as they made no overt use of arms. On December seventeenth he observed further:

"But if even seven or eight states send agents to Washington to say 'We want to get out of the Union,' we shall feel constrained by our devotion to human liberty to say, 'Let them go.' And we do not see how we could take the other side without coming in direct conflict with those rights of men we hold paramount to all political arrangements, however convenient or advantageous.''

On the twenty-fourth the subject was considered with this conclusion:

''Most certainly we believe that governments are made for the peoples, not peoples for governments; that the latter derive their just powers from the consent of the governed; and whenever a portion of this Union, large enough to form an independent, self-sustaining nation, shall show that, and say authentically to the residue, 'We want to get away from you,' I shall say—and we trust self-respect, if not regard for the principles of self-government will constrain the residue of the American people to say—'Go.' ''

Four days later he had this to say:

''Nor is it treason for the state to hate the Union and seek its disruption. A state, a whole section, may come to regard the Union as a blight upon its prosperity, an obstacle to its progress, and be fully justified in seeking its dissolution. And in spite of adverse clamor we insist that, if ever a third or even a fourth of these states shall have deliberately concluded that the Union is injurious to them, and that their vital interests require their separation from it, they have a perfect right to seek such separation; and should they do so with reasonable patience, and due regard for the rights and interests of those they leave behind, we shall feel bound to urge and insist that their wishes be gratified, their demand conceded.''

When a great organ of public opinion could so view the necessities of consistency, can it be wondered that James Buchanan, much abused President, knew not what to do, or that the President-elect and his counselors did nothing more than await events?

The popular impression has been that it was Greeley who uttered the phrase: "Wayward sisters, let them go in peace." This distinction belongs to Major-General Winfield Scott, Commander-in-Chief of the Army, upon whom devolved the duty of dealing with treason, if that was to be the meaning of secession, which was actively under way at the time he made the utterance.

In the 847,514 who voted for Breckinridge, Greeley saw the actual strength of the forces of disunion, divided, however, into the following classes:

"I. The Disunionists, pure and simple, who, believing slavery the only natural and stable basis of social order, and noting the steady advance of the free states in relative wealth, population, and power, deemed the secession and confederation of the slaveholding states the only course consistent with their interests or their safety. I doubt whether this class numbered half a million of the fifteen hundred thousand legal voters residing in the slave states, while it could count no open adherents in the free states.

"II. Those who, while they perceived neither safety nor sense in secession, did not choose to be stigmatized as abolitionists nor hooted as cowards, but preferred the remote, contingent perils even of civil war to the imminent certainty of persecution and social outlawry, if they should be pointed out as lacking the courage or the will to risk all in defiance of "southern rights."

"III. Those who, while at heart hostile to disunion,—deeming it no remedy for existing ills, while it opened a new vista of untold, awful calamities,—yet regarded the menace of secession with complacency, as certain to frighten "the North" into any and every required concession and restriction to avert the threatened disruption."

In his *Recollections* he asserts:

"I had forty years been listening, with steadily diminishing patience, to southern threats of disunion. Whatever an awakened conscience, or an enlightened apprehension of national interest, commended to a majority of the North as just—was apt to be met by the bravado, 'Do what you propose, and we will dissolve the Union!' I had become weary of this, and desirous of ending it. In my cherished conception, the Union was no boon conferred on the North by the South, but a voluntary partnership, at least as advantageous to the latter as to the former. I desired that the South should be made to comprehend and respect this truth. I wished her to realize that the North could do without the South quite as well as the South could do without the North.

"For the first breath of disunion from the South fanned into vigorous life the old spirit of compromise and cringing at the North. 'What will you do to save the Union?' was asked of us Republicans, as if we had committed some enormity in voting for and electing Lincoln, which we must now atone by proffering concessions and disclaimers to the justly alarmed and irritated South."

So much for the South. As to the North:

"At once the attitude of the North became alarmed, deprecatory, self-abasing. Every local election held during the two months succeeding our national tri-

umph showed great 'Conservative' gains. Conspicuous abolitionists were denied the use of public halls,
or hooted down if they attempted to speak. Influential
citizens, through meetings and letters, denounced the
madness of 'fanaticism,' and implored the South
to stay her avenging arm until the North could have
time to purge herself from complicity with 'fanatics,'
and demonstrate her fraternal sympathy with her
southern sister,—that is, attest her unshaken loyalty
to the Slave Power. An eminent southern conservative [John J. Crittenden] having proposed, as a new
Union-saving compromise, the running of the line of
36 degrees, 30 minutes North latitude through our new
territories to the Pacific, and the positive allotment
and guaranty of all south of that line to slavery forever, the suggestion was widely grasped as an olive
branch, even the veteran Thurlow Weed commending
the proposal to popular favor and acceptance as fair
and reasonable. The Republican party—which had
been called into existence by the opening of free soil
to slavery—seemed in positive danger of signalizing
its advent to power by giving a direct assent to the
practical extension of slavery over a region far larger
and more important than that theoretically surren-
dered by the Kansas-Nebraska Bill. In fact, the
attitude of the North, during the two last months of
1860, was foreshadowed in four lines of Collins' *Ode
to the Passions:*

> " 'First, fear his sand, its skill to try,
>   Amid the chords bewildered laid;
> And back recoiled, he knew not why,
>   E'en at the sound himself had made.'

And the danger was imminent that, if a popular vote
could have been had (as was proposed) on the Crittenden Compromise, it would have prevailed by an
overwhelming majority. Very few Republicans would
have voted for it; but very many would have refrained

from voting at all; while their adversaries would have brought their every man to the polls in its support, and carried it by hundreds of thousands.

"My own controlling conviction from first to last was—There must, at all events, be no concession to slavery. Disunion, should it befall, may be calamity; but complicity in slavery extension is guilt, in which the Republicans must in no case concur. It had for an age been the study of slaveholding politicians to make us of the North partners with them in the maintenance, diffusion and profit or loss of their industrial system. 'Slavery is quite as much your affair as ours,' they were accustomed to say in substance: 'we own and work the negroes; you buy the cotton and sugar produced by their labor, and sell us in return nearly all we and they eat, drink and wear. If they run away, you help catch and return them; now set us off a few hundred thousand miles more of territory whereon to work them, and help us to acquire Cuba, Mexico, etc., as we shall say we need them, and we will largely extend our operations, to our mutual benefit.' It was this extension that I was resolved at all hazards to defeat."

Requests for discussion and warnings that the Union could not be dissolved by force, characterized Greeley's course toward the South. "We said in substance," he observes, "you Disunionists claim to be the southern people, and rest your case on the vital principle proclaimed in our fathers' immortal Declaration of Independence,—'Governments derive their just powers from the consent of the governed.' We admit the principle—nay, we affirm, we glory in it; but your case is not within it. You are not the southern people; you are a violent, unscrupulous minority, who have conspired to clutch power and wield it for ends which the overawed, gagged, paralyzed majority, of heart condemn. Secure us a fair opportunity to state our case, and to argue the points at issue before your people, and we will abide their decision. We disclaim a union of force,—a union held together by bayonets; let us be fairly heard; and, if your people decide that they choose to break away from us, we will interpose no obstacle to their peaceful withdrawal from the Union.''

In this attitude he had plenty of company. Doctor Lyman Abbott in his *Reminiscences* recalls how ''in every community were found Republicans who lamented that they had voted for Mr. Lincoln, and frankly confessed that they would never have done so could they have foreseen the consequences.'' Seward, then a United States Senator, observed truly enough: ''No one has any system, or any courage or confidence in the Union.'' Fernando Wood, now Mayor of New York for the second time after a two-year interval, came out for a fantastic scheme to establish the city as an independent entity apart from the state and the United States. He had the German free cities in mind. So far as the new President was concerned, no one appeared to have any confidence in him at all.

Lincoln himself seemed serenely unmoved. Greeley recites that he saw the President-elect about a fortnight before his inauguration (at Springfield, Illinois), but could discern ''nothing that indicated or threatened belligerency on our part.'' On the contrary ''the President sat listening to the endless whine of officeseekers, and doling out village post-offices to importunate or lucky partisans, just as though we were sailing before land breezes on a smiling summer sea, and to my inquiry: 'Mr. President! Do you know

that you will have to *fight* for the place in which you
sit?' he answered pleasantly, I will not say lightly—
but in words that intimated his disbelief that any
fighting would transpire or be needed. . . . He . . .
clung to the delusion that forbearance, patience and
soft words would yet obviate all necessity for deadly
strife.'' The President, thought Greeley, never came
to a full realizing sense until ''that halting, desolating,
stumbling advance to Bull Run was made'' by ''half
the force that should have been sent forward.''

Of Lincoln's opinion at the moment Donn Piatt
has left this record: ''I soon discovered that this
strange and strangely gifted man, while not at all
cynical, was a skeptic. His view of human nature was
low, but good-natured. I could not call it suspicious,
but he believed only what he saw. This low estimate
of humanity blinded him to the South. He could not
understand that men would get up in their wrath and
fight for an idea. He considered the political movement South as a sort of game of bluff, gotten up by
politicians, and meant as solely to frighten the North.
He believed that when the leaders saw their efforts
in that direction were unavailing, the tumult would
subside. 'They won't give up the offices,' I remember
he said, and added, 'Were it believed that vacant
places could be had at the North Pole, the road there
would be lined with dead Virginians.' ''

When the fact became plain that the South was
intent upon the use of arms, Greeley voiced his alarm
at Lincoln's supineness in no uncertain terms. This
found small support. William Cullen Bryant often
wrote to the President from the office of the New York
Evening Post, urging him not to be moved by
Greeley's ''vagaries.''

On behalf of Lincoln it must be remembered that important states in the North, like New Jersey and Pennsylvania, together with the city of New York, were Democratic; that Lincoln was in the minority, by about one million votes, a fact that made his ability to control the situation and "fight for his seat" very doubtful. If the South departed unanimously he was still to face over fifty per cent. of the northern vote in opposition to himself and his party. It well might have made him pause, as it no doubt did, and wisely, as the event proved, for the provocation was not his when the clash came. Though the North rose, it did not do so as one man. Copperheads and skedaddlers were all too plentiful to make his success certain. Thurlow Weed, in the Albany *Evening Journal,* expressed the belief that: "Mad, however, as the South is, there is a Union sentiment there worth cherishing." Weed realized the seriousness of the situation, and believed the South was in earnest so far as seven states were concerned. He called for wisdom on the part of the Republican party to maintain and uphold the supremacy of the Constitution and the laws, and not to abuse the confidence or disappoint the expectations of the people.

The New York *Herald* expressed a very general view, April 10, 1861, just as the guns were about to begin playing on Fort Sumter:

"Anticipating, then, the speedy inauguration of civil war at Charleston, at Pensacola, or in Texas, or, perhaps, at all these places, the inquiry is forced upon us, what will be the probable consequences? We apprehend that they will be: first, the secession of Virginia and the other border slave states, and their union with the Confederate States; secondly, the organization of an army for the removal of the United States ensign and authorities from every fortress or public building within the Confederate States, including the White House, the Capitol and other buildings of Washington. After the secession of Virginia from the United States, it is not likely that Maryland can be restrained from the same decisive act. She will follow the fortunes of Virginia, and will undoubtedly claim that, in withdrawing from the United States, the District of Columbia reverts into her possession under the supreme right of revolution. Here we have verge and scope enough for a civil war of five, ten or twenty years' duration.

"What for? To 'show that we have a Government'—to show that the seceded states are still in our Union, and are still subject to its laws and authorities. This is the fatal mistake of Mr. Lincoln, and his Cabinet, and his party. The simple truth—patent to all the world—is, that the seceded states are out of the Union, and are organized under an independent government of their own. The authority of the United States, within the borders of this independent Confederacy, had been completely superseded, except in a detached fort here and there. We desire to restore this displaced authority in its full integrity. How is this to be done? By entering into a war with the seceded states for the continued occupation of those detached forts? No. A war will only widen the breach, and enlarge and consolidate this Southern Confederacy, on the one hand; while, on the other, it will bring ruin upon the commerce, the manufactures, the financial and industrial interests of our northern cities and states, and may end in an oppressive military despotism.

"How then are we to restore these seceded states to the Union? We can do it only by conciliation and compromise."

One suggested way out of the momentary confusions was that the government should buy all slaves. Greeley rather favored this idea. No one paid any attention to it.

All this philandering came to an end when South Carolina fired on Fort Sumter, April 12, 1861. Three days later Greeley expressed himself in the *Tribune* to this effect:

"Fort Sumter is lost, but freedom is saved. There is no more thought of bribing or coaxing the traitors who have dared to aim their cannon balls at the flag of the Union, and those who gave their lives to defend it. [No one was killed.] It seems but yesterday that at least two-thirds of all the journals of this city were the virtual allies of the secessionists, their apologists, their champions. The roar of the great circle of batteries pouring their iron hail upon the devoted Sumter has struck them all dumb. It is as if one had made a brilliant and effective speech, setting forth the innocence of murder, and, having just bidden adieu to the cheers and the gaslights, were to be confronted by the gray form and staring eyes of a victim of assassination, the first fruit of his oratorical success.

"For months before the late presidential election a majority of our journals predicted forcible resistance to the government as the natural and necessary result of a Republican triumph; for months since, they have been cherishing and encouraging the Slaveholders' Rebellion, as if it were a natural and proper proceeding. Their object was purely partisan—they wished to bully the Republican administration into shameful recreancy to Republican principle, and then call upon the people to expel from power a party so profligate and so cowardly. They did not succeed in this; they have succeeded in enticing their southern

protégés and sometime allies into flagrant treason. . . . Most of our journals lately parading the
pranks of the secessionists with scarcely disguised ex-
ultation, have been suddenly sobered by the culmina-
tion of the slaveholding conspiracy. They would evidently like to justify and encourage the traitors
further, but they dare not; so the Amen sticks in their
throat. The aspect of the people appals them. Democrat as well as Republican, Conservative and Radical,
instinctively feel that the guns fired at Sumter were
aimed at the heart of the American Republic. Not
even in the lowest groggery of our city would it be
safe to propose a cheer for Beauregard and Governor
Pickens. The Tories of the Revolution were relatively
ten times as numerous here as are the open sympathizers with the Palmetto Rebels. It is hard to lose
Sumter; it is a consolation to know that in losing it
we have gained a united people. Henceforth, the loyal
states are a unit in uncompromising hostility to treason, wherever plotted, however justified.

"Fort Sumter is temporarily lost, but the country
is saved. Long live the Republic!"

That the editor of the *Tribune* himself had been one
of the leaders in the dilly-dallying was swept out of
his memory. From that time on Greeley was unremit-
ting in urging energetic effort to stamp out revolt—
far more so than the government seemed either able
or willing to be. His view of the assault on Sumter
was that the chief conspirators of the Confederacy saw
their strength slipping away and treated the South to
a shower of blood deliberately, to keep Alabama and
other lukewarm states from abandoning the cause in
favor of a common-sense adjustment.

So long as Simon Cameron remained secretary of
war, everything wabbled. George B. McClellan became head of the Army of the Potomac in July. He

was an engineer officer, capable but professional, and could not comprehend that raw troops against raw troops were about the same as trained against trained in the final result. The rout at Bull Run gave him an excuse to sit down and "organize," instead of following N. B. Forrest's maxim to "git over thar and git to fitin'." There was definite clamor for setting Lincoln aside and putting affairs in the hands of a dictator. McClellan, in a letter to his wife, admitted a willingness to take on the task and to "die" after he had saved the country.

From New York came a demand that George Law, a successful transportation magnate, be put in the President's place. This suggestion probably grew out of a rather insolent letter the millionaire sent Lincoln under date of April 25, 1861, in which he complained of the interruption of traffic through Baltimore. In it he said:

"The public mind is already excited to the highest point that this state of things has been so long tolerated; and the people are determined that free and uninterrupted communication with the seat of government shall be immediately established, not by circuitous routes, but by the direct lines of communication that they have heretofore traveled over. And it is demanded of the government that they at once take measures to open and establish those lines of communication, and that they protect and preserve them from any further interruption. Unless this is done, the people will be compelled to take it into their own hands, let the consequences be what they may, and let them fall where they will. It is certainly desirable that this be done through the regularly constituted authorities at Washington; and the government is earnestly desired to act without delay.

"There is entire unanimity on the part of the people of the free states to sustain the government and maintain the Union.

"I trust, Mr. President, that this letter will not be received unkindly; as, in writing it, I simply do what I feel it to be my duty as a citizen to do in this extraordinary state of things."

The southern position was satirized by Orpheus C. Kerr in these mocking lines:

REPUDIATION

" 'Neath a ragged Palmetto a Southerner sat
A-twisting the band of his Panama hat,
And trying to lighten his mind of a load
By humming the words of the following ode:
  'Oh! for a nigger, and oh! for a whip;
  Oh! for a cocktail, and oh! for a nip;
  Oh! for a shot at old Greeley and Beecher;
  Oh! for a crack at a Yankee school-teacher;
  Oh! for a captain and oh! for a ship;
  Oh! for a cargo of niggers each trip.'
And so he kept oh-ing for what he had not,
Not contented with owing for all he had got."

The era of action in the war did not begin until the Secretary of War was forced out of office, on January 15, 1862, and sent off into the sub-Arctic as minister to Russia. Simon Cameron had run his office more in the interest of contractors than of victory. In his stead came Edwin M. Stanton, Democrat, a man of inflexible purpose and unfaltering courage. One does not need to like him to say this. He had been for a brief time attorney-general in Buchanan's crumbling Cabinet. The country took heart at the change and so did Greeley. The *Tribune* ran true and bold again. February 18, 1862, it said:

"While every honest heart rises in gratitude to God for the victories which afford so glorious a guaranty of the national salvation, let it not be forgotten that it is to Edwin M. Stanton, more than to any other individual, that these auspicious events are now due. Our generals in the field have done their duty with energy and courage; our officers, and with them the noble democracy of the ranks, have proved themselves worthy sons of the Republic; but it is by the impassionate soul, the sleepless will, and the great practical talents of the Secretary of War, that the vast power of the United States has now been hurled upon their treacherous and perjured enemies to crush them to powder. Let no man imagine that we exalt this great statesman above his deserts, or that we would detract an iota from that share of glory which in this momentous crisis belongs to every faithful participator in the events of this war. But we can not overlook the fact that whereas but the other day all was doubt, distrust and uncertainty; the nation despairing almost of its own restoration to life; Congress the scene of bitter imputations and unsatisfactory apologies; the army sluggish, discontented, and decaying; and the abyss of ruin and disgrace yawning to swallow us—now all is inspiration, merriment, victory and confidence. We seem to have passed into another state of existence, to live with distinct purposes, and to find the certainty of their realization."

To this Stanton modestly entered a disclaimer. All the same he eschewed politics and "ran" the conflict to a successful end.

One of the first moves made by Stanton was to take Greeley's managing editor and make him assistant secretary of war. In a way this was a favor to Greeley. Dana had become dominant in the *Tribune* office and made much trouble for his superior, altering and suppressing his articles in accordance with his own journalistic judgment, which was generally good. In the course of his duties Dana was sent out into the field of combat to "observe" operations, to the considerable distaste of commanding officers, and became noted for getting badly panic-stricken at Chickamauga.

The lives of Greeley and his family and the safety of the home at Chappaqua, New York, not to mention the property of the *Tribune* in New York, were placed in great peril by the draft riots of July, 1863. To replenish the army, the President had decreed the enforced selection of recruits by lot. The drawings began on Saturday, July eleventh, under Federal supervision, Robert Nugent, Assistant Provost-Marshal-General being in charge, under orders from his chief, General Joseph B. Fry. It was contended that New York and Brooklyn were unfairly listed and the draft numbers out of all proportion to the share of men available in the two cities. There was no trouble at the beginning, but the Sunday papers published the lists of the Saturday drawings. These drew heavily upon mechanics and laborers, many of them Irish, who had joined the Democratic party, which, under its then leadership, was, to say the least, conservative in attitude toward the prosecution of the conflict.

The lists being widely read the next day, Sunday, roused a spirit of resentment and resistance, though the drawings were resumed on Monday, with no apparent suspicion on the part of the authorities that trouble was brewing. It started at the station for the Ninth District, at Forty-sixth Street and Third Avenue, a tenement-house and Irish "shanty" section.

The wheel began turning at ten o'clock, and in half an hour the blindfolded official who drew the names had extracted about a hundred. These were duly read off in a room crowded with anxious men, mainly workers of the lower grade. Outside a crowd had been gathering—laborers from the Second and Third Avenue street railways and workers from factories in the neighborhood who left their tasks to slake their anxiety and so formed a mob of a thousand or more that crowded about the corner. About ten-thirty o'clock a pistol shot was fired into the station, followed by a shower of stones through the windows. A rush resulted. The wheel was smashed, the deputy marshals were driven out, the building was set on fire, and soon the whole block was blazing.

Mobs formed in many parts of the city intent upon resisting the hated impressment and filled with vengeance toward the negroes and the New York *Tribune,* the two factors held mainly responsible for the war. Marching rioters improvised verses to the tune of *John Brown's Body,* with a refrain affirming their purpose to "hang Horace Greeley to a sour apple tree." The police battled against odds, and a special guard of bluecoats was stationed in Printing House Square, under George W. Walling, to protect all the newspapers there printed and especially the detested *Tribune.* Leonard W. Jerome, father of Lady Randolph Churchill and grandfather of the brilliant Winston Churchill, sat through the first night beside a Gatling gun placed in the doorway of the New York *Times,* of which he was a stockholder, cornerwise across from the *Tribune.* Later the *Tribune* added a cannon to its equipment.

Greeley rather wanted to take the risk of facing the rioters. "It doesn't make much difference," was his remark. "I've done my work. I might as well be killed by this mob as to die in bed. Between now and the next time is only a little while."

Greeley's foes took the trouble to charge him with pusillanimous conduct during the riots—another falsehood. He made response in the *Tribune* to their flings:

"On the 13th of July, 1863 (the first day of the Draft Riots in our city), the editor of the *Tribune* was visited in his office about midday by a devoted friend, who urged and entreated him to accompany the said friend to his home, a few miles distant. That friend assured him that he knew that the life of said editor was to be taken forthwith—that it had been plotted and settled that he should be an early and certain victim of the ruffian mob then howling about the *Tribune* office, and inciting each other to the assault, which they actually made at dusk that night, when they smashed the windows, furniture, etc., and set fire to the building, but were promptly routed and expelled by the police. Riot, arson, and pillage were then rife in different sections of our city, of which the rebel mob appeared to have undisputed possession. The editor (who writes this) informed his friend that nothing would induce him to leave the city—that he was where he had a right to be—and where he should remain. That friend, after exhausting remonstrance and entreaty, left him to his fate, not expecting to see him again. After five p. m. of that day, the editor, having finished his work at the office, went over to Windust's eating-house for his dinner, passing through the howling mob for nearly the entire distance, and recognized by several of them. Two friends accompanied him, but not at his invitation or suggestion. Neither of the three was harmed. At Windust's dinner was ordered and eaten exactly as on other days, but in the largest room in the house, without the shadow of hiding or concealment of any kind. Dinner finished, the editor took a carriage and drove to his lodging, where he resumed writing for the *Tribune,* and continued it through the evening, sending down his copy to the office, and being visited thence by friends who informed him of the mob's assault, and the narrow escape of the building and contents from destruction. Remaining all night at his lodging, he returned next morning to the office (now being armed), saw from a window the mob howling in its front, hastily repaired to the City Hall Park, there to listen to a harangue from Horatio Seymour, and remained there nearly to the close of the day [Tuesday], when he was finally induced to leave by the representation of the good and true soldier who commanded it as fortress, that he would prefer that the mob should not be provided with the extra inducements for assault which the known presence of Mr. Greeley in the building would afford. He returned to the office next morning, though the first hackman to whom he applied refused to let him enter his carriage; and he was in the office nearly throughout each day of that memorable week up to Friday evening, when he (as usual) took the Harlem cars for home at Chappaqua, where he spent the Saturday, as he has done nearly every Saturday, save in winter, for the last fifteen years. And whoever asserts that he at any time that week 'was hiding under Windust's table,' is a branded liar and villain, as Mr. Windust, Mr. William A. Hall, and other surviving and most credible witnesses will gladly attest.''

The mob subsided on the third day. Meanwhile Mrs. Greeley and her young daughters, Ida and Gabrielle, were in peril at Chappaqua, something that apparently did not occur to Greeley. Living almost hermitlike, Mrs. Greeley was unaware of the disturbance. No papers had come, but this was not unusual with a poor postal service, and she was going about her affairs with no thought of danger, when a Quaker neighbor, named Quinby, came to tell her that a gang of some three hundred ruffians from Sing Sing and other river towns were drinking at the tavern in an effort to fire up their courage to sack the Greeley home and kill the family. He besought her to abandon the place and come with the children to safe shelter in his home.

This the resolute lady refused to do. The farm laborers were showing signs of drunkenness and disorder, and were more than likely to join the mob if it came. They were sent to a distant part of the farm, while Clark, the superintendent, a bold and resourceful Englishman, joined Mrs. Greeley in preparation to receive the assailants. The valuables were packed in a wagon covered with hay, and driven to the Quinby house. The pictures and books were removed to a stone stable, half built into the hillside some distance away.

Clark had been hurried to Sing Sing for a keg of gun-powder, which he brought. Its head was knocked out and a train laid to a point some distance from the house. Mrs. Greeley's plan was certainly heroic. She intended to remain in her home and warn off the mob, while Clark and Quinby were to slip out the back way with the children and make for safety in the woods. She intended to wait until the rioters had broken in, then she was going to run for it and fire the train. The results would no doubt have been glorious.

THE GREELEY HOUSE, CHAPPAQUA

The peaceful Quaker, while assenting to the preliminaries, felt it wise to prevent the tragedy. Accordingly he went to the tavern and informed members of the mob that a warm welcome awaited them at Chappaqua; that the editor was absent, but his wife was very much at home. "Heed my warning, my brethren," he pleaded. "Horace Greeley is a peace man, but Mary Greeley will fight to the last."

That evening the crowd came to the farm gates, which were barred. It howled and threatened for a time, then faded away. Mrs. Greeley put the children to bed and slept peacefully through the night.

The draft was temporarily suspended on the plea of Governor Horatio Seymour. Errors and injustices in it were corrected, and the drawing was resumed on August nineteenth, when a garrison of ten thousand troops and three batteries of artillery attended the ceremonies. There was no further trouble, nor did any great accession to the ranks result, evasions and substitutes working the draft down to its lowest terms. The exact number of killed and wounded in these riots was never known. The estimate is a thousand. About one million, five hundred thousand dollars' worth of property was destroyed, including the Colored Orphan Asylum, which stood on Fifth Avenue across Fifty-first Street from the present St. Patrick's Cathedral. Serious damage also befell the reputation of Governor Seymour for addressing a body of rioters as "my friends."

The peril to the Greeley family was very real throughout the disturbance. In one instance the home of a well-known citizen was invaded and wrecked under a mob-impression that it was their home.

Of his own opinions Greeley gives a further glance in the preface of the second volume of *The American Conflict,* completed July 21, 1866, in which he observes that up to the draft riots of 1863 ''I had not been habitually confident of an auspicious immediate issue from our momentous struggle. Never doubting that the ultimate result would be such as to vindicate emphatically the profoundly wise beneficence of God, it had seemed to me more probable—in view of the protracted and culpable complicity of the North in whatever guilt or shame, of immorality or debasement, was inseparable from the existence and growth of American slavery—that a temporary triumph might accrue to the Confederates. The real danger of the Republic was not that of permanent division, but of general saturation by and subjugation to the despotic ideas and aims of the slaveholding oligarchy. Had the Confederacy proved able to wrest from the federal authorities an acknowledgment of its independence, and had peace been established and ratified on that basis, I believe the Democratic party in the loyal states would have forthwith taken ground for 'restoration' by the secession of their respective states, whether jointly or severally, from the Union, and their adhesion to the Confederacy, under its Montgomery Constitution—making slavery universal and perpetual. And, under the moral influence of southern triumph and northern defeat, in full view of the certainty that thus only could reunion be achieved, there can be little doubt that the law of political gravitation, of centripetal force, thus appealed to, must have ultimately prevailed. Commercial and manufacturing thrift would have gradually vanquished moral repugnance. It might have required some years to heal the wounds of war and secure a popular majority in three or four of the border states in favor of annexation; but the geographic and economic incitements to Union are so urgent and palpable, that state after state would have concluded to go to the mountain, since it stubbornly refused to come to Mahomet: and all the states that the Confederacy would consent to accept, on conditions of penitence and abjuration, would, in time, have knocked humbly at its grim portals for admission and fellowship. That we have been saved from such a fate is due to the valor of our soldiers, the constancy of our ruling statesmen, the patriotic faith and courage of those citizens who, within a period of three years, loaned more than two billions to their government when it seemed to many just tottering on the brink of ruin; yet, more than all else, to the favor and blessing of Almighty God. They who, whether in Europe or America, from July, 1862, to July, 1863, believed the Union death-stricken, had the balance of material probabilities on their side; they erred only in underrating the potency of those intellectual, moral and providential forces, which in our age operate with accelerated power and activity in behalf of liberty, intelligence and civilization.''

In this same volume Greeley made these his concluding words:

"The revolution had failed and gone down but the Rebel Army of Virginia and its commander had *not* failed. Fighting sternly against the Inevitable—against the irrepressible tendencies, the generous aspirations of the age—they had been proved unable to succeed where success would have been a calamity to their children, to their country and the human race. And, when the transient agony of defeat had been endured and passed, they all experienced a sense of relief, as they crowded about their departing chief, who, with streaming eyes, grasped and pressed their outstretched hands, at length finding words to say: 'Men, we have fought through the war together. I have done the best that I could for you.' There were few dry eyes among those who witnessed the scene; and our soldiers hastened to divide their rations with their late enemies, now fellow countrymen, to stay their hunger until provisions from our trains could be drawn for them. Then, while most of our army returned to Burkesville, and thence, a few days later, to Petersburg and Richmond, the work of paroling went on, under the guardianship of Griffin's and Gibbon's infantry, with McKenzie's cavalry; and, so fast as paroled, the Confederates took their way severally to their respective homes; many of them supplied with transportation, as well as food, by the government they had fought so long and so bravely to subvert and destroy.''

CHAPTER X

GREELEY AND LINCOLN

WHEN Abraham Lincoln came to Congress from Illinois in 1847, Horace Greeley had become the recognized trumpeter of the Whig party. The Mexican War had been fought and won, though the treaty of Guadeloupe-Hidalgo was not yet signed. Neither Greeley nor Lincoln approved of the conflict, commenced by one Whig general, Zachary Taylor, and completed by another, Winfield Scott. The treaty when made, February 2, 1848, fixed the Rio Grande as the boundary. Mexico had placed the boundary of Texas at the Nueces. It was Taylor's move to the former stream in time of peace that provoked the war. The controversy did not die with the treaty. Some comment by Greeley during the aftermath brought him this letter from Lincoln, under date of June 27, 1848:

"Friend Greeley: In the *Tribune* of yesterday I discovered a little editorial paragraph in relation to Colonel Wentworth, of Illinois, in which, in relation to the boundary of Texas, you say: 'All Whigs and many Democrats having ever contended it stopped at the Nueces.' Now this is a mistake which I dislike to see go uncorrected in a leading Whig paper. Since I have been here, I know a large majority of such Whigs of the House of Representatives as have spoken on the question have not taken that position. Their position, and in my opinion the true position, is that the boundary of Texas extended just so far as American settlements taking part in her revolution extended; and that as a matter of fact these settlements did extend, at one or two points, beyond the Nueces, but not anywhere near the Rio Grande at any point. The 'stupendous desert' between the valleys of those two rivers, and not either river, has been insisted on by the Whigs as the true boundary.

"Will you look at this? By putting us in the position of insisting on the line of the Nueces, you put us in a position which, in my opinion, we can not maintain, and which therefore gives the Democrats an advantage of us. If the degree of arrogance is not too great, may I ask you to examine what I said on this very point in the printed speech I send you.

"Yours truly,

"A. LINCOLN."

Lincoln, it will be perceived, was a born politician. Greeley was not. He could never leave a bridge standing to escape by; Lincoln was ever thoughtful in this particular, as the letter shows. Upon his retirement from Congress, the Whigs went into an eclipse in Illinois, but not Lincoln. He grew until the Douglas debates, in 1858, brought him prominently before the country as one of the leading lights in the new Republican party.

In 1868 Greeley wrote a lecture on Lincoln, which was not often delivered, it would appear. The manuscript fell into the hands of his old friend and neighbor, Joel Benton, who deciphered it, and the whole was printed in the *Century Magazine* for July, 1891. "I first met Mr. Lincoln," he notes, "late in 1848, at Washington [when Greeley was serving his own brief

term in Congress], as a representative in the Thirtieth
Congress—the only one to which he was ever elected.
His was, as apportioned under the census of 1840, a
Whig district, and he was elected from it in 1848 by
the largest majority ever given any one. [He defeated
Peter Cartwright, the celebrated evangelist.] He was
then not quite forty years old; a genial, cheerful,
rather comely man, noticeably tall, and the only
Whig from Illinois—not remarkable, otherwise, to
the best of my recollection. He was generally liked
on our side of the House; he made two or three moderate and sensible speeches that attracted little attention; he voted generally to forbid the introduction of
slavery into the still untainted territories; but he did
not vote for Mr. Galt's resolve looking to the immediate abolition of slavery in the Federal District [of
Columbia], being deterred by the somewhat fiery pre-
amble thereto. He introduced a counter-proposition
of his own, looking to abolition by a vote of the people [Douglas' proposition in after years]—that is,
by the whites of the District—which seemed to me
much like submitting to the inmates of the peniten-
tiary a proposition to double the lengths of their
respective terms of imprisonment. In short, he was
one of the very mildest type of Wilmot Proviso Whigs
from the free states—not nearly so pronounced as
many who long since found a congenial rest in the
ranks of the pro-slavery Democracy.'' Not one of his
associates, Greeley observes, would have picked Lincoln as the man among them who would be first to
attain the presidency.

"He seemed," Greeley wrote on another occasion,
"a quiet, good-natured man, who did not aspire to

leadership and seldom claimed the floor. I think he made but one set speech during that session, and this speech was by no means a long one. Though a strong partisan he voted against the bulk of his party once or twice, when that course was dictated by his convictions. He was one of the most moderate, though firm, opponents of slavery extension, and notably of a buoyant, cheerful spirit. It will surprise some to hear that, though I was often in his company thenceforward till his death, and long on terms of friendly intimacy with him, I never heard him tell an anecdote or story.''

When it became known that Lincoln was to oppose Douglas for the senatorship, the *Tribune* did not thrill at the news. Greeley was more than fair in presenting Douglas to his readers, so much so that Lincoln wrote to Charles L. Wilson from Springfield, on June 1, 1858: ''I have believed—I do believe now—that Greeley, for instance, would be rather pleased to see Douglas reelected over me, or any other Republican; and yet I do not believe it is so because of any secret arrangement with Douglas. It is because he thinks Douglas's superior position, reputation, experience, ability, if you please, would more than compensate for his lack of a pure Republican position and therefore do the cause of Republicanism more good than would the election of any one of our better undistinguished pure Republicans. I do not know how you estimate Greeley, but I consider him incapable of corruption or falsehood. He denies that he directly is taking part in favor of Douglas, and I believe him. Still, his feeling constantly manifests itself in his paper, which, being so extensively read in Illinois, is and will continue to be a drag upon us. I have also thought that Governor Seward, too, feels about as Greeley does, but not being a newspaper editor, his feeling in this respect is not much manifested. I have no idea that he is, by conversation or by letter, urging Illinois Republicans to vote for Douglas.''

Lincoln knew, of course, that the man who could beat Stephen A. Douglas would become a formidable figure in the next Republican convention. Things political did not happen to Abraham Lincoln by chance. He was an apt player at the great game; knew Seward was in the field, and that Greeley would not be averse to the honor. Yet it is hard to conceive of Greeley "killing" off a candidate by direct or indirect action in his own interest. That he could complain because things did not come his way did not mean he had been trying to maneuver them.

In the light of cold study it is quite possible that Greeley thought Douglas's definite and unmistakable program was better for the country than Lincoln's vague phrasings. The latter said some things that live, but committed himself squarely on nothing that dealt with the pressing problem of slavery. He could charge Douglas with digging up a question which had been put to sleep, but could not or did not tell what he would do with it now that it was awake. He would not even say flatly that he favored the abolition of slavery in the District of Columbia, about which there was little difference of opinion, north or south, but only that he wanted it done "gradually." He went some distance with Douglas on leaving all questions to the people, but held that Douglas was going too far— departing from the ways of the fathers, which, had they been followed, would, he believed, have brought about the bloodless extinction of the evil.

Douglas, on his part, urged that this was the trouble; the country had been made rigidly half slave and half free by the Missouri Compromise of 1850. He wanted it put in a position where it could elect by states the course it cared to adopt through the ballot. Here was where he departed from "the ways of the fathers," who had fixed slavery in the Constitution by protecting the right of the owner to reclaim his bondman. Lincoln had "never hesitated to say" that "under the Constitution of the United States, the people of the southern states are entitled to a congressional fugitive slave law." So far as the existing law went he thought "it should have been framed so as to be free from some of the objections that pertain to it, without lessening its efficiency."

Horace Greeley could hardly be expected to endorse such sentiments with very loud cheers. He regarded Lincoln as an able man, playing politics ably. Lincoln modified his famous statement that the country could not endure "half slave and half free" in the course of the third debate with Douglas at Jonesboro, on September 5, 1858: "I have said I supposed it could not," he remarked, in stating his reasons for having asserted it as a fact. "I insist upon this government being placed where our fathers originally placed it."

Thus he put his feet on the very platform of the southern bolters who refused to accept Douglas in 1860 and nominated James C. Breckinridge. And the same bolt elected Lincoln on quite a different platform!

In one of the notes he jotted down for use during the debates, Lincoln recorded this thought: "I believe the declaration that 'all men are created equal' is the great fundamental principle upon which our free institutions rest. That negro slavery is violative of that principle, but that by our form of government that principle has not been made one of legal obligation. That by our form of government the states which have slavery are to retain or disuse it, at their own pleasure, and that all others—individuals, free states, and National Government—are constitutionally bound to leave them alone about it."

There is not much of the ring of the "great emancipator" about this. It could not fit into any line of Horace Greeley's thoughts about the rights of man. Douglas charged that Lincoln in a caucus of Illinois Whigs in 1847 had urged the throwing overboard of Henry Clay: "that the Whigs had fought long enough for principle and ought to begin to fight for success." This was not refuted. And it would weigh with Greeley, who cared nothing for success and everything for principle.

Summing up the result of the debates and Douglas's success in keeping in the Senate, Greeley made himself authority for the statement that Lincoln spent no more than one thousand dollars, while Douglas lavished money to the amount of eighty thousand dollars, accumulating a burden of debt that followed him to the grave.

In his *Recollections of a Busy Life,* Greeley frankly avowed his sympathies with Douglas. "It seemed to me," he wrote, "that not only magnanimity, but policy, dictated to the Republicans of Illinois that they should promptly and heartily tender their support to Mr. Douglas. They did not concur, however, but received

the suggestion with passionate impatience. Having
for a quarter of a century confronted Mr. Douglas as
the ablest, most alert, most effective of their adversaries, they could not now be induced to regard him in
a different light; and, besides, their hearts were set on
the election, as his successor, of their own special
favorite and champion Abraham Lincoln, who, though
the country at large scarcely knew him . . . was endeared to them by his tested efficiency as a canvasser
and his honest worth as a man. . . . They did not
for a while incline to forgive me for the suggestion
that it would have been wise and better not to have
opposed Mr. Douglas's return; but I still abide in that
conviction.'' He considered Douglas ''the readiest
man I ever knew,'' and regarded his death so soon
after the outbreak of the war as a ''most grievous and
irreparable'' loss.

To presidents and politicians the aggressive editor
is much of a nuisance. Greeley, with his prying, persistent prescience, was more; he was a pest. His keen
insight, his strength of purpose, his unwillingness to
temporize, all combined to make him an undesirable
with the shapers of policies and the executors of plans.
So it fell about that Greeley was a thorn in the side
of Lincoln as soon as Lincoln became the head of the
State.

The rush of office-seekers fairly overwhelmed the
President at the start. They swarmed like locusts.
The impending crisis in the nation, the fast seceding
of the southern states, did not arrest their hunger.
Lincoln was goaded almost to madness. He was in a
state of siege at Springfield and mail claims came in
by the cart-load. In New York the election of a sen-

STEPHEN A. DOUGLAS

(From the Statue by Leonard W. Volk)

ator was pending, and naturally the new President was besought to lend a hand. Greeley was a candidate. Thurlow Weed put a cloven hoof in the door, and writing to Lincoln, drew this response:

"Springfield, Illinois, February 4, 1861.

"Dear Sir: I have both your letter to myself and that to Judge Davis, in relation to a certain gentleman in your state claiming to dispense patronage in my name, and also to be authorized to use my name to advance the chances of Mr. Greeley for an election to the United States Senate.

"It is very strange that such things should be said by any one. The gentleman you mention did speak to me of Mr. Greeley in connection with the senatorial election, and I replied in terms of kindness toward Mr. Greeley, which I really feel, but always with an expressed protest that my name must not be used in the senatorial election in favor of, or against, any one. Any other representation of me is a misrepresentation.

"As to the matter of dispensing patronage, it perhaps will surprise you to learn that I have information that you claim to have my authority to arrange that matter in New York. I do not believe that you have so claimed, but still so some men say. On that subject you know all I have said to you is 'Justice to all,' and I said nothing more particular to any one. I say this to reassure you that I have not changed my position. In the hope, however, that you will not use my name in the matter, I am,

"Yours truly,

"A. LINCOLN."

The clashings over patronage evoked this grim note from Lincoln on May 8, 1861, to Salmon P. Chase, Secretary of the Treasury: "I am told there is an office in your department called 'The Superintending

Architect of the Treasury Department' connected with the Bureau of Construction, which is now held by a man of the name of Young, and wanted by a gentleman of the name of Christopher Adams. Ought Mr. Young to be removed, and if yes, ought Mr. Adams to be appointed? Mr. Adams is magnificently recommended; but the great point in his favor is that Horace Greeley and Thurlow Weed join in recommending him. I suppose the like never happened before and never will again; so that it is now or never. What say you?''

Lincoln's victory at the polls, as well as at Chicago, was largely attributed to Greeley, who had thus been expected to have great influence with the administration. He was depicted in a popular cartoon as carrying the new President into the White House on his shoulders, followed by all the faddists of the day. To the contrary, Greeley neither exercised nor attempted to exercise any ''pull'' with the Chief Executive, save as he pleaded or criticized in the columns of the *Tribune*. He took no office from Lincoln, nor would he ask favors from him for others, though much besought. His brother, Barnes Greeley, who had remained at home with the old folks on the farm, being somewhat weary of living by the sweat of his brow, thought a thousand dollar job as mail agent would be a desirable relief. He accumulated some local recommendations and sent them to Horace with a request for further aid, incidentally adding that he needed his backing because another man had offered to fill the place for five hundred dollars a year. He got this reply: ''If another man offers to do this service for five hundred dollars, and you expect one thousand dollars, that is an excellent reason why you should not have it. If you had it, the Government would be losing five hundred dollars a year.''

Of Lincoln's first inaugural, Greeley said in his 1868 lecture: ''The man evidently believed with all his soul that, if he could but convince the South that he would arrest and return her fugitive slaves, and offered to slavery every support required by comity, or by the letter of the Constitution, he would avert her hostility, dissolve the Confederacy, and restore throughout the Union the sway of Federal authority and laws. There was never a wilder delusion. . . . I apprehend that Mr. Lincoln was very nearly the last man in the country, whether North or South, to relinquish his rooted convictions that the growing chasm might be closed and the Union fully restored without the shedding of blood.''

Discussing the inaugural later, in the *American Conflict*, Greeley said:

''Mr. Lincoln's rejection of disunion as physically impossible—as forbidden by the geography and topography of our country—is a statesmanlike conception that had not before been so clearly apprehended or so forcibly set forth. And, in truth, not one-tenth of the then active Secessionists ever meditated or intended disunion as permanent. They proposed to destroy the Union in order to reconstitute it according to their own ideas, with slavery as its corner-stone. To kick out the New England States, rural New York, and that 'fanatical' section of the West that is drained by the Great Lakes and the St. Lawrence—such was the constant inculcation of pro-slavery journalists and politicians throughout that eventful winter and spring. Free states were to be admitted into the Confederacy, on condition of their fully abjuring all manner of anti-slavery sentiment and inculcation evermore, and

becoming slave states. A few southern fanatics, who
deemed nothing needed but the reopening of the African Slave-Trade to render 'the South' the mistress of
the world, wished to be rid of all 'Yankee' association
and contamination evermore; but the great mass, even
in the cotton states, regarded secession but as a device
for bringing the North to its knees, and binding it over
to future docility to every exaction of the slave power.

"Mr. Lincoln fondly regarded his inaugural as a
resistless proffering of the olive-branch to 'the
South'; the conspirators everywhere interpreted it as
a challenge to war."

It is not surprising that Greeley should have regarded the selection of William H. Seward as secretary of state without much enthusiasm, and to have
felt it put a stamp upon the administration—as it certainly did. Moncure D. Conway relates that "Greeley
earnestly denied any ill will toward Seward, but said
he had no faith in him as a minister." Greeley said
to Conway: "Seward always has, and must have, a
policy; a policy is just what we don't want. We want
manliness." Conway continues: "He was haunted
by fear of slave power; and he remarked, 'We may
wake up some fine morning and find the Democratic
party wheeled around, and united on some base and
ruinous concession for peace.' "

According to Conway (this in July, 1861), "the
pain and responsibility of editing the *Tribune* were
telling on him sadly." The editor gave Conway an
article by Whitelaw Reid, who wrote over the pen
name of "Agate," and "in talking it over he deplored
his own connection with journalism." Conway quotes
him as saying further: "A man had better be a hod-
carrier than a journalist."

This conversation was held in Washington, and there was more behind it than Conway knew. Greeley was really lamenting his fate to be held responsible for journalistic matters over which he had no control. The policy of turning the *Tribune* over to a stock company had been a mistake. It brought other voices and interests into the management and these made themselves felt in checking what were thought to be Greeley's mistakes. His willingness to let the states depart had reacted unfavorably upon the paper, which was now clamoring for a move against Richmond, where the Confederate Congress was to meet on July 20, 1861, and establish that city as the Confederate capital. The able and aggressive managing editor, Dana, was really editing the paper, and, in Greeley's absence, ran for a week this besom at the head of the editorial page:

THE NATION'S WAR CRY

Forward to Richmond! Forward to Richmond! The Rebel Congress mnst not be allowed to meet there on the 20th of July! By that date the place must be held by the National Army!

Now the editor did not provoke or approve this. It was done by others in the *Tribune* office to offset his peace policy. Fitz Henry Warren, Washington correspondent, was the author. The result of the nagging was the ill-advised movement that brought on the battle of Bull Run, with its defeat and shame, July 21, 1861. Most of the Union forces engaged did not stop running until they reached Washington the next day. Congressmen and others who had driven out in carriages to witness the expected triumph, joined in the frantic flight of the soldiers. The account written for the London *Times* by Sir William H. Russell, who thereby earned the sobriquet "Bull Run" Russell, put a sneering stamp upon our military prowess that Europe apparently accepted as its standard until taught differently in the great World War. The Union loss at Bull Run was 481 killed, 1,011 wounded and 1,400 missing—mostly taken prisoners. The astonished Confederates lost 269, and 1,480 were wounded.

Russell was compelled to leave the country for accurately reporting the affair, but the chief blame fell upon the editor of the *Tribune*. The mischievous Bennett, in the New York *Herald,* held high the accusing finger. Greeley felt it necessary to decry the foolish move in the *Tribune* of July twenty-fifth under the caption, "Just Once," saying:

"An individual's griefs or wrongs may be of little account to others; but when the gravest public interests are imperiled through personal attacks and the coarsest imputations of base motives, the assailed, however humble, owes duties to others which can not be disregarded. I propose here to refute months of persistent and envenomed defamation by the statement of a few facts.

"I am charged with having opposed the selection of Governor Seward for a place in President Lincoln's Cabinet. That is utterly, absolutely false, the President himself being my witness. I might call many others, but one such is sufficient.

"I am charged with what is called 'opposing the administration' because of that selection, and various paragraphs which have from time to time appeared in the *Tribune* are quoted to sustain this inculpation.

The simple fact that not one of those paragraphs was either written or in any wise suggested or prompted by me suffices for that charge. It is true—I have no desire to conceal or belittle it—that my ideas as to the general conduct of the war for the Union are those repeatedly expressed by myself and others through the *Tribune,* and, of course, are not those on which the conduct of that war has been based. It is true that I hold and have urged that this war can not, must not, be a long one; that it must be prosecuted with the utmost energy, promptness and vigor, or it will prove a failure; that every week's flying of the secession flag defiantly within a day's walk of Washington renders the suppression of the revolt more difficult, if not doubtful. It is true that I think a government that begins the work of putting down a rebellion by forming 'camps of instruction,' or anything of that sort, is likely to make a very long job of it. It is true that I think our obvious policy, under the circumstances, would have been to be courteous and long-suffering toward foreign powers, but resolute and ready in our dealings with armed rebels; and it seems to me that the opposite course has been taken. But the watchword, 'Forward to Richmond,' is not mine, nor anything of like import. I wish to evade no responsibility, but to repel a personal aspersion. So with regard to the late article urging a change in the Cabinet. While I know that some of the best material in the country enters into the composition of that Cabinet, I yet feel that changes might be made therein with advantage to the public service. Yet I did not write, and I did not intend to have published, the article calling for a change of Cabinet, which only appears through a misapprehension. I shrunk from printing it in part because any good effect it might have was likely to be neutralized by the very course which had been taken— that of assailing me as its supposed author.

"I have no desire in the premises but that what is best for the country shall be done. If the public judge

that this great end—an energetic and successful prosecution of the war—will be most surely subserved by
retaining the Cabinet as it is, I acquiesce in that decision. The end being secured, the means are to me
utterly indifferent.

"I wish to be distinctly understood as not seeking
to be relieved from any responsibility for urging the
advance of the Union grand army into Virginia,
though the precise phrase, 'Forward to Richmond!' is
not mine, and I would have preferred not to iterate it.
I thought that that army, one hundred thousand
strong, might have been in the rebel capital on or
before the twentieth instant, while I felt that there
were urgent reasons why it should be there if possible.
And now, if any one imagine that I, or any one connected with the *Tribune*, ever commanded or imagined
such strategy as the launching of barely thirty thousand of the one hundred thousand Union volunteers
within fifty miles of Washington against ninety thousand rebels enveloped in a labyrinth of strong en-
trenchments and unreconnoitered masked batteries,
then demonstration would be lost on his closed ear.
But I will not dwell on this. If I am needed as a
scapegoat for all the military blunders of the last
month, so be it. Individuals must die that the nation
may live. If I can serve her best in that capacity, I
do not shrink from the ordeal.

"Henceforth I bar all criticism in these columns on
army movements, past or future, unless somebody
should undertake to prove that General Patterson is a
wise and brave commander. He seems to have none
to speak his praises; so, if there is anything to be said
in his behalf, I will make an exception in his favor.
Other than this, the subject is closed and sealed. Correspondents and reporters may state facts, but must
forbear comments. I know there is truth that yet
needs to be uttered on this subject, but this paper has
done its full share—all that it ought, and perhaps
more than it could afford to do—and henceforth stands

back for others. Only I beg it to be understood—once for all—that if less than half the Union armies directly at hand are hurled against all the rebel forces that could be concentrated—more than double their number—on ground specially chosen and strongly fortified by the traitors, the *Tribune* does not approve and should not be held responsible for such madness. Say what you will of the past, but remember this for the future, though we keep silence.

"Henceforth it shall be the *Tribune's* sole vocation to rouse and animate the American people for the terrible ordeal which has befallen them. The great republic eminently needs the utmost exertions of every loyal heart and hand. We have tried to serve her by exposing breakers ahead and around her; henceforth be it ours to strengthen, in all possible ways, the hands of those whose unenviable duty it is to pilot her through them. If more good is thus to be done, let us not repine that some truth must be withheld for a calmer moment, and for less troubled ears.

"The journal which is made the conduit of the most violent of these personal assaults on me attributes the course of the *Tribune* to resentment 'against those who have ever committed the inexpiable offense of thwarting Mr. Greeley's raging and unsatiated thirst for office.'

"I think this justifies me in saying that there is no office in the gift of the government or of the people which I either hope, wish, or expect ever to hold. I certainly shall not parade myself as declining places that are not offered for my acceptance; but I am sure that the President has always known that I desired no office at his hands; and this, not through any violation of my rule above stated, but through the report of mutual and influential friends, who at various times volunteered to ask me if I would take any place whatever under the government, and were uniformly and conclusively assured that I would not.

"Now let the wolves howl on. I do not believe they

can goad me into another personal notice of their ravings.

"Horace Greeley."

This statement he followed up with a letter to Lincoln, reading:

"New York, Monday, July 29, 1861. Midnight.

"Dear Sir: This is my seventh sleepless night—yours, too, doubtless—yet I think I shall not die, because I have no right to die. I must struggle to live, however bitterly. But to business. You are now considered a great man, and I am a hopelessly broken one. You are now undergoing a terrible ordeal, and God has thrown the gravest responsibilities upon you. Do not fear to meet them. Can the rebels be beaten after all that has occurred, and in view of the actual state of feeling caused by our late awful disaster? If they can—and it is your business to ascertain and decide—write me that such is your judgment, so that I may know and do my duty. And if they can not be beaten—if our recent disaster is fatal—do not fear to sacrifice yourself to your country. If the rebels are not to be beaten—if that is your judgment in view of all the light you can get—then every drop of blood henceforth shed in this quarrel will be wantonly, wickedly shed, and the guilt will rest heavily on the the soul of every promoter of the crime. I pray you to decide quickly, and let me know my duty.

"If the Union is irrevocably gone, an armistice for thirty, sixty, ninety, one hundred and twenty days—better still for a year—ought at once to be proposed with a view to a peaceful adjustment. Then Congress should call a national convention, to meet at the earliest possible day. And there should be an immediate and mutual exchange or release of prisoners and a disbandment of forces. I do not consider myself at present a judge of anything but the public sentiment. That seems to me everywhere gathering and deepening against a prosecution of the war. The gloom in this city is funereal—for our dead at Bull Run were many, and they lie unburied yet. On every brow sits sullen, scorching, black despair. It would be easy to have Mr. Crittenden move any proposition that ought to be adopted, or to have it come from any proper quarter. The first point is to ascertain what is best that can be done—which is the measure of our duty—and do that very thing at the earliest moment.

"This letter is written in the strictest confidence, and is for your eye alone. But you are at liberty to say to members of your Cabinet that you know I will second any movement you may see fit to make. But do nothing timidly nor by halves. Send me word what to do. I will live till I can hear it, at all events. If it is best for the country and for mankind that we make peace with the rebels at once, and on their own terms, do not shrink even from that. But bear in mind the greatest truth: 'Whoso would lose his life for my sake shall save it.' Do the thing that is the highest right, and tell me how I am to second you.

"Yours, in the depth of bitterness,

"HORACE GREELEY."

This letter did not become public until late in 1887. Samuel Sinclair then wrote to the *Tribune* in extenuation, January 1, 1888: "When that letter was written, Mr. Greeley had been and was still severely ill with brain fever; the entire letter, in my judgment, revealed that he was on the verge of insanity when he wrote it."

The attack of brain fever followed the undue excitement, surely enough. It lasted two weeks, during which Greeley was delirous and unconscious most of the time. Ill-nourished and overworked, he recovered as by a miracle. His anguish at the untoward fix he found himself in is depicted in the following letter to Conway:

"New York, Aug. 17, 1861.

"My dear Conway: I have yours of the thirteenth. I have been very ill, and am yet too weak to work, yet am doing so because I must. I scarcely slept at all for a week; now the best I can do is to get two or three hours' uneasy oblivion every night. But I hope I shall mend. The *Tribune* did suffer considerably by the truth told by Warren, etc., about the want of purpose and management at Washington, and I think would have been ruined had I not resolved to bend to the storm. I did it very badly, for I was all but insane, yet I hope all will yet be well with us. You see that everybody is now saying that we were right originally with regard to Scott, etc., and that the Cabinet ought to be reconstituted. My strong objection to the attack on the Cabinet was that it would (because of the momentary fury against the *Tribune)* keep them in when they want to go out. No president could afford to have it said that a newspaper had forced him to give battle and then turned out his Cabinet because he lost that battle.

"My friend, the hour is very dark; but I have not lost my faith in God. If this people is worthy to fight and win a battle for Liberty and Law, that battle will be won; if they are not, I do not see that there is any more a place for so weak and poor an instrument as I am. If our baseness requires the humiliation of utter discomfiture, that will be our portion, and the Father of all Good will work out His holy ends through other and purer agencies. In any case, and however the end may be postponed and obscured, *this infernal Rebellion seals the doom of slavery.*

"And so, asking your prayers that my unworthiness may no wise hinder or postpone the fulfillment of God's benign purposes, I remain,

"Yours,

"Horace Greeley."

Greeley was both upset and unfairly criticized. He had never advocated the sending of a single corps against the entire Confederate Army. He had called for a force of 100,000 men, and properly enough criticized the gathering of the forces.

That Greeley had little confidence in Lincoln's ability to end the war by force of arms is apparent from his attitude in openly encouraging foreign intervention as a means of bringing the contest to a close. Collector of Customs Hiram Barney was authority for a statement made to Henry J. Raymond, that Greeley was in touch with Clement L. Vallandigham about such a measure to end the fighting. Raymond himself wrote in his journal, excerpts from which were printed in *Scribner's Magazine* for March, 1890, that, meeting Greeley on the Albany boat, the latter asserted to him his purpose "to carry out the policy of foreign mediation" and so end the conflict, which had become bloody and exhausting. "You'll see," Raymond quotes Greeley as saying, "that I'll drive Lincoln into it." Raymond communicated this to one of the *Tribune's* trustees and received assurances that Greeley would not be permitted to persist in the policy. Besides Vallandigham, he was discussing intervention with the French Minister, Monsieur Mercier, at Washington, and Raymond records that at dinner with Secretary of State Seward in Washington, January 26, 1863, the latter reviewed Greeley's activities and said he had rendered himself liable to prosecution under the so-called "Logan" Act that forbids American citizens from meddling with affairs of state involving foreign nations. (This act is still on the statute books.) Monsieur Mercier was allowed to stay in Washington, though an open sympathizer with the Confederacy who had advised Napoleon III to recognize its government. Lincoln never believed in digging up more snakes than he could kill.

A crowded assembly in the lecture-room of the Smithsonian Institution at Washington, on January 4, 1862, listened to an address by Greeley on the subject of "The Nation." President Lincoln, Salmon P. Chase, Secretary of the Treasury, and several senators and congressmen, ornamented the platform. The speaker declared himself then against compromise, because it implied concessions to armed treason. The misfortune of the country had been in its reluctance to meet its antagonist in the eye. Slavery as the aggressor had earned a rebel's doom. The contest, he was certain, would result in enduring benefits to the cause of human freedom. These sentiments were greeted with great applause, though the President is not reported as having joined in.

A proposition providing for the gradual emancipation of slaves, which, of course, could only be put into effect in the border states that had not seceded, was defeated in Congress in March, 1862. The President called the delegates from these commonwealths together on July 12, 1862, and addressed them. He told them that if they had voted for the measure, "the war would now be substantially ended," adding, "and the plan therein proposed is yet one of the most potent and swift means of ending it." He thought the acceptance of gradual, compensated emancipation by the border states would be a notice to those in arms that they could expect no aid or accession from these and would be inclined to give in. The idea carried with it the migration of the negroes. "Room in South America for colonization," he went on to say, "can be obtained cheaply and in abundance, and when numbers shall be large enough to be company and encouragement for one another, the freed people will not be so reluctant to go."

To support his desire to keep the border states satisfied, he had overruled the emancipating acts of General John C. Fremont in Missouri, and of General David Hunter in Virginia. Only General Benjamin F. Butler was sustained, because of his device of holding escaped negroes as "contraband of war" and keeping them at work for the army.

"You are patriots and statesmen," Lincoln informed his hearers. This was mere flattery. They were neither, and by their failure to conform to the President's request, gave Greeley and the abolitionists more reasons for their demand for absolute emancipation with no pay to any one who held property in human flesh. These now became most impatient at the delay.

That Greeley forced Lincoln's hand in the matter of the Emancipation Proclamation is fairly established. The President had been hard pressed toward emancipation by Chase, Secretary of the Treasury, and by Stanton, Secretary of War. That he did not act sooner was due to several reasons—not all good. He feared the effect on the half loyal border states; cherished, in a way, some hope of a compromise that might save the Union and leave slavery to some later adjustment, and was wary of the effect of yielding to abolition sentiment on many people in the North. Lincoln's political sense was his guide, not his emotion.

He was not worrying about the slave; his concern was for either conquering or conciliating the master. That slavery might emerge triumphant from the conflict was one of the worries uppermost in Greeley's mind. In this humor he wrote an open letter to the President, which was printed in the *Tribune* of August 19, 1862. It was entitled "The Prayer of Twenty Millions," and bore the editor's signature. The concluding paragraphs contain the gist of the matter. These read:

"On the face of this wide earth, Mr. President, there is not one disinterested, determined, intelligent champion of the Union cause who does not feel that all attempts to put down the Rebellion, and at the same time uphold its inciting cause, are preposterous and futile—that the Rebellion, if crushed out to-morrow, would be renewed within a year if slavery were left in full vigor—that army officers, who remain to this day devoted to slavery, can at best be half-way loyal to the Union—and that every hour of deference to slavery is an hour of added and deepened peril to the Union. I appeal to the testimony of your ambassadors in Europe. It is freely at your service, not mine. Ask them to tell you candidly whether the seeming subserviency of your policy to the slave-holding, slavery-upbuilding interest, is not the perplexity, the despair, of statesmen of all parties; and be admonished by the general answer!

"I close as I began, with the statement that what an immense majority of the loyal millions of your countrymen require of you is a frank, declared, unqualified, ungrudging execution of the laws of the land, more especially of the Confiscation Act. That act gives freedom to the slaves of rebels coming within our lines, or whom those lines may at any time enclose—we ask you to render it due obedience by publicly requiring all your subordinates to recognize and obey it. The rebels are everywhere using the late anti-negro riots of the North—as they have long used your officers' treatment of negroes in the South—to convince the slaves that they have nothing to hope from a Union success—that we mean in that case to sell them into a bitter bondage to defray the cost of the war. Let them impress this as a truth on the great mass of their ignorant and credulous bondmen, and the Union will never be restored—never. We can not conquer ten millions of people united in solid phalanx against us, powerfully aided by northern sympathizers and European allies. We must have scouts, guides, spies, cooks, teamsters, diggers, and choppers, from the blacks of the South—whether we allow them to fight for us or not—or we shall be baffled and repelled. As one of the millions who would gladly have avoided this struggle at any sacrifice but that of principle and honor, but who now feel that the triumph of the Union is indispensable not only to the existence of our country but to the well-being of mankind, I entreat you to render a hearty and unequivocal obedience to the law of the land."

No president had ever been "called" in this resonant fashion before. Greeley made the issue between man and man, between compromise and direct action. It was a challenge that could not be overlooked or set aside. Lincoln answered by telegraph, on August 22, 1862, in these terms:

> "Executive Mansion, Washington,
> "Aug. 22, 1862.

"Honorable Horace Greeley:
  "Dear Sir: I have just read yours of the 19th instant, addressed to myself through the New York *Tribune*.
  "If there be in it any statements or assumptions of fact which I may know to be erroneous, I do not now and there controvert them.
  "If there be any inference which I may believe to

be falsely drawn, I do not now and here argue against them.

"If there be perceptible in it an impatient and dictatorial tone, I waive it in deference to an old friend whose heart I have always supposed to be right.

"As to the policy I 'seem to be pursuing,' as you say, I have not meant to leave any one in doubt. I would save the Union. I would save it in the shortest way under the Constitution.

"The sooner the national authority can be restored, the nearer the Union will be the Union as it was.

"If there be those who would not save the Union unless they could at the same time save slavery, I do not agree with them.

"If there be those who would not save the Union unless at the same time destroy slavery, I do not agree with them.

"*My paramount object is to save the Union, and not to save or destroy slavery.*

"If I could save the Union without freeing any slave, I would do it—if I could save it by freeing all the slaves, I would do it—and if I could do it by freeing some and leaving others alone, I would also do that.

"What I do about slavery and the colored race, I do because I believe it helps to save this Union; and what I forbear, I forbear because I do not believe it would help me to save the Union.

"I shall do less whenever I shall believe what I am doing hurts the cause; and I shall do more whenever I believe doing more will help the cause.

"I shall try to correct errors when shown to be errors; and I shall adopt new views so fast as they shall appear to be true views.

"I have here stated my purpose according to my views of official duty; and I intend no modification of my oft-expressed personal wish that all men everywhere could be free.   "Yours,

"A. LINCOLN."

Though ostensibly an answer to his "Prayer of Twenty Millions," this letter was nothing of the sort, Greeley maintained in the lecture quoted earlier: "I had not besought him to proclaim a general emancipation; I had only urged him to give full effect to the laws of the land, which prescribed that slaves employed with their master's acquiescence in support of rebellion should thenceforth be treated as free by such employment, and by the general authority. I have no doubt that Mr. Lincoln's letter was prepared before he ever saw my 'Prayer' and that this was merely used by him as an opportunity, an occasion, an excuse, for setting forth his own altered opinion—changed not by his volition, but by circumstances—fairly before the country."

One month later, on September 22, 1862, the Emancipation Proclamation was made public. Lincoln did not credit Greeley with building the fire under him, but is quoted as having said: "I made a solemn vow before God, that if General Lee should be driven back from Pennsylvania, I would crown the result by a declaration of freedom of the slaves." Inconsistent with this is the fact that, while General Robert E. Lee had been checked at Antietam on September sixteenth-seventeenth, Major-General George B. McClellan, of the Army of the Potomac, was not credited with the victory, but had his command taken from him and given to the incompetent Ambrose E. Burnside. Presumably to reward the man who did the driving back was not included in the "solemn vow before God."

Coldly analyzed, the Proclamation was not a note of thanksgiving, but one of political necessity. Mc-

Clellan was taken out of the path to the presidency, while emancipation silenced Greeley and his abolitionist supporters. The excuse for shelving McClellan was that he had not followed up his success. With all allowance for his vanity and lack of team work with Lincoln, he was an able officer and had no defeats on his record. Greeley and McClellan combined could have defeated Lincoln for reelection in 1864, had the one grown in glory and the other been allowed to remain critical as to the main issue. Lincoln cleverly disposed of both.

Moreover, the proclamation, now rated as a glorious action, met with nothing like full Republican favor. Thurlow Weed wrote John Bigelow: "I greatly fear that the Proclamation has 'done for us.' I do dislike to say this, even to you, but I can not help it. In the very strongest and broadest sense of language, I assure you that it has strengthened the South and weakened the North. . . . I have done with Greeley. He is no longer troublesome. There is a mutiny in the *Tribune* Building and it is possible his own hounds will turn upon him"

A bit of feeling concerning Greeley crept into a speech Lincoln made before a Chicago delegation which had called on him, September 13, 1862, to urge emancipation. He was plainly bothered and replied rather lamely to their petition. "Would my word free the slaves?" he asked. He did not want to issue a mandate that the whole world would see must be necessarily inoperative, "like the Pope's bull against the comet." The negroes freed by General Benjamin F. Butler as contraband of war ate more than his army, and there was nothing to prevent the rebels from enslaving them as fast as caught. When this happened "I am very ungenerously attacked for it. For instance, when, after the late battles at and near Bull Run, an expedition went out from Washington to bury the dead and bring in the wounded, and the rebels seized the blacks sent along to help and sent them into slavery, Horace Greeley said in his paper that the Government would probably do nothing about it. What could I do?"

Greeley records that he did not see the President between January, 1862, and February, 1863, when the latter remarked to him that emancipation had not done the expected good at home, but "had helped us abroad"—it had been indorsed by British workmen.

While Grant, now in full charge of the war, had proclaimed his purpose to "fight it out on this line if it takes all summer," the month of July, 1864, came in upon a despondent country. The Wilderness, Spottsylvania and Cold Harbor had taken a terrible toll, and Grant was blocked before Petersburg, having shifted his line to the south of Richmond instead of "fighting it out" on the one determined upon. McClellan loomed large for the presidency, and the general outlook for the Republicans and their administration was dark. In the South Lee's victories cost more than they gained and were exhibitions of courage rather than accomplishment. The war was taking on a savage aspect. Northern men were starving in southern prison camps, and southern ones dying of smallpox and pneumonia in camps of the North. Grant had stopped exchanges as strengthening Lee. All this bred sorrow, depression and lack of faith.

On both sides there grew a feeling that some way

out should be found that would not require going on to the bitter end. North Carolina developed a strong sentiment for truce and settlement, making the matter an issue in the state gubernatorial campaign. Sundry southerners undertook to open negotiations through northern Democrats. These were under way, in early July, when Greeley saw fit to intervene. His account of his own proceedings follows:

"Sometime since it was announced by telegraph from Halifax that Messrs. C. C. Clay, of Alabama; Jacob Thompson, of Mississippi [ex-United States Senators] Professor J. P. Holcombe, of the University of Virginia, and George N. Sanders, of Kentucky, had reached that city from Dixie via Bermuda, on important business, and all of these but Mr. Thompson (who was in Toronto) were soon quartered at the Clifton, on the Canada side of Niagara Falls. I heard soon after of confidential interviews between some or all of those gentlemen and leading Democrats, from our own and neighboring states, and there were telegraphic whispers of overtures for reconstruction, and conditions were set forth as those on which the Confederates would consent to reunion. (I can not say that any of these reports were authentic.) At length, after several less direct intimations, I received a private letter from Mr. Sanders, stating that Messrs. Clay, Holcombe, himself, and another, desired to visit Washington, upon complete and qualified protection being given by the President or the Secretary of War.

"As I saw no reason why the opposition should be the sole recipients of these gentlemen's overtures, if such they were (and it is stated that Mr. Clay aforesaid is preparing or to prepare an important letter to the Chicago Convention), I wrote the President, urging him to invite the rebel gentlemen aforesaid to Washington, there to open their budget. I stated expressly that I knew not what they would propose if so invited; but I could imagine no offer that might be made by them which would not conduce, in one way or another, to a restoration of the integrity and just authority of the Union.

"The President ultimately acquiesced in this view so far as to consent that the rebel agents should visit Washington, but directed that I should proceed to Niagara, and accompany them thence to the capital. This service I most reluctantly undertook, feeling deeply and observing that almost any one else might better have been sent on this errand. But time seemed precious, and I immediately started."

The man to whom Greeley appealed for an opening was W. C. (Colorado) Jewett, who replied to his intimation of a willingness to start something, in these terms:

"Niagara Falls, July 5, 1864.

"My dear Mr. Greeley: In reply to your note, I have to advise having just left Honorable George N. Sanders, of Kentucky, on the Canada side. I am authorized to state to you, for your use only, not the public, that two ambassadors of Davis & Co. are now in Canada, with full and complete powers of a peace, and Mr. Sanders requests that you come on immediately to me, at Cataract House, to have a private interview; or if you will send the President's protection for him and two friends, they will come on and meet you. He says the whole matter can be consummated by you, them, and President Lincoln. Telegraph me in such form that I may know if you are to come here, or they to come on with me.

"Yours,
"W. C. JEWETT."

Greeley laid the letter before President Lincoln immediately upon its receipt, writing him this explanation:

"New York, July 7, 1864.

"My dear Sir: I venture to enclose you a letter and telegraphic despatch that I received yesterday from our irrepressible friend, Colorado Jewett, at Niagara Falls. I think they deserve attention. Of course I do not indorse Jewett's positive averment that his friends at the Falls have 'full power' from J. D., though I do not doubt that he thinks they have. I let that statement stand as simply evidencing the anxiety of the Confederates everywhere for peace. So much is beyond doubt. I therefore venture to remind you that our bleeding, bankrupt, almost dying country also longs for peace—shudders at the prospect of fresh conscriptions, of further wholesale devastations, and of new rivers of human blood; and a wide-spread conviction that the government and its prominent supporters are not anxious for peace, and do not improve proffered opportunities to achieve it, is doing great harm now, and is morally certain, unless removed, to do far greater in the approaching elections. It is not enough that we anxiously desire a true and lasting peace; we ought to demonstrate and establish the truth beyond cavil. The fact that A. H. Stephens was not permitted a year ago to visit and confer with the authorities at Washington has done us harm which the tone of the late national convention at Baltimore is not calculated to counteract. I entreat you, in your own time and manner, to submit overtures for pacification to the southern insurgents, which the impartial must pronounce frank and generous. If only with a view to the momentous election soon to occur in North Carolina, and of the draft to be enforced in the free states, this should be done at once. I would give the safe conduct required by the rebel envoys at Niagara, upon their parole to avoid observation and to refrain from all communication with their sympathizers in the loyal states; but you may see reasons for declining it. But whether through them or otherwise, do not, I entreat you, fail to make the southern people comprehend that you, and all of us, are anxious for peace, and prepared to grant liberal terms. I venture to suggest the following plan of adjustment:

"1. The Union is restored and declared perpetual.
"2. Slavery is utterly and forever abolished throughout the same.
"3. A complete amnesty of all political offenses, with a restoration of all the inhabitants of each state to all the privileges of citizens of the United States.
"4. The Union to pay four hundred million dollars ($400,000,000) in five per cent. United States stock to the late slave states, loyal and secession alike, to be apportioned pro rata, according to their slave population respectively, by the census of 1860, in compensation for the losses of their loyal citizens by the abolition of slavery. Each state to be entitled to its quota upon the ratification by its legislature of this adjustment. The bonds to be at the absolute disposal of the legislature aforesaid.
"5. The said slave states to be entitled henceforth to representation in the House on the basis of their total, instead of their Federal population, the whole now being free.
"6. A national convention, to be assembled as soon as may be, to ratify this adjustment, and make such changes in the Constitution as may be deemed advisable.
"Mr. President, I fear you do not realize how intently the people desire any peace consistent with the national integrity and honor, and how joyously they will hail its achievement and bless its authors. With United States stocks worth but forty cents in gold per dollar, and drafting about to commence on the third million of Union soldiers, can this be wondered at? I do not say that a just peace is now attainable, though I believe it to be so; but I do say that a frank offer by you to the insurgents of terms which the impartial say ought to be accepted, will, at the worst, prove an im-

mense and sorely needed advantage to the national cause. It may save us from a northern insurrection.
"Yours truly,
"HORACE GREELEY.
"P. S. Even though it should be deemed unadvisable to make an offer of terms to the rebels, I insist that, in any possible case, it is desirable that any offer they may be disposed to make should be received, and either accepted or rejected. I beg you to invite those now at Niagara to exhibit their credentials and submit their ultimatum.

"H. G."

The President was probably tired himself, discouraged by military defeats, bedeviled by both the opposition and the meddlers in his own party. He therefore did not kick the proposition out or invoke the Logan Act. His response was pointed, shrewd and wise. It read:

"Washington, D. C., July 9, 1864.
"Honorable Horace Greeley: Dear Sir:—Your letter of the 7th, with inclosures, received. If you can find any person anywhere professing to have any proposition of Jefferson Davis in writing, for peace, embracing the restoration of the Union and the abandonment of slavery, whatever else it embraces, say to him he may come to me with you; and that if he really brings such proposition, he shall, at the least, have safe conduct with the paper (and without publicity if he chooses) to the point where you shall have met him. The same if there be two or more persons.
"Yours truly,
"A. LINCOLN."

Greeley saw the neat trap set for him and replied rather tartly:

"Office of The Tribune, New York, July 10, 1864.

"My dear Sir: I have yours of yesterday. Whether there be persons at Niagara (or elsewhere) who are empowered to commit the rebels by negotiation, is a question; but if there be such, there is no question at all that they would decline to exhibit their credentials to me, much more to open their budget and give me their best terms. Green as I may be, I am not quite so verdant as to imagine anything of the sort. I have neither purpose nor desire to be made a confidant, far less an agent, in such negotiations. But I do deeply realize that the rebel chiefs achieved a most decided advantage in proposing, or pretending to propose, to have A. H. Stephens visit Washington as a peacemaker, and being rudely repulsed; and I am anxious that the ground lost to the national cause by that mistake shall somehow be regained in season for effect on the approaching North Carolina election. I will see if I can get a look into the hand of whomsoever may be at Niagara; though that is a project so manifestly hopeless that I have little heart for it, still I shall try.

"Meantime I wish you would consider the propriety of somehow apprising the people of the South, especially those of North Carolina, that no overture or advance looking to peace and reunion has ever been repelled by you, but that such a one would at any time have been cordially received and favorably regarded, and would still be.

"Yours,

"HORACE GREELEY.

"Honorable A. Lincoln."

He proceeded, however, to hold the door open. The first result was a letter from Sanders, which said:

"Clifton House, Niagara Falls, C. W., July 12, 1864.

"Sir: I am authorized to say that Honorable

Clement C. Clay, of Alabama, Professor James P. Holcombe, of Virginia, and George N. Sanders, of Dixie, are ready and willing to go at once to Washington, upon complete and unqualified protection being given, either by the President or Secretary of War. Let the permission include the three names and one other.

"Very respectfully,
"GEORGE N. SANDERS.
"To Honorable Horace Greeley."

On the strength of this, Greeley wrote Lincoln:

"Office of The Tribune, New York, July 12, 1864.

"My dear Sir: I have now information upon which I can rely, that two persons duly commissioned and empowered to negotiate for peace are at this moment not far from Niagara Falls, in Canada, and are desirous of conferring with yourself, or with such persons as you may appoint and empower to treat with them. Their names (only given in confidence) are Honorable Clement C. Clay, of Alabama, and Honorable Jacob Thompson, of Mississippi. If you should prefer to meet them in person, they require safe conduct for themselves and for George N. Sanders, who will accompany them. Should you choose to empower one or more persons to treat with them in Canada, they will of course, need no safe conduct; but they can not be expected to exhibit credentials save to commissioners empowered as they are. In negotiating directly with yourself, all grounds of cavil would be avoided, and you would be enabled at all times to act upon the freshest advices of the military situation. You will of course understand that I know nothing and have proposed nothing as to terms, and that nothing is conceded or taken for granted by the meeting of persons empowered to negotiate for peace. All that is assumed is a mutual desire to terminate this wholesale slaughter, if a basis of adjustment can be mutually agreed on; and it seems to me high time that an effort

to this end should be made. I am, of course, quite
other than sanguine that a peace can now be made, but
I am quite sure that a frank, earnest, anxious effort
to terminate the war on honorable terms would im-
mensely strengthen the government in case of its failure, and would help us in the eyes of the civilized
world, which now accuses us of obstinacy and indispo-
sition even to seek a peaceful solution of our san-
guinary, devastating conflict.

"Hoping to hear that you have resolved to act in
the premises, and to act so promptly that a good influence may even yet be exerted on the North Carolina
election next month,

"I remain yours,

"HORACE GREELEY.

"Honorable A. Lincoln, Washington."

The President's reply was short: "I have just
received yours of the thirteenth [twelfth] and am disappointed by it. I was not expecting you to send me
a letter, but to bring me a man or men. Mr. Hay goes
to you with my answer to yours of the thirteenth
[twelfth]."

"Mr. Hay" was Colonel (then Major) John Hay,
who was later to join Greeley's staff. The letter he
brought was, of course, official. The President wrote:

"Executive Mansion, Washington, July 15, 1864.
"Honorable Horace Greeley: My dear Sir:—
Yours of the thirteenth [twelfth] is just received, and
I am disappointed that you have not already reached
here with those commissioners. If they would consent
to come on being shown my letter to you of the ninth
inst., show that and this to them; and if they will
come on the terms stated in the former, bring them.
I not only intend a sincere effort for peace, but I in-

tend that you shall be a personal witness that it is made.

"Yours truly,
"A. LINCOLN."

Hay reached New York on the morning of July sixteenth, and went at once to see Greeley, reporting back to Lincoln after the interview: "Arrived this morning at six A. M. and delivered your letter a few minutes after. Although he thinks some one less known would create less excitement and be less embarrassed by public curiosity, still, he will start immediately, if he can have an absolute safe conduct for four persons to be named by him. Your letter he does not think will guard them from arrest, and with only those letters, he would have to explain the whole matter to any officer who might choose to hinder him. If this meets your approbation I can write the order in your name as A. A. G., or you can send it by mail."

Hay put up at the Astor House, where the President replied by wire: "Write the safe conduct as you propose, without waiting for one by mail from me. If there is or is not anything in the affair, I wish to know it without unnecessary delay." Accordingly Hay wrote out the safe conduct. It read:

"The President of the United States directs that the four persons whose names follow, to-wit: Honorable Clement C. Clay, Honorable Jacob Thompson, Professor James P. Holcombe, George N. Sanders, shall have safe conduct to this city of Washington, in company with the Honorable Horace Greeley, and shall be exempt from arrest or annoyance of any kind from any officer of the United States during their journey to the city of Washington. By order of the President."

Armed with the document, Greeley proceeded at once to Niagara Falls, and began negotiations across the chasm. He notified the awaiting Confederates of his presence in this fashion:

"Niagara Falls, N. Y., July 17, 1864.

"Gentlemen: I am informed that you are duly accredited from Richmond as the bearers of propositions looking to the establishment of peace; that you desire to visit Washington in the fulfillment of your mission, and that you further desire that Mr. George N. Sanders shall accompany you. If my information be thus far substantially correct, I am authorized by the President of the United States to tender you his safe conduct on the journey proposed, and to accompany you at the earliest time that will be agreeable to you."

Clay and Holcombe replied:

"Clifton House, Niagara Falls, July 18, 1864.
"Sir: We have the honor to acknowledge your favor of the seventeenth inst., which would have been answered on yesterday but for the absence of Mr. Clay. The safe conduct of the President of the United States has been tendered us, we regret to state, under some misapprehension of facts. We have not been accredited to him from Richmond as bearers of propositions looking to the establishment of peace. We are, however, in the confidential employment of our government, and are entirely familiar with its wishes and opinions on that subject; and we feel authorized to declare that, if the circumstances disclosed in this correspondence were communicated to Richmond, we would be at once invested with the authority to which your letter refers; or other gentlemen, clothed with full powers, would be immediately sent to Washington with the view of hastening a consummation so

much to be desired, and terminating at the earliest possible moment the calamities of the war. We respectfully solicit, through your intervention, a safe conduct to Washington, and thence by any route which may be designated, through your lines to Richmond. We would be gratified if Mr. George N. Sanders was embraced in this privilege.

"Permit us, in conclusion, to acknowledge our obligations to you for the interest you have manifested in the furtherance of our wishes, and to express the hope that in any event you will afford us the opportunity of tendering them in person before you leave the Falls.

"We remain, very respectfully,
"C. C. CLAY, JR.,
"J. F. HOLCOMBE."

This was not at all what Greeley had anticipated. He therefore responded:

"International Hotel, Niagara, N. Y., July 18, 1864.

"Gentlemen: I have the honor to acknowledge the receipt of yours of this date by the hand of Mr. W. C. Jewett. The state of facts therein presented being materially different from that which was understood to exist by the President when he entrusted me with the safe conduct required, it seems to me on every account advisable that I should communicate with him by telegraph, and solicit fresh instructions, which I shall at once proceed to do. I hope to be able to transmit the results this afternoon; and at all events I shall do so at the earliest moment.

"Yours truly,
"HORACE GREELEY."

The telegram sent to the White House was as follows:

"Niagara Falls, July 18, 1864.

"Honorable Abraham Lincoln, President: I have communicated with the gentlemen in question, and do not find them so empowered as I was previously assured. They say that 'We are, however, in the confidential employment of our government, and entirely familiar with its wishes and opinions on that subject; and we feel authorized to declare that, if the circumstances disclosed in this correspondence were communicated to Richmond, we would at once be invested with the authority to which your letter refers, or other gentlemen, clothed with full powers, would immediately be sent to Washington with the view of hastening a consummation so much to be desired, and terminating at the earliest possible moment the calamities of war. We respectfully solicit, through your intervention, a safe conduct to Washington, and thence by any route which may be designated to Richmond.' Such is the more material portion of the gentlemen's letter. I will transmit the entire correspondence, if desired.

"Awaiting your further instructions, I remain yours,

"HORACE GREELEY."

The "commissioners" sent word to Greeley by Jewett, who was on the ground, that they would await word from Washington, July nineteenth. Greeley had informed them that he had received, later the night before, a message from Washington to the effect that further instructions were under way which he felt "confident" would enable him "to answer definitely your note of yesterday morning" and regretting the delay. He thought the "instructions" would arrive by noon on the twentieth. The "commissioners" graciously promised to be on hand to receive them. Colonel Hay was bringing the "instructions" in person, to the relief of Greeley, who sorely needed something solid to stand on. He duly arrived on the twentieth, and in company with Greeley, crossed the river to Clifton, where Hay handed to Holcombe this note in Lincoln's handwriting:

"Executive Mansion, Washington, D. C., July 18, 1864. "To Whom it may Concern: Any proposition which embraces the restoration of peace, the integrity of the whole Union, and the abandonment of slavery, and which comes by and with an authority that can control the armies now at war against the United States, will be received and considered by the Executive Government of the United States, and will be met by liberal terms on other substantial and collateral points, and the bearer thereof shall have safe conduct both ways.

"ABRAHAM LINCOLN."

"I left the Falls by the next train," records Greeley in his account of the affair, "leaving Major Hay to receive any response to the President's proffer should any be made, but there was none." Hay, on Greeley's departure, despatched this formal note to Holcombe:

"Major Hay would respectfully inquire whether Professor Holcombe and the gentlemen associated with him desire to send to Washington by Major Hay any messages in reference to the communication delivered to him on yesterday, and in that case when he may expect to be favored with such messages."

To this Holcombe replied with equal formality:

"Mr. Holcombe presents his compliments to Major Hay, and greatly regrets if his return to Washington has been delayed by any expectation of an answer to the communication which Mr. Holcombe received from him on yesterday, to be delivered to the President of the United States. That communication was accepted as the response to a letter of Messrs. Clay and Holcombe to the Honorable H. Greeley, and to that gentleman an answer has been transmitted.''

Greeley advised Jewett of his departure in a note, which read:

"In leaving the Falls I feel bound to state that I have had no intercourse with the Confederate gentlemen at the Clifton House, but such as I was fully authorized to hold by the President of the United States, and that I have done nothing in the premises but in fulfillment of his injunctions. The notes, therefore, which you have interchanged between those gentlemen and myself, can in no case subject you to the imputation of unauthorized dealing with public enemies.''

To Jewett the commissioners wrote, in acknowledging the news:

"We are in receipt of your note admonishing us of the departure of Honorable Horace Greeley from the Falls, that he regrets the sad termination of the initiatory steps taken for peace, in consequence of the change made by the President in his instructions to convoy commissioners to Washington for negotiations unconditionally, and that Mr. Greeley will be pleased to receive any answer we may have to make through you. We avail ourselves of this offer to enclose a letter to Mr. Greeley, which you will oblige us by delivering. We can not take leave of you without expressing our thanks for your courtesy and kind offices as the intermediary through whom our correspondence with Mr. Greeley has been conducted.''

The "commissioners" cleared their skirts in the letter to Greeley, summing themselves up in this fashion:

"The paper handed to Mr. Holcombe on yesterday in your presence by Major Hay, Assistant Adjutant-General, as an answer to the application in our note of the 18th inst., is couched in the following terms:

" 'Executive Mansion, Washington, D. C., July 18, 1864.

" 'To Whom It May Concern:

" 'Any proposition which embraces the restoration of peace, the integrity of the whole Union, and the abandonment of slavery, and which comes by and with an authority that can control the armies now at war against the United States, will be received and considered by the Executive Government of the United States, and will be met by liberal terms on other substantial and collateral points, and the bearer or bearers thereof shall have safe conduct both ways.

" 'ABRAHAM LINCOLN.'

"The application to which we refer was elicited by your letter of the seventeenth instant, in which you inform Mr. Jacob Thompson and ourselves that you were authorized by the President of the United States to tender us his safe conduct, on the hypothesis that we were 'duly accredited from Richmond as bearers of propositions looking to the establishment of peace,' and desired a visit to Washington in the fulfillment of this mission. This assertion, to which we then gave, and still do, entire credence, was accepted by us as the evidence of an unexpected but most gratifying change in the policy of the President—a change which we felt authorized to hope might terminate in the conclusion of a peace mutually just, honorable, and advantageous to the North and to the South, exacting no condition but that we should be 'duly accredited from Richmond as bearers of propositions looking to the establishment of peace.'

"Thus proffering a basis for a conference as comprehensive as we could desire, it seemed to us that the President opened a door which had previously been closed against the Confederate States for a full interchange of sentiments, free discussion of conflicting opinions, and untrammeled effort to remove all causes of controversy by liberal negotiations. We, indeed, could not claim the benefits of a safe conduct which had been extended to us in a character we had no right to assume and had never affected to possess; but the uniform declarations of our Executive and Congress, and their thrice repeated and as often repulsed attempts to open negotiations, furnish a sufficient pledge that this conciliatory manifestation on the part of the President of the United States would be met by them in a temper of equal magnanimity. We had, therefore, no hesitation in declaring that if this correspondence was communicated to the President of the Confederate States he would promptly embrace the opportunity presented for seeking a peaceful solution of this unhappy strife.

"We feel confident that you must share our profound regret that the spirit which dictated the first step toward peace had not continued to animate the counsels of your President. Had the representatives of the two governments met to consider this question—the most momentous ever submitted to human statesmanship—in a temper of becoming moderation and equity, followed as their deliberations would have been by the prayers and benedictions of every patriot and Christian on the habitable globe, who is there so bold as to say that the frightful waste of individual happiness and the public prosperity which is daily saddening the universal heart might not have been terminated, or if the desolation and carnage of war must still be endured through weary years of blood and suffering, that there might not at least have been infused into its conduct something more of the spirit which softens and partially redeems its brutalities?

"Instead of the safe conduct which we solicited, and which your first letter gave us every reason to suppose would be extended for the purpose of initiating a negotiation in which neither government would compromise its rights or its dignity, a document had been presented which provoked as much indignation as surprise. It bears no feature of resemblance to that which was originally offered and is unlike any paper which ever before emanated from the constitutional executive of a free people. Addressed 'To whom it may concern,' it precludes negotiation, and prescribes in advance the terms and conditions of peace. It returns to the original policy of 'no bargaining, no negotiations, no truces with rebels, except to bury their dead, until every man shall have laid down his arms, submitted to the government, and sued for mercy.'

"What may be the explanation of this sudden and entire change in the views of the President, of this rude withdrawal of a courteous overture for negotiation at the moment it was likely to be accepted, of this emphatic recall of words of peace just uttered, and fresh blasts of war to the bitter end, we leave for the speculation of those who have the means or inclination to penetrate the mysteries of his Cabinet, or follow the caprice of his imperial will. It is enough for us to say that we have no use whatever for the paper which has been placed in our hands. We could not transmit it to the President of the Confederate States without offering him an indignity, dishonoring ourselves, and incurring the well-merited scorn of our countrymen.

"Whilst an ardent desire for peace pervades the people of the Confederate States, we rejoice to believe that there are few, if any, among them who would purchase it at the expense of liberty, honor and self-respect. If it can be secured only by their submission to terms of conquest, the generation is yet unborn which will witness its restitution. If there be any military autocrat in the North who is entitled to proffer the conditions of this manifesto, there is none in the South authorized to entertain them. Those who control our armies are the servants of the people, not their masters; and they have no more inclination than they have right to subvert the social institutions of the sovereign states, to overthrow their established constitutions, and to barter away their priceless heritage of self-government.

"This correspondence will not, however, we trust, prove wholly barren of good results.

"If there is any citizen of the Confederate States who has clung to a hope that peace was possible with this administration of the Federal Government, it will strip from his eyes the last film of such delusion; or if there be any whose hearts have grown faint under the suffering and agony of this bloody struggle, it will inspire them with fresh energy to endure and brave whatever may yet be requisite to preserve to themselves and their children all that gives dignity and value to life or hope, and consolation to death. And if there be any patriots or Christians in your land who shrink appalled from the illimitable vista of private misery and public calamity which stretches before them, we pray that in their bosoms a resolution may be quickened to recall the abused authority and vindicate the outraged civilization of their country.

"For the solicitude you have manifested to inaugurate a movement which contemplates results the most noble and humane, we return our sincere thanks."

The vexed and humiliated Greeley came back to the *Tribune* office to meet the customary contumely that goes with meddling and failure. He was stung by the state in which he found himself, and to get clear of much misrepresentation, asked Lincoln's permission to print the correspondence, addressing John Hay to that effect. Lincoln replied direct, on August 6, 1864: "Yours to Major Hay about the publication of our correspondence received. With the suppression of a few passages in your letters in regard to which I think you and I would not disagree, I should be glad of the publication. Please come over and see me."

The suggestion of suppression of parts of his letters did not appeal to Greeley. He wanted all or none made public. In the impasse thus caused, Lincoln called in Henry J. Raymond, editor of the New York *Times,* a staunch standby, writing him on August fifteenth:

"I have proposed to Mr. Greeley that the Niagara correspondence be published, suppressing only the parts of his letters over which the red pencil is drawn in the copy which I herewith send. He declines giving his consent to the publication of his letters unless these parts be published with the rest. I have concluded that it is better for me to submit for the time to the consequences of the false position in which I consider he has placed me, than .to subject the country to the consequences of publishing their discouraging and injurious parts. I send you this and the accompanying copy, not for publication, but merely to explain to you, and that you may preserve them until their proper time shall come."

It will be perceived that Lincoln is disingenuous in this statement. He permits the impression that he "proposed to Mr. Greeley" that the correspondence be published, whereas the initiative came from Greeley. At all events, Greeley proceeded to make the whole affair public, including the correspondence in full.

The fizzle did not end the efforts of the cornered Confederacy to find a way out by compromise. Things began coming the way of the North. While Lee had headed Grant, and the mine disaster at Petersburg had further dampened northern optimism, Farragut's great naval victory at Mobile Bay and Sherman's march to the sea followed with stunning success, cutting the Confederate food lines to Lee's army.

The hopes of the Confederacy were further dashed by the result of the election in the North. Lincoln's victory over McClellan was a conclusive endorsement of his policies, reinforced as they were by the adoption of the Thirteenth Amendment forever abolishing slavery.

Intimations reached Lincoln that the Confederates were again willing to treat if they could find some one who would talk to them. He accordingly, on December 28, 1864, gave Frank P. Blair, Sr., a pass to Richmond, and there, on January 12, 1865, Blair received from Jefferson Davis an offer to send a commission to confer with one appointed by "the United States Government," as he put it, "and renew the effort to enter into a conference with the view to secure peace between the two countries."

Lincoln's answer was a willingness to confer "with a view of securing peace to the people of our common country." Accordingly, Alexander H. Stephens, Vice-President of the Confederacy, R. M. T. Hunter and J. A. Campbell were detailed upon a mission to ascertain "after a free interchange of ideas and information, upon what principles and terms, if any, a just and honorable peace can be established, without the further effusion of blood."

President Lincoln met the three on board a steamer in Hampton Roads on the morning of February 3, 1865. The President and Stephens, who were known to each other, conferred a long time apart. The attention of the Confederates was called to the fact that the Thirteenth Amendment was in unalterable effect and would have to be accepted as part of any terms to be made. The commissioners returned to Richmond and reported this result. President Davis advised the Confederate Congress on February 5, 1865, that "the enemy refused to enter into any negotiations with the Confederate States, or any one of them separately, or to give to our people any other terms or guarantees than those which the conqueror may grant, or to permit us to have peace on any other basis than our unconditional submission to their rule."

Lincoln had had to play shrewd politics to secure his reelection in 1864. Greeley was not the only force against him. Secretary of the Treasury Chase was hostile, and John C. Fremont, who had been stripped of his feathers in Missouri and West Virginia, was deeply antagonistic, not so much against Lincoln as against his Postmaster-General, Montgomery Blair, of Missouri, to whom Fremont laid his downfall. Chase threatened to bolt, and Fremont was put in nomination at Cleveland, May 31, 1864, as an independent candidate, with General John Cochrane, of New York, a war Democrat, as running mate. The convention met pursuant to a call signed, among others, by so good a man as the Reverend George B. Cheever, D. D., B. Gratz Brown, of Missouri, and Lucius Robinson, later Democratic Governor of New York. The chief plank advocated a single term for the President. Lincoln undertook to clear his own road. He pushed Hannibal Hamlin off the tail of the ticket, replacing him with Andrew Johnson, Democrat, Military Governor of Tennessee. He found that Fremont could be placated by the retirement of Montgomery Blair from the postmaster-generalship, and requested his resignation rather rawly on September twenty-fourth. Fremont and Cochrane retired from the race. Chase was worked back into line by the promise of the chief justiceship as soon as the venerable Roger Brooke Taney should die. It seems odd to look back and observe that the author of the Dred Scott decision should have sat serenely on the Supreme Court bench until October 12, 1864!

In New York state affairs Greeley, in 1864, had allied himself with Reuben E. Fenton, of Chautauqua County, an anti-Weed Republican. Lincoln, disturbed by Greeley's offishness, sought a way to get hold of him, using Fenton as a contact. Fenton had for an active agent George G. Hoskins, of Wyoming County, who kept in touch with Greeley. Finding him chilly, Hoskins so reported to Fenton, who was then in Congress, and Fenton advised the President. The outcome was a direct invitation asking for a meeting, Lincoln, with his usual meekness, offering to make the trip to New York. His letter read:

"Dear Mr. Greeley: I have been wanting to see you for several weeks, and if I could spare the time I should call upon you in New York. Perhaps you may be able to visit me. I shall be very glad to see you.
"Yours truly,
"A. Lincoln."

To this Greeley had made no reply when Hoskins dropped in to see how things were coming on. Greeley showed him the note, said he had not replied to it, and declared that he would not. Hoskins urged a showing of respect for the President, but Greeley was unmoved. His visitor then boldly advised that he, Hoskins, should act as a messenger by word of mouth. He proceeded to the White House and asked to see the President as Greeley's representative. Here is what followed, as set down by D. S. Alexander, in the Lyons, New York, *Republican* for August 3, 1921:

"The doorkeeper, glancing at the letter, bade the caller take a seat and quickly disappeared. He returned in a moment or two, saying that the President, half-clad, was in the toilet shaving himself, but 'he says if you will excuse his appearance, you should come up at once.' Thereupon he led the way to the second floor and pointed to a half-open door. A slight rap brought the response 'Come in.' As Hoskins entered, the President, clad in undershirt, trousers and slippers, put down the razor and extended his hand, saying, 'Mr. Hoskins, I am very glad to see you. Take that chair,' pointing to one near the entrance. The President, continuing to stand, began at once to express his lifelong admiration of Mr. Greeley, asserting that he had been a constant reader of the *Tribune* since its establishment, and that he regarded him as the ablest editor in the United States, if not in the world, and believed he exerted more influence in the country than any other man, not excepting the President of the United States. He declared him the equal if not the superior of Benjamin Franklin.

"The mention of Franklin seemed to open the way to business. 'You know, Mr. Hoskins, that Benjamin Franklin was the first postmaster-general and I have always regretted that I could not in 1861 appoint Mr.

Greeley to that office. But I have determined, Mr.
Hoskins, if I am reelected and reinaugurated, to appoint him postmaster-general. Seward wants to go to
England, and that will give me the opportunity. But,
in any event, Mr. Hoskins, I shall appoint him. He is
worthy of it and my mind is made up.'

"At this point Hoskins, quite overcome with astonishment at the President's frankness, asked if he was
at liberty to inform Mr. Greeley of his intentions.
'Certainly,' replied the President. 'This is what I
intended to tell him if he had come himself. I shall
not fail, if God spares my life, to keep this solemn
promise.'

"This seemed to close the interview, and as Hoskins rose to go the President took his hand and bade
him convey to Mr. Greeley expressions of his high
esteem.

"Hoskins reached New York the same evening, and
going directly to Greeley's office conveyed the result of
his interview. When he had finished, Greeley asked,
in his high-keyed tone, 'Hoskins, do you believe that
lie?' The latter asserted his belief that Mr. Lincoln
would do exactly what he had promised. 'I don't,'
retorted Greeley. Hoskins said, 'I will stake my life
upon it.' Thereafter Greeley remained silent, his eyes
fixed on the floor as if in deep thought, and Hoskins
quietly retired. The next morning the *Tribune* blew
the long wished for blast that ended its languishing
campaign. An editorial, nearly two columns in length,
closed as follows (September 6, 1864):

" 'Henceforth, we fly the banner of ABRAHAM
LINCOLN for the next president. Let the country
shake off its apathy; let it realize what is the price of
defeat—a price neither we nor the world can afford;
let it be understood how near we are to the end of the
Rebellion, and that no choice is left us now but the instrument put into our hands, and with that we CAN
and MUST finish it. . . . Mr. Lincoln has done sev-

en-eighths of the work after his fashion; there must be vigor and virtue enough left in him to do the other fraction. The work is in his hands. We MUST reelect him, and, God helping us, we will.' ''

Hoskins became speaker of the New York Assembly as a result of the state election, and often met Greeley. On April fourteenth they were together, and the editor, referring to the fact that the Cabinet had not been reconstructed or himself in any way recognized, burst out with:

"Hoskins, didn't I tell you that was a lie?"

Hoskins promised to run over to Washington that night and see what the trouble was. As he stepped out of the sleeper on the morning of the fifteenth he heard the clarion cry of a newsboy: "The President is assassinated! The President is dead!"

Whatever his doubts, Greeley supported Lincoln after he once took his stand. That he became deeply concerned is shown by a letter written to Moncure D. Conway, who was in England, and writing special articles for the *Tribune,* reproving him for not coming home to help in the campaign. English public opinion, by the way, offered interesting material throughout the whole war period. It was consistently adverse to the North, and more than adverse to Lincoln. *Punch* lampooned Lincoln until his death, and then recanted by printing Tom Taylor's poem, with its scathing lines:

"You lay a wreath on murdered Lincoln's bier,
    You who with mocking pencil were wont to trace,
Broad for the self-complacent British sneer,
    His length of shambling limb, his furrowed face."

Greeley's letter to Conway said of the future election:

"There was no year of our great trial that was not one of intense agony to me, as to thousands besides, who would gladly have been buried in the darkest corner of Siberia, only that we know it would not do. And we are still in the whirlpool with no assurance of a safe deliverance. It is by no means certain that the Copperheads will not choose the next president—being enabled to choose him because many are in Europe who should be here in the thickest of the fight."

Conway did not return. He did not consider "the Union apart from emancipation worth one man's blood. So despite Horace Greeley's reproach, reason bade me stay where I was wanted for tasks to which I felt I could bring some competency. So it was that, having gone to England for a few months, I remained more than thirty years."

The Lincoln shrewdness in dealing with men worked better with James Gordon Bennett, of the New York *Herald,* than it did with Greeley. Bennett was cold, not to say hostile, during the campaign, and was continuing his line of stabbing the President, when the latter wrote him on February 20, 1865: "Dear Sir: I propose, at some convenient and not distant day, to nominate you to the United States Senate as minister to France." Bennett declined the honor, but the hitherto hostile *Herald* became a devoted supporter of the administration for the few months it was to endure.

Many men of might in the Republican party, not to say the President himself, were doubtful of a reelection, and uncertain of its advisability. In retrospect, after Lincoln's death, Greeley said of his own attitude:

"I did not favor his renomination for president, for I wanted the war driven onward with vehemence, and this was not his nature. Always dreading that the National Credit would fail or the National Resolution falter, I feared that his easy ways would allow the rebellion to obtain European recognition and achieve ultimate success. But that 'Divinity that shapes our ends' was quietly working out for us a larger and fuller deliverance than I had dared hope for, leaving to such short-sighted mortals as I, no part but to wonder and adore. We have had chieftains who would have crushed out the rebellion in six months and restored 'the Union as it was'; but God gave us the one leader whose control secured not only the downfall of the rebellion, but the eternal overthrow of human slavery under the flag of the Great Republic."

Greeley said in ending his lecture of 1868:

"I believed then, I believe this hour, that a Napolean I, a Jackson, would have crushed secession out in a single short campaign—almost in a single victory. I believed that an advance on Richmond 100,000 strong, might have been made by the end of June, 1861, that would have insured a counter-revolution throughout the South, and the voluntary return of every state, through a dispersion and disavowal of its rebel chiefs, to the counsels and the flag of the Union; but such would have left slavery intact—it would have established it on a firmer foundation than ever before. . . . Looking back through the mists of seven eventful, tragic, trying, glorious years, I clearly discern that the one providential leader, the indispensable hero of the great drama—faithfully reflecting even in his hesitation and seeming vacillations the sentiments of the masses—fitted by his very defects and shortcomings for the burden laid upon him, the good to be wrought through him, was Abraham Lincoln.''

After Lincoln's assassination Greeley said also:

''He was no inspired Elijah or John the Baptist, emerging from the awful desert, sanctified by lonely fastings and wrestlings with Satan in prayer, to thrill a loving, suppliant multitude with unwonted fires of penitence and devotion. He was no loyal singer of Israel, touching at will his heart and sweeping all chords of emotion and inspiration in the general heart—he was simply a plain, true, earnest, patriotic man, gifted with eminent common sense, which, in its wide range, gave a hand to shrewdness on the one hand, humor on the other, and which allied him intimately, warmly, with the masses of mankind.''

Surely this is a fair and just conclusion about Abraham Lincoln. Greeley observed further:

''There are those who say that Mr. Lincoln was fortunate in his death as in his life; I judge otherwise. I hold him most inapt for the leadership of a people involved in a desperate, agonizing war; while I deem few men better fitted to guide a nation's destinies in time of peace. Especially do I deem him fitted to soothe, to heal, and to unite in bonds of true, fraternal affection a people just lapsing into peace after years of distracting, desolating internal strife. His true career was just opening when an assassin's bullet quenched his light of life.''

CHAPTER XI

What promised to be the crowning cataclysm in Horace Greeley's career was his signing the bail bond which released Jefferson Davis, late President of the Southern Confederacy, from his durance in Fortress Monroe. Davis had been captured by a squadron of Michigan cavalry belonging to Major-General James H. Wilson's division on May 10, 1865, near Irwinsville, Georgia. It was claimed that he was caught dressed in his wife's skirts, and much was made of this story. It was not true. He did have a shawl and a feminine water-proof cloak over his shoulders, which gave rise to the yarn. Feeling was high over the assassination of Lincoln, and Davis was suspected of being responsible. He was accordingly sent to Fortress Monroe, on the steamer *William P. Clyde,* where Major-General Nelson A. Miles, then a most dashing young officer, caused irons to be placed on his ankles to prevent his wandering. Davis resisted, and four men held him while shackles were adjusted by the blacksmith. He was then locked in a cell. Four days later Secretary of War Stanton ordered the irons removed. Davis was, however, kept in a cell from May 22 to October 2, 1865, where General Miles took great pride in exhibiting him to visitors, to the captive's deep humiliation.

It might be recalled that when Black Hawk, the Sac Chief, was taken at the end of his "war" in 1837, he was started down the river from Keokuk to St. Louis by steamer, and was made a show of on the way; that it was Lieutenant Jefferson Davis, then of the Regular Army, who came on board at one of the landings, took charge of the prisoner, stopped the practise, and treated Black Hawk as he deserved to be treated—as a warrior and gentleman.

Released from his cell, Davis was given four comfortable rooms, where Mrs. Davis kept him company. He was then indicted for treason by a Virginia jury and held in duress until the spring of 1867. Considerable northern dissent arose over his treatment. Davis had many friends above Mason and Dixon's Line. He had spent several summers in Portland, Maine, and was popular there. Bowdoin College had given him an LL. D., though withholding one from William Pitt Fessenden because of his anti-slavery leanings. A movement was inaugurated to secure his release from Fortress Monroe under bail, the courts having held that the Act of 1862 permitted this in case of alleged treason.

Therefore, in May, 1867, Horace Greeley, Gerrit Smith, Augustus Schell, Horace Clarke, Cornelius Vanderbilt, and D. J. Jackson, of New York; Aristides Walsh, of Pennsylvania; W. H. MacFarland, R. B. Hoxall, Isaac Davenport, Thomas R. Price, Abram Warwick, Gustavus A. Myers, W. W. Crump, James Lyons, James Thomas, J. A. Meredith, William Allen, W. H. Lyons, John Minor Botts and T. A. Doswell, of Virginia, met at Richmond and signed a bond for $100,000, under which the ex-President of the Con-

federacy went free. The great Charles O'Conor, of
New York, and Robert Ould, of Richmond, volunteered as counsel and pressed for trial. Meanwhile
an appalling storm broke about the head of Horace Greeley. Friends of a lifetime turned against him
and he was execrated all over the nation. The first
volume of *The American Conflict* had been an enormous success. The second was issued in time to
coincide with the bailing of Davis. Thousands of subscribers canceled their contracts and the consequences to the *Tribune* were colossal. The weekly was
refused at post-offices by the carload. It had a circulation around two hundred and fifty thousand; about
two hundred thousand of this was lost. The daily
suffered, too, though New York did not get as excited
as the country at large. Magnanimity had proved too
swift a reversal of form for men whose passions had
not cooled, or who had lost sons and brothers by the
war. That a noble and sensible thing had been done
was not within their power to see. Davis represented
treason and rebellion, just as John Brown, to the
same minds, represented liberty.

Greeley's financial interest in the *Tribune* had
become small by repeated selling of stock. His fellow-
shareholders were now proportionately concerned at
the effect of his latest act.

At this moment the Union League Club of New
York decided to put Greeley on the carpet. He had
become a member of this body when it organized for
patriotic purposes after the outbreak of the war. It
now experienced the impulse to sit grand-jurylike
upon his conduct. Accordingly, thirty-six of the club's
members united in a call for a special meeting, before
which the editor was to be cited to answer for his deed.

To the Union Leaguers Greeley flung back a noble reply. It filled two columns in the *Tribune* of May 23, 1867, with masterly invective, and follows in full:

BY THESE PRESENTS, GREETING

"To Messrs. George W. Blunt, John A. Kennedy, John O. Stone, Stephen Hyatt and thirty-two other members of the Union League Club:

"Gentlemen: I was favored, on the 16th inst., by an official note from our over-courteous President, John Jay, notifying me that a requisition had been presented to him for 'a special meeting of the Club at an early day, for the purpose of taking into consideration the conduct of Horace Greeley, a member of the Club, who has become a bondsman for Jefferson Davis, late chief officer of the Rebel Government.' Mr. Jay continues:

" 'As I have reason to believe that the signers, or some of them, disapprove of the conduct which they propose the Club shall consider, it is clearly due, both to the Club and to yourself, that you should have the opportunity of being heard on the subject; I beg, therefore, to ask on what' evening it will be convenient for you that I call that meeting,' etc., etc.

"In my prompt reply I requested the President to give *you* reasonable time for reflection, but assured him that *I* wanted none; since I should not attend the meeting, nor ask any friend to do so, and should make no defense, nor offer aught in the way of self-vindication. I am sure my friends in the Club will not construe this as implying disrespect; but it is not my habit to take part in any discussions which may arise among other gentlemen as to my fitness to enjoy their society. That is their affair altogether, and to them I leave it.

"The single point whereon I have any occasion or wish to address you is your virtual implication that there is something novel, unexpected, astounding, in my conduct in the matter suggested by you as the basis of your action. I choose not to rest under this assumption, but to prove that you, being persons of ordinary intelligence, must know better. On this point I cite you to a scrutiny of the record:—

"The surrender of General Lee was made known in this city at eleven P. M. of Sunday, April 9, 1865, and fitly announced in the *Tribune* of next morning April tenth. On that very day, I wrote, and next morning printed in these columns, a leader entitled 'Magnanimity in Triumph,' wherein I said:—

" 'We hear men say: "Yes, forgive the great mass of those who have been misled into rebellion, but punish the leaders as they deserve." But who can accurately draw the line between leaders and followers in the premises? By what test shall they be discriminated? . . . Where is your touchstone of leadership? We know of none.

" 'Nor can we agree with those who would punish the original plotters of secession, yet spare their ultimate and scarcely willing converts. On the contrary, while we would revive or inflame resentment against none of them, we feel far less antipathy to the original upholders of "the resolutions of '98,"—to the disciples of Calhoun and McDuffie, to the nullifiers of 1832, and the "State Rights" men of 1850,—than to the John Bells, Humphrey Marshalls, and Alexander H. H. Stuarts, who were schooled in the national faith, and who, in becoming disunionists and Rebels, trampled on the professions of a lifetime, and spurned the logic wherewith they had so often unanswerably demonstrated that secession was treason. . . . We consider Jefferson Davis this day a less culpable traitor than John Bell.

" 'But we can not believe it wise or well to take the life of any man, who shall have submitted to the national authority. The execution of even one such would be felt as a personal stigma by every one who had aided the Rebel cause. Each would say to himself, "I am as culpable as he; we differ only that I

am deemed of comparatively little consequence.'' A
single Confederate led out to execution would be evermore enshrined in a million hearts as a conspicuous
hero and martyr. We can not realize that it would
be wholesome or safe—we are sure it would not be
magnanimous—to give the overpowered disloyalty of
the South such a shrine. Would the throne of the
house of Hanover stand more firmly had Charles Edward been caught and executed after Culloden? Is
Austrian domination in Hungary more stable to-day
for the hanging of Nagy Sandor and his twelve compatriots after the surrender of Vilagos?

   '' 'We plead against passions certain to be at this
moment fierce and intolerant; but on our side are the
ages and the voice of history. We plead for a restoration of the Union, against a policy which would afford
a momentary gratification at the cost of years of perilous hate and bitterness. . . .

   '' 'Those who invoke military execution for the
vanquished, or even for their leaders, we suspect will
not generally be found among the few who have long
been exposed to unjust odium as haters of the South,
because they abhorred slavery. And as to the long-
oppressed and degraded blacks,—so lately the slaves,
destined still to be the neighbors, and (we trust) at
no distant day the fellow-citizens of the southern
whites,—we are sure that their voice, could it be
authentically uttered, would ring out decidedly, sono-
rously, on the side of clemency, of humanity.'

   ''On the next day I had some more of this spirit,
and on the thirteenth, an elaborate leader, entitled
'Peace,—Punishment,' in the course of which I said:—

   '' 'The New York *Times,* doing injustice to its own
sagacity in a characteristic attempt to sail between
wind and water, says: ''Let us hang Jefferson Davis
and spare the rest.'' . . . We do not concur in the
advice. Davis did not devise nor instigate the Re-

bellion; on the contrary he was one of the latest and most reluctant of the notables of the cotton states to renounce definitively the Union. His prominence is purely official and representative; the only reason for hanging him is that you therein condemn and stigmatize more persons than in hanging any one else. There is not an ex-Rebel in the world—no matter how penitent—who will not have unpleasant sensations about the neck on the day when the Confederate President is to be hung. And to what good end?

" 'We insist that this matter must not be regarded in any narrow aspect. We are most anxious to secure the assent of the South to emancipation; not that assent which the condemned gives to being hung when he shakes hands with his jailer and thanks him for past acts of kindness; but that hearty assent which can only be won by magnanimity. Perhaps the Rebels, as a body, would have given, even one year ago, as large and as hearty a vote for hanging the writer of this article as any other man living; hence, it more especially seems to him important to prove that the civilization based on free labor is of a higher and humaner type than that based on slavery. We can not realize that the gratification to enure to our friends from the hanging of any one man, or fifty men, should be allowed to outweigh this consideration.'

"On the following day I wrote again:—

" 'We entreat the President promptly to do and dare in the cause of magnanimity. The southern mind is now open to kindness, and may be magnetically affected by generosity. Let assurance at once be given that there is to be a general amnesty and no general confiscation. This is none the less the dictate of wisdom, because it is also the dictate of mercy. What we ask is, that the President say in effect, "Slavery having, through rebellion, committed suicide, let the North and the South unite to bury the carcass, and then clasp hands across the grave." ' '

"The evening of that day witnessed that most appalling calamity, the murder of President Lincoln, which seemed in an instant to curdle all the milk of human kindness in twenty millions of American breasts. At once insidious efforts were set on foot to turn the fury thus engendered against me, because of my pertinacious advocacy of mercy to the vanquished. Chancing to enter the Club House the next (Saturday) evening, I received a full broadside of your scowls, ere we listened to a clerical harangue intended to prove that Mr. Lincoln had been providentially removed because of his notorious leanings toward clemency, in order to make way for a successor who would give the Rebels a full measure of stern justice. I was soon made to comprehend that I had no sympathizers—or none who dared seem such—in your crowded assemblage. And some maladroit admirer having, a few days afterward, made the Club a present of my portrait, its bare reception was resisted in a speech from the chair by your then President,—a speech whose vigorous invective was justified solely by my pleadings for lenity to the Rebels.

"At once a concerted howl of denunciation and rage was sent up from every side against me by the little creatures whom God, for some inscrutable purpose, permits to edit a majority of our minor journals, echoed by a yell of 'Stop my paper!' from thousands of imperfectly instructed readers of the *Tribune*. One impudent puppy wrote me to answer categorically whether I was or was not in favor of hanging Jefferson Davis, adding that I must stop his paper if I were not! Scores volunteered assurances that I was defying public opinion; that most of my readers were against me; as if I could be induced to write what they wished said rather than what they needed to be told. I never before realized so vividly the baseness of the editorial vocation, according to the vulgar conception of it. The din raised about my ears now is nothing to that I then endured and despised. I am humiliated by the reflection that it is (or was) in the power of such insects to annoy me, even by pretending to discover with surprise something that I have for years been publicly, emphatically proclaiming.

"I must hurry over much that deserves a paragraph, to call your attention distinctly to occurrences in November last. Upon the Republicans having, by desperate effort, handsomely carried our state against a formidable-looking combination of recent and venomous apostates with our natural adversaries, a cry arose from several quarters that I ought to be chosen United States senator. At once, kind, discreet friends swarmed about me, whispering, 'Only keep still about universal amnesty, and your election is certain. Just be quiet a few weeks, and you can say what you please thereafter. You have no occasion to speak now.' I slept on the well-meant suggestion, and deliberately concluded that I could not, in justice to myself, defer to it. No man should be enabled to say to me, in truth, 'If I had supposed you would persist in your rejected, condemned amnesty hobby, I would not have given you my vote.' So I wrote and published, on the twenty-seventh of that month, my manifesto entitled *The True Basis of Reconstruction,* wherein, repelling the idea that I proposed a dicker with the ex-Rebels, I explicitly said:

" 'I am for universal amnesty, so far as immunity from fear of punishment or confiscation is concerned, even though impartial suffrage should, for the present, be defeated. I did think it desirable that Jefferson Davis should be arraigned and tried for treason; and it still seems to me that this might properly have been done many months ago. But it was not done then; and now I believe it would result in far more evil than good. It would rekindle passions that have nearly burned out or been hushed to sleep; it would fearfully convulse and agitate the South; it would arrest the progress of reconciliation and kindly feeling there; it would cost a large sum directly; and a far larger indirectly; and, unless the jury were scandalously packed, it would result in a non-agreement or no verdict. I can imagine no good end to be subserved by such a trial; and, holding Davis neither better nor worse than several others, would have him treated as they are.'

"Is it conceivable that men who can read, and who were made aware of this declaration,—for most of you were present and shouted approval of Mr. Fessenden's condemnation of my views at the Club, two or three evenings thereafter,—can now pretend that my aiding to have Davis bailed is something novel and unexpected?

"Gentlemen, I shall not attend your meeting this evening. I have an engagement out of town, and shall keep it. I do not recognize you as capable of judging or even fully apprehending me. You evidently regard me as a weak sentimentalist, misled by a maudlin philosophy. I arraign you as narrow-minded blockheads, who would like to be useful to a great and good cause, but don't know how. Your attempts to base a great, enduring party on the hate and wrath necessarily engendered by a bloody civil war, is as though you should plant a colony on an iceberg which had somehow drifted into a tropical ocean. I tell you here, that out of a life earnestly devoted to the good of human kind, your children will select my going to Richmond and signing that bail-bond as the wisest act, and will feel that it did more for freedom and humanity than all of you were competent to do, though you had lived to the age of Methuselah.

"I ask nothing of you, then, but that you proceed to your end by a direct, frank, manly way. Don't sidle off into a mild resolution of censure, but move the expulsion which you purposed, and which I deserve, if I deserve any reproach whatever. All I care for is, that you make this a square, stand-up fight, and record your judgment by yeas and nays. I care not how few vote with me, nor how many vote against me; for I know that the latter will repent it in dust and ashes before three years have passed. Understand, once for all, that I dare you and defy you, and that I propose to fight it out on the line that I have held from the day of Lee's surrender. So long as any man was seeking to overthrow our government, he was my enemy; from the hour in which he laid down his arms, he was my formerly erring countryman. So long as any is at heart opposed to the national unity, the federal authority, or to that assertion of the equal rights of all men which has become practically identified with loyalty and nationality, I shall do my best to deprive him of power; but whenever he ceases to be thus, I demand his restoration to all the privileges of American citizenship. I give you fair notice, that I shall urge the reenfranchisement of those now proscribed for rebellion so soon as I shall feel confident that this course is consistent with the freedom of the blacks and the unity of the Republic, and that I shall demand a recall of all now in exile only for participating in the Rebellion, whenever the country shall have been so thoroughly pacified that its safety will not thereby be endangered. And so, gentlemen, hoping that you will henceforth comprehend me somewhat better than you have done, I remain

"HORACE GREELEY."

The Union Leaguers curled up under this blast and resolved that there was nothing in the member's conduct that called for action.

Nobody tried to court-martial Commodore Vanderbilt—he was so very rich. There was no assault on Gerrit Smith, though he was a pioneer abolitionist. Augustus Schell was a Democrat and so immune. The attempt to discipline Greeley went no further, but he continued to be brutally and wantonly assailed. In the stanza beginning "We'll hang Jeff Davis to a sour apple tree" which had been appended to *John Brown's Body* and was much sung in the army and later throughout the country, Greeley's name now took the place of Davis's. Writing to W. H. Huntington, long Paris correspondent of the *Tribune*, under date of May 27, 1867, John Bigelow observed, after expressing his pity for both the makers and readers of New York morning papers: "I think of subscribing for the *Tribune*, however, for the sake of reading your letters and old Horace Greeley's. His letter to the Union League was the best thing he ever wrote, as the act on his part which provoked the correspondence was probably the silliest thing he ever did. I think public sentiment at the North at present would delight in hanging old H. G. to a sour apple tree in place of his bailee." In another note written the same day to N. M. Beckwith, Bigelow reiterates his views: "At last a man has turned up who is more unpopular than Jeff Davis, and that is Horace Greeley. I think if Greeley could be hung now they would be content to let Jeff run."

Bigelow had just returned from a long stay in Paris, where he had represented the United States during the war and after, so he was looking at events with fresh and amazed eyes. Huntington responded from Paris on June 11, 1867: "If you see the *Revue des Deux Mondes* of June first, or your servant's letter in the *Tribune* of June seventh, you will observe that [Eugene] Forcade puts a very different and high estimation of Greeley and his act of bailing out that broken cistern, J. Davis, from what the weaker vessels at home do. Without thinking much of it at first, one way or the other, I was rather disposed to find Greeley rather right than wrong in the business, but on learning of the geniality and warmth of the popular outburst against him for his share in it, I more firmly concluded he was right. The very violence of this attack of indignation shows that it is not likely to last, or to be based upon the operation of reason.''

The bitterness died down, but not out. Greeley lost much of his hold, which he never regained, nor did the weekly *Tribune* ever come back to its former proportions in either circulation or influence.

The Davis case was called for trial in Richmond in December, 1868, with Chief Justice Salmon P. Chase and Justice John C. Underwood sitting on the circuit. O'Conor and Ould moved to quash the indictment. The two judges divided, Chase favoring the motion and Underwood dissenting. The difference was testified to the United States Supreme bench, but before it could be reached, the general amnesty of December 25, 1868, went into effect. In February, 1869, a *nolle prosequi* entered by the counsel for Davis ended his ordeal and released the bondsmen.

Greeley's account of his share in the bail episode is very simple. Andrew Johnson "from an intemperate denouncer of the beaten Rebels as deserving of severe punishment, became their protector and patron. Jefferson Davis, in Fortress Monroe . . . was an ugly elephant on Johnson's hands, and thousands were anxious that he should remain there. Their views of the matter did not impress me as statesmanlike or even sagacious.'' Accordingly, when George Shea, of New York, "son of an old friend,'' who was the attorney of record for the imprisoned ex-Presi-

dent, consulted Greeley as to the feasibility of securing his release under bail, he suggested several "conspicuous unionists" who would cheerfully "stand
security," adding after reflection: "If my name
should be found necessary, you may use that."
Months went by before he "was apprised" that his
name would be needed. When Davis was brought to
the bar in Richmond "I was there by invitation, and
signed the bond in due form." He continues:

"It was telegraphed all over the North that I had
a very affectionate meeting and greeting with the
prisoner when he had been bailed; when, in fact, I
had never before spoken nor written to him any message whatever, and did not know him even by sight
when he entered the court room. After the bond was
signed one of the counsel asked me if I had any objection to being introduced to Mr. Davis, and I replied
that I had none; whereupon we were introduced and
simply greeted each other. I made, at the request of
a friend, a brief call on his wife that evening, as they
were leaving for Canada; and there our intercourse
ended."

Again: "I believe no one has yet succeeded in
inventing an unworthy motive for my act that could
impose on the credulity of a child or even of my bit-
terest enemy. I was quite aware that what I did would
be so represented as to alienate for a season some
valued friends, and set against me the great mass
of those who know little and think less; thousands
of those who rejoiced in Davis's release, nevertheless
joining full-voiced in the howl against me. I knew
that I should outlive the hunt, and could afford to
smile at the pack even when the cry was loudest. So
I went quietly on my way; and in due time the storm
gave place to calm."

The mass can not change its mind as suddenly as the individual, even though the individual makes up the mass. The accumulated hatred of six vexing and wretched years had concentrated on Jefferson Davis. He was the figurehead, the symbol. It was enough. The man's high qualities, his undoubted faith in his cause, meant nothing to those who had suffered, as they believed, from his actions. The sour apple tree, in one form or other, becomes a sacred scaffold in such circumstances, and a Davis or a Greeley is always bound to be hanged on it.

CHAPTER XII

QUITE outside of journalism, Horace Greeley's activities were enormous. He took an interest in everything that was going on, and a part in a deal of it. His labors, joined with those of his profession, were colossal. It seems, in surveying his career, impossible for one individual to have done so much. This, too, before the day of the stenographer, the typewriter, and the dictaphone. He penned all of his own writings, did his own researching, read his own proofs and attended to about everybody else's affairs besides. Traveling, lecturing, exhorting and communing without cessation, it is no wonder that when disease befell him it seized upon the brain. He detested laziness: "A lazy man, in my view, is always the pitiable victim of mis-education." Had there been in him even a little laziness it might have saved the wastage of much excellent energy.

A semi-country home on Turtle Bay, an indentation on the shore of the East River opposite the south end of Blackwell's Island as it was then known, became his property in 1844. Here he had eight acres of ground, on which he feebly exercised his desire to "farm it," as they say in Vermont. It was once the residence of Isaac Lawrence, head of the local branch of the United States Bank, then out of business, and had been allowed to run down. Down-at-the-heel places seem to have had a special appeal for Horace Greeley.

"The place," wrote Margaret Fuller, who spent much time there during her engagement on the *Tribune*, "is to me entirely charming; it is so completely in the country, and all around is so bold and free. It is two miles or more from the thickly settled parts of New York, but omnibuses and cars give me constant access to the city, and, while I can readily see what and whom I will, I can command time and retirement. Stopping on the Harlem road, you enter a lane nearly a quarter of a mile long, and going by a small brook and pond that locks in the place, and ascending a slightly rising ground, get sight of the house, which, old-fashioned and of mellow tint, fronts on a flower garden filled with shrubs, large vines and trim box-borders. On both sides of the house are beautiful trees standing fair, full-grown and clear. Passing through a wide hall you come out upon a piazza, stretching the whole length of the house, where one can walk in all weathers."

Nine years later the editor bought a tract of rough sour land at Chappaqua, Westchester County, New York, packed between hills, so that frost was apt to settle down with perilous lateness and earliness, so wet as to drown out the crops. "The choice," he wrote in his *Recollections*, "was substantially directed by my wife, who said that she insisted on but three requisites . . . 1—A peerless spring, of pure, soft living water; 2—A cascade or brawling brook; 3—Woods largely composed of evergreens."

He had some difficulty in finding the spot. "Those

who object," he said in reply to some carping friends,
"to my taste in choosing for my home a rocky,
wooded hillside, sloping to the north or west, with
a bog at its foot, can not judge me fairly unless they
consider the above requirements."

The "farm" so acquired was about thirty-five
miles from his New York office, and was reached by
the Harlem railroad, on which he commuted, or
rather, week-ended. In all, the property covered
about seventy-five acres. The place afforded him
diversion and cost a lot of money. About twenty-five
acres were covered with standing timber, in which he
loved to whack about with an ax, lopping off limbs
and cutting out crowded trees. Here, too, he got an
inspiration for *What I Know About Farming,* the last
book to come from his pen. Nevertheless his experiences were more on the line of the comment made by
Josh Billings: "What i kno about farming is kussed
little." The best crop farmer Greeley ever raised
was turnips. He drained the bog and his pocketbook
at the same time. Lazy hired men and cheating "su-
perintendents" added to his difficulties, but could not
diminish his ardor. "Some day" he meant to gather
his treasures at Chappaqua and retire there, but the
moment never came. "As yet I am a horse in a bark-
mill, and tread his monotonous round, never finding
time to do to-day what can possibly be postponed to
the morrow."

In 1848, through the unseating of David S. Jackson, there befell a ninety-day vacancy in the outlying
city congressional district, which was then all of New
York above Fourteenth Street and three wards below
it. It was filled at a general election by the familiar

method used to kill off an obligation. The Whigs named Greeley for the short term, and the more politically useful James Brooks, of the New York *Express,* for the full one, thus hitting two editorial birds with one stone. Greeley was not specially gratified, but served out the time apportioned to him. This made him a member of the Thirtieth Congress. John Quincy Adams had recently died in his seat in the House, and there were no commanding Whigs on the floor. The big guns of the party were in the Senate. James K. Polk was president, and James Buchanan secretary of state. Abraham Lincoln was an unobtrusive fellow-member.

The new member was promptly in hot water from the unlucky duality of being a member of Congress and editor of the *Tribune.* His fellow representatives were not slow in resenting his advantage over them. They could only speak from the floor of the House; he had all outdoors at his command. He was active in a movement, unsuccessful, to abolish flogging in the United States Navy, the abuse continuing until public sentiment was aroused by the publication of Herman Melville's *White Jacket* two years later. Offsetting this, the new member tried to stop the navy grog ration, but failed. He prevented the passage of a bill paying seven dollars and fifty cents per column to the *Union* and the *National Intelligencer* for printing the debates of Congress, which made him more than unpopular with their editors. Odium was increased by his efforts to stop the practise of giving each congressional employee a bonus of two hundred and fifty dollars at the end of the session. An attempt to limit the disposal of public lands to actual settlers won him further disfavor, but it became the basis of the Homestead Act in after years. Another motion that failed was one to use the navy's ships for transport of passengers to California, the gold boom being under way.

The crowning row grew out of his exposing the "mileage" fraud both on the floor and in the columns of the *Tribune*. One place or the other would have been enough, but both were too much for those criticized. Mileage had become a pleasant form of graft, by reason of the development of steamboat and railroad routes. This made it comfortable and convenient to take long roundabout roads for reaching Washington, instead of the old way by stage across country. It also fattened the congressman's pocketbook—in some instances very substantially. The *Tribune* figured out that by this practise the government was paying for a hundred and eighty thousand miles of excess mileage. For this Greeley was challenged on the floor and admitted the authorship of the article, which characterized some of his associates in terms more picturesque than polite. He had a few defenders, Amos Tuck, of New Hampshire, being the most valorous. A bill which Greeley introduced requiring mileage to be computed by the most direct road was defeated, but thereafter congressional peregrinations became much less circuitous. The congressman was repeatedly called to acount on the floor for charges made in the *Tribune*—not unjustly, it would often appear. The two positions were entirely out of harmony, and inconsistent with good taste.

Later in life Greeley concluded that the Congress he had sat in was pretty honest, containing not more than ten or twelve black sheep, and these clearly known.

Another activity of Greeley's was signalized when he became, on January 29, 1850, the first president of the New York Printers' Union, now Typographical Union No. 6, serving one year. He was always a friend of the working printer and stood high in the affection of the men. He believed in unionism and cooperation, as well as protection, his views being expressed in the *Tribune* of August 13, 1853:

"We believe that the wages of Labor should be liberal—that the true interest of all classes requires this—and that they have generally been lower than they should be.

"We believe that unregulated, unrestricted competition—the free trade principle of 'every man for himself' and 'buy where you can the cheapest'—tends everywhere and necessarily to the depression of wages and the concentration of wealth. Capital can wait—Labor can not—but must earn or famish. Without organization, concert and mutual support, among those who live by selling their labor, its price will get lower and lower as naturally as water runs down-hill. Consequently, we are in favor of trades unions or regular associations of workers in the several callings for the establishment and maintenance of fair and just rates of wages in each.

"We believe employers have rights as well as journeymen—that they, too, should hold meetings and form societies or appoint delegates to confer with like delegates on the part of the journeymen; and that by the joint action of these conferrers, fair rates of wages in each calling should be established and maintained.

"We believe that the rates thus established are and should be morally binding upon all who see fit to engage in these callings respectively—that he who can not afford them has no right to be an employer, and he who will not ought to be shunned alike by journeymen and customers—and that whenever employers or journeymen believe that the circumstances of their trade require an increase or reduction of wages they ought to assemble their own class and procure its sanction to a new conference of delegates as aforesaid, and that its decision should be conclusive.

"We believe that strikes, or refusals of journeymen to work at such wages as they can command, are seldom necessary—that proper representations and conciliatory action on the part of journeymen would secure all requisite modifications of wages without striking—and that the aggregate of wasted time, misdirected energy, embittered feeling and social anarchy which a strike creates is seldom compensated by any permanent enhancement of wages thus obtained.

"We believe that the primary and most culpable authors of strikes and the mischiefs thence arising are those employers who refuse to unite in any efforts for the systematic adjustment of wages, but insist on fixing and paying such rates of wages as they choose, without reference to the established regulations or current usages of the vocation. If these would but desist from their evil practises, the claims of journeymen alone to regulate wages without asking the concurrence of employers would be easily proved untenable and speedily abandoned. While the journeymen's scales of prices are the only ones, they ought, for want of better, to be respected and adhered to. But to secure a conference and a mutual agreement as to wages, the employers in any trade have but to ask it. In short—we believe the present fermentation among the trades of our city a salutary and hopeful one—that it is based on a just idea of the existing regulations of Labor to Capital, and rightly affirms the wages should increase as currency is expanded and living becomes nominally dearer; and we hold that, should it result in disastrous collisions between employers and employed, paralyzing whole departments of industry, the fault will mainly lie at the door of those employers who refuse to cooperate in establishing and upholding just rates of wages in their several vocations. If journeymen alone regulate the prices of labor, they will be likely to fix them too high; if employers alone fix them (as they virtually do under the free-trade system) they will naturally fix them too low; but let journeymen and employers in each trade unite in framing, upholding and from time to time modifying their scale, and it will usually be just about right.''

In 1851, Greeley treated himself to a trip to Europe, induced by the heralded wonders of the first World's Fair, held in the Crystal Palace at Hyde Park, London. He had been named chairman of the jury appointed to award premiums to a class called Number Ten, which brought him into touch with leading people and gave him a wider welcome than a simple sojourner would have received. Among other attentions, he was called in as a witness before a committee of Parliament, which sat to consider the removal of the stamp tax on newspapers and advertising. Richard Cobden was one of his questioners. His replies were clear but evidently not convincing, because it was ten years before the onerous excise was taken off the journals and it became finally possible to print publications for the masses in Great Britain.

After the duties of juryman were completed, Greeley journeyed to the continent, visiting France, Italy and Switzerland. He wrote copious observations for the *Tribune*, caustically criticizing European institutions, as was deemed the duty of good Americans in his day. St. Peter's in Rome he described as "the Niagara of edifices," but was not allowed to observe the art treasures in the Vatican, at which he was plainly miffed. On the return road he took in more of England and much of Scotland, peeping in at the Universal Peace Conference in London, which he thought would have to do a good deal of fighting before it accomplished its purpose. He was more than glad to get home, after four busy months of absence. His chief discovery seems to have been that the usual Englishman, "though cold and even repulsive out-of-doors, is tender and truthful in his home."

Not to be outdone by Britons, New York built a Crystal Palace, covering the ground between Fortieth and Forty-second Streets on Sixth Avenue, now known as Bryant Park. Greeley was one of the directors. This got him into a scrape and jail four years later, when he again went abroad, this time to take in the French Exposition. A French exhibitor who had met some losses at the New York show brought a suit for damages, under which Greeley was arrested and lodged in the prison of Clichy, instead of attending a dinner party to which he had been invited by M. B. Field. John Y. Mason was American Minister. He did his best to get the prisoner out, but did not succeed. Greeley found an American in the jail who knew him by sight, and this fellow-countryman bestirred himself to convince the prison warden that some one had made a mistake. Nevertheless, the great editor was kept under lock and key two days before being released, and put to great annoyance before he got rid of the claim—two thousand, five hundred dollars. Elihu B. Washburne, afterward

Minister to France, chanced to be in Paris, and his efforts helped to rid Greeley of responsibility for the unprofitable venture in America. The Crystal Palace show lost all the money its stockholders put in and poorly secured its bondholders. It was too far uptown, Greeley held, in explaining its troubles. He and P. T. Barnum did their best to pull it out of the hole, failed, and the luckless enterprise came to an end by the burning of the "Palace" in 1858.

The traveler, returning to New York, was met by the news that his mother had died on the day he departed from Liverpool. She was "but sixty-eight years old," her son noted in mentioning her demise, and "had long been worn out in mind and body by hard work and rugged cares." Zaccheus, her husband, survived until 1867. His years numbered eighty-seven.

The field of book authorship became Greeley's in 1850, when sundry of his lectures and articles were put into a volume called *Hints Toward Reforms,* by Harper and Brothers, then the leading American publishers. The volume comprised mainly discussions of social topics, in which he excelled, one being "Alcoholic Liquors," the commodity which he detested. Moral force rather than law was invoked to stop their abuse. Of palliations he wrote in 1868:

"While I look with interest at all attempts to substitute American wines and malt liquors for the more maddening decoctions of the still, I have noted no such permanent triumphs in the thousand past attempts to cast out big devils by the incantations of little ones as would give me reason to put faith in the principle, or augur success for this latest experiment."

He had previously edited the *Whig Almanac,* which finally became merged in that published by the *Tribune.* Thanks to his admiration of Henry Clay, he was selected to edit Sargent's life of that worthy, for which he furnished an account of Clay's death and funeral. In it he recounts his final interview with his hero:

"Learning from others how ill and feeble he was, I had not intended to call upon him, and remained two days under the same roof without asking permission to do so. Meantime, however, he was casually informed of my being in Washington, and sent me a request to call at his room. I did so, and enjoyed a half-hour's free and friendly conversation with him, the saddest and the last! His state was even worse than I feared; he was already emaciated, a prey to a severe and distressing cough, and complained of spells of difficult breathing. I think no physician could have judged him likely to live two months longer. Yet his mind was unclouded and brilliant as ever, his aspirations for his country's welfare as ardent; and, though all personal ambition had long been banished, his interest in the events and impulses of the day was nowise diminished. He listened attentively to all I had to say of the repulsive aspects and revolting features of the Fugitive Slave Law and the necessary tendency of its operation to excite hostility and alienation on the part of our northern people, unaccustomed to slavery, and seeing it exemplified only in the brutal arrest and imprisonment of some humble and inoffensive negro whom they had learned to regard as a neighbor. I think I may, without impropriety, say that Mr. Clay regretted that more care had not been taken in its passage to divest this act of features needlessly repulsive to northern sentiment, though he did not deem any change in its provisions now practicable."

Glances at Europe, published in 1853, was a selection of letters covering his first voyage overseas, for which he received five hundred dollars for the copyright. The growing issue of Free Soil and the abolition of slavery caused him to compile and publish, in 1856, a very concrete history of it from the beginning of independence to that date. In association with his brother-in-law, John F. Cleveland, he published a campaign book for 1860 which proved useful.

Greeley's most important work, *The American Conflict,* was written in part during 1864. He made a contract with O. D. Case and Company, of Hartford, subscription book publishers, who secured an enormous list of subscribers. The author hired a room in the Bible House, at Fourth Avenue and Ninth Street, New York, and there worked like a beaver until the first huge volume was done. It is more a feat of journalism than literature, and naturally had to deal much with undigested or undetermined events. The result on the whole, however, was a work of great value as a source. Something like one hundred and fifty thousand copies were sold, and the author profited largely in spite of terms that were more favorable to the publishers than himself. The second volume, coming out in 1867 in face of his bailing of Jefferson Davis, was much less successful.

A liberal offer from Robert Bonner, publisher of the *New York Ledger,* drew from Greeley in 1868 for that interesting weekly a series of sketches which took book form in *Recollections of a Busy Life.* It abounded in reminiscence and more in comment on men and things, and proved very popular.

Lecture travels provided strenuous diversion. On

one trip the lecturer was blocked at Erie, Pennsylvania, his old home town, by a fight between the town and the Erie railroad. The railroad had its terminus there and was narrowing its six-foot gauge to fit a connecting line to the West, to the resentment of the inhabitants, who had profited by the necessary transfer of freight and passengers. The citizens stopped the work and defied a court order, so that for some time the affair looked like a small rebellion. In the midst of it Greeley had to ride seven miles in an open sleigh, exposed to a winter's storm. This made him break forth: "Let Erie be avoided by all travelers until grass shall grow in her streets and until her piemen in despair shall move to some other city"—as he himself had done years before, from the office of the *Gazette!* And in a further blast: "Let Erie have her way, and all passengers and all freight must change cars before her pie-shops." He was fond of pie, by the way. "The whole world is to be taxed, as in the days of Cæsar Augustus, in order that Erie may clutch a sixpence for every dollar of expense she imposes on others. Is it strange that so mean and selfish an exaction should be enforced by mobs, arson, devastation and ostentatious defiance of judicial mandates?" He wanted President Pierce to deal with the lawless performance, remarking rather unreasonably: "Had a runaway negro been somehow mixed up with the matter, we should have had half of the United States army in Erie a month ago."

A memorable journey to California by stage across the great plains was made by Greeley in 1859. He left New York on the ninth of May, going by rail to St. Joseph, Missouri, and thence by stage. He reached

Denver when that aspiring town was six months old, and interviewed Brigham Young in Salt Lake City, where he found comfort after days of hardship. The Prophet was grading a section for the Pacific railroad, that was to be ten years longer in finding rails. He saw no idlers, and Brigham assured him there was none in all Utah. The habits of industry and thrift among the Mormons won his "hearty admiration."

Silver had not yet made Nevada a bonanza, and the traveler spent five weary days and nights traversing its desolation. Descending into California, he visited the big trees of Calaveras, the Yosemite Valley, and the Mariposa grove, then part of Colonel John C. Fremont's vast estate. California gave him a cordial reception. He arrived at San Francisco in mid-August, became the guest of the city and made a number of addresses, one at a meeting held to promote the Pacific Railroad. The *Bulletin* report noted that, though nearly fifty, he had no wrinkles on his face, which bore a "general expression of mildness and benignity." The "famous white hat had been discarded for one of dun-colored wool." His overcoat was without buttons, these having been snipped off by admiring dwellers in the Sierras for souvenirs. He had also gained weight on the trip despite its rough discomforts. The crowning event of the trip, however, was his celebrated *Ride to Placerville*, veraciously chronicled by Charles Farrar Browne (Artemus Ward) who visited the coast soon after Greeley. Ward's sketch follows in full:

"When Mr. Greeley was in California ovations awaited him at every town. He had written powerful leaders in the *Tribune* in favor of the Pacific Rail-

MR. GREELEY AND BRIGHAM YOUNG

(From Harper's Weekly, Sept. 3, 1859)

road, which had greatly endeared him to the citizens of the Golden State. And therefore they made much of him when he went to see them.

"At one town the enthusiastic populace tore his celebrated white coat to pieces, and carried the pieces home to remember him by.

"The citizens of Placerville prepared to fête the great journalist, and an extra coach, with extra relays of horses, was chartered of the California Stage Company to carry him from Folsom to Placerville—distance, forty miles. The extra was in some way delayed, and did not leave Folsom until late in the afternoon. Mr. Greeley was to be fêted at seven o'clock that evening by the citizens of Placerville, and it was altogether necessary that he should be there at that hour. So the Stage Company said to Henry Monk, the driver of the extra, 'Henry, this great man must be there at seven to-night.' And Henry answered, 'The great man shall be there.'

"The roads were in an awful state, and during the first few miles out of Folsom slow progress was made.

"'Sir,' said Mr. Greeley, 'this is not a trifling matter. I *must* be there at seven!'

"Again came the answer, 'I've got my orders!'

"But the speed was not increased, and Mr. Greeley chafed away another half-hour; when, as he was again about to remonstrate with the driver, the horses suddenly started into a furious run, and all sorts of encouraging yells filled the air from the throat of Henry Monk.

"'That is right, my good fellow!' cried Mr. Greeley. 'I'll give you ten dollars when we get to Placerville. Now we *are* going!'

"They were indeed, and at a terrible speed.

"Crack, crack! went the whip, and again 'that voice' split the air. 'Git up! Hi yi! G'long! Yip—yip!'

"And on they tore over the stones and ruts, up hill and down, at a rate of speed never before achieved by stage horses.

"Mr. Greeley, who had been bouncing from one end of the coach to the other like an India-rubber ball, managed to get his head out of the window, when he said:

" 'Do—on't—on't—on't you—u—u think we—e—e—e shall get there by seven if we do—on't—on't go so fast?'

" 'I've got my orders!' That was all Henry Monk said. And on tore the coach.

"It was becoming serious. Already the journalist was extremely sore from the terrible jolting, and again his head 'might have been seen' at the window.

" 'Sir,' he said, 'I don't care—care—*air,* if we don't get there at seven!'

" 'I have got my orders!' Fresh horses. Forward again, faster than before. Over rocks and stumps, on one of which the coach narrowly escaped turning a summerset.

" 'See here!' shrieked Mr. Greeley. 'I don't care if we don't get there at all!'

" 'I've got my orders! I work for the Californay Stage Company, I do. That's wot I work for. They said, "Git this man through by seving." An' this man's goin' through. You bet! Gerlong! Whoo-ep!'

"Another frightful jolt, and Mr. Greeley's bald head suddenly found its way through the roof of the coach, amidst the crash of small timbers and the ripping of strong canvas.

" 'Stop, you—maniac!' he roared.

"Again answered Henry Monk:

" 'I've got my orders! *Keep your seat, Horace!*'

"At Mud Springs, a village a few miles from Placerville, they met a large delegation of the citizens of Placerville, who had come out to meet the celebrated editor, and escort him into town. There was a military company, a brass band, and a six-horse wagonload of beautiful damsels in milk-white dresses, representing all the states in the Union. It was nearly dark now, but the delegation were amply provided with

torches, and bonfires blazed all along the road to
Placerville.

"The citizens met the coach in the outskirts of
Mud Springs, and Mr. Monk reined in his foam covered steeds.

" 'Is Mr. Greeley on board?' asked the chairman
of the committee.

" 'He was, a few miles back!' said Mr. Monk. 'Yes,'
he added, after looking down through the hole which
the fearful jolting had made in the coach-roof—'yes,
I can see him! He is there!'

" 'Mr. Greeley,' said the chairman of the committee, presenting himself at the window of the coach,
'Mr. Greeley, sir! We are come to most cordially
welcome you, sir—why, God bless me, sir, you are
bleeding at the nose!'

" 'I've got my orders!' cried Mr. Monk. 'My orders is as follers: Git him there by seving! It wants
a quarter to seving. Stand out of the way!'

" 'But, sir,' exclaimed the committee-man, seizing
the off leader by the reins—'Mr. Monk, we are come
to escort him into town! Look at the procession, sir,
and the brass band, and the people, and the young
women, sir!'

" 'I've got my orders!' screamed Mr. Monk. 'My
orders don't say nothin' about no brass bands and
young women. My orders says, "Git him there by
seving!" Let go them lines! Clear the way there!
Whoo-ep! Keep your seat, Horace!' and the coach
dashed wildly through the procession, upsetting a portion of the brass band, and violently grazing the wagon
which contained the beautiful young women in white.

"Years hence, gray-haired men, who were little
boys in this procession, will tell their grandchildren
how this stage tore through Mud Springs, and how
Horace Greeley's bald head ever and anon showed
itself like a wild apparition, above the coach roof.

"Mr. Monk was on time. There is a tradition that
Mr. Greeley was very indignant for a while; then he

laughed, and finally presented Mr. Monk with a brand new suit of clothes.''

Ward's narrative of the incident has never been contradicted, and it gave Henry Monk a fame that lasted as long as he lived, which was a good while. When, in the early 'nineties, Nate Saulsbury and Buffalo Bill were running the Wild West in its greatest glory, Monk drove the ''Overland Stage'' for a season. I recall him as a blond, thick-set, square-faced man, who could be trusted to ''git'' Horace or any one else ''there by seving.''

The return trip to New York was made by water, via Panama. Greeley based many letters upon it, coming out strongly for the completion of the cross-continent railroad. Unfortunately, whatever pleasure there might have been in the trip was soon taken away by the sudden crisis of events in the South.

The *Tribune* sanctum furnished the staff with many a diverting encounter. One of the editor's great interests was the American Institute, sometimes called the ''Farmer's Club.'' Greeley was president of this body for years, during which time it held an annual fair in a big ramshackle building at Third Avenue and Sixty-fifth Street. This lived for a quarter of a century after his death. The *Tribune* one day contained an amusing report of a meeting of the board of trustees, in which their proceedings were prettily burlesqued. Nobody seemed to know how it got into the paper, but investigation showed that Stanley Huntley, a very new reporter from Brooklyn, had committed the act.

The youth was summoned into the presence.

"How did this thing get into the paper?" squawked the chief in a rage.

"When I brought in the copy," answered the youth, "they told me to put it in that box. So I just poked it in and went home."

"That box" was the copy conveyor to the composing-room, and by the simple process of following the suggestion, the article had not been seen by any editor, and so made its sacrilegious way into the *Tribune*.

The reporter expected to be slaughtered. Instead, Greeley looked at him tenderly. "You shouldn't have written it that way, my dear boy," he said. "Don't you know I'm the president of that society?"

Huntley afterward made some reputation as a humorist with his *Spoopendyke Papers* in the Brooklyn *Daily Eagle*.

A strange outcome of Greeley's vigorous journalism was the libel suit brought against him by James Fenimore Cooper, the novelist. Cooper had returned from abroad after a long absence, venting much disapproval of "Home as Found," in a book of that title. For this and the tactless exclusion of the people of Cooperstown, where he set up a baronial home, from a favorite beach on Otsego Lake, he was vigorously assailed, first locally and then widely throughout the state, James Watson Webb, Colonel William L. Stone and Thurlow Weed joining the chorus of criticism. Cooper at once started a series of libel suits and won most of them. The one against Weed was brought at Fonda, a small Mohawk Valley town which Weed failed to reach on trial day in time to prevent the entering of a judgment by default that in the end cost him two thousand, five hundred dollars. Weed wrote a letter to the *Tribune* in resentment, which was printed anonymously. It read:

"*Mr. Fenimore Cooper and His Libels.*
"Fonda, Nov. 27, 1841.
"To the Editor of the *Tribune*—

"The circuit court now sitting here is to be occupied chiefly with the legal griefs of Mr. Fenimore Cooper, who was determined to avenge himself upon the Press for having contributed by its criticisms to his waning popularity as a novelist.

"The 'handsome Mr. Effingham' has three cases of issue here, two of which are against Mr. Weed, Editor of the Albany *Evening Journal*.

"Mr. Weed not appearing on Monday (the first day of court), Cooper moved for judgment by default, as Mr. Weed's counsel had not arrived. Colonel Webb, who, on passing through Albany, called at Mr. Weed's house and learned that his wife was seriously and his daughter dangerously ill, requested Mr. Sacia to state the facts to the Court, and ask a day's delay. Mr. Sacia made, at the same time, an appeal to Mr. Cooper's humanity. But that appeal, of course, was an unavailing one. The novelist pushed his advantage. The Court, however, ordered the cause to go over until the next day, with the understanding that the default should be entered then if Mr. Weed did not appear. Colonel Webb then despatched a messenger to Mr. Weed with this information. The messenger returned with a letter from Mr. Weed, stating that his daughter lay very ill, and that he would not leave her while she was suffering or in danger. Mr. Cooper, therefore, immediately moved for his default. Mr. Sacia interposed again for time, but it was denied. A jury was empanelled to assess Mr. Effingham's damages. The trial, of course, was ex parte, Mr. Weed being absent and defenseless. Cooper's lawyer made

a wordy, windy, abusive appeal for exemplary damages. The jury retired, under a strong charge against
Mr. Weed from Judge Willard, and after remaining
in their room until twelve o'clock at night, sealed a
verdict for four hundred dollars for Mr. Effingham,
which was delivered to the Court this morning.

"This meager verdict, under the circumstances, is
a severe and mortifying rebuke to Cooper, who had
everything his own way.

"The value of Mr. Cooper's character, therefore,
has been judicially ascertained.

"It is worth exactly four hundred dollars.

"Colonel Webb's trial comes on this afternoon;
his counsel, A. L. Jordan, Esq., having just arrived
in the up-train. Cooper will be blown sky high. This
experiment upon the Editor of the *Courier and Enquirer*, I predict, will cure the 'handsome Mr. Effingham' of his monomania for libels."

The *Tribune* was promptly sued by the combative
Cooper. The case was tried at Ballston, New York,
and resulted in a verdict for two hundred dollars, with
one hundred dollars costs. Greeley defended himself,
and got his money back by writing an eleven-column
account of the farcical trial for the *Tribune*. He was
rather proud of the report, accounting it "the best
day's work I ever did."

For this Cooper sued him anew, but the case never
came to trial and the legislature, as one result, took
some of the rigor out of libel laws. On the whole, the
Tribune got off easy in this respect, Greeley recording
that only "twice in the course of my thirty-odd years
of editorship, I have encountered human beings base
enough to require me to correct a damaging statement,
and, after I had done so to the extent of their desire,
to sue me upon that retracted statement for libel."

In 1868 Charles Dickens, then at the living summit of his fame, paid America his second and last visit. The rancor that had followed the publication of his notes on America twenty-five years before had pretty well died out—he had only told the truth—and he was widely welcomed. The New York Press Club, then a thing of consequence, gave him a dinner at Delmonico's on April eighteenth. It was Greeley who presided over a distinguished company that included Henry J. Raymond, Samuel Bowles, William Henry Hurlbut, George William Curtis, James Parton, Charles F. Briggs ("Harry Franco"), Murat Halstead, James T. Fields, Doctor Henry M. Field, David G. Croly, General Joseph R. Hawley, Colonel T. B. Thorpe, John R. G. Hassard, Augustus Maverick, S. S. Conant, Albert D. Richardson, F. B. Carpenter, E. H. Clements, Thomas McElrath, Samuel Sinclair, William Orton, J. F. Cleveland, Thomas Nast and Whitelaw Reid, all shining names in American journalism. The chair was in fine form. He proposed the toast to the guest in this fashion:

"It is now a little more than thirty-four years since I, a young printer, recently located in the city of New York, had the audacity to undertake the editing and publishing of a weekly newspaper for the first time. Looking around at that day for materials with which to make an engaging appearance before the public, among the London magazines which I purchased for the occasion was the old *Monthly*, containing a story by a then unknown writer—known to us only by the quaint description of 'Boz.' That story, entitled, I think, at that time *Delicate Attentions*, but in its present form entitled *Mr. Watkins Tottle*, I selected and published in the first number of the first journal with which my name was connected. Pickwick was then an unchronicled, if not uncreated character. Sam Weller had not yet arisen to increase the mirth of the Anglo-Saxon race. We had not heard, as we have since heard, of the writer of those sketches, whose career then I may claim to have in some sort commenced with my own [*great laughter*] and the relation of admirer and admired has continued from that day to the present. I am one of not more than twenty of the present company who welcomed him in this country, on an occasion much like this, a quarter of a century ago. When I came to visit Europe, now seventeen years ago, one of my most pleasant experiences there, and one of my pleasantest recollections of Europe, is that of buying in the farthest city I visited—the city of Venice, on the Adriatic—an Italian newspaper, and amusing myself with what I could not read—a translation of *David Copperfield*, wherein the dialogue between Ham and Peggotty, with which I was familiar in English, was rendered into very amusing Italian. . . . Friends and fellow laborers, as I am to set you an example to-night of a short speech, I will, without further prelude, ask you to join me in this sentiment: 'Health and happiness, honor and generous, because just, recompense to our friend and guest, Charles Dickens.' ''

On the early evening of November 25, 1869, Daniel Frohman, aged perhaps eighteen, was the obliging mail clerk in the business office of the New York *Tribune*. He and his brother Charles had come to New York from Sandusky, Ohio, to seek the fortune that both found. The gas was lit, and a handsome bearded man stepped up to the counter to ask for his mail. The boy knew him as Albert D. Richardson, next to Horace Greeley the most famous of the *Tribune's* staff. He was proud to talk to him for a few minutes while the caller sorted his letters.

The conversation was interrupted by a pistol shot fired by Daniel McFarland, who had been loitering in the lobby awaiting the coming of his man. The shot took effect, though Richardson, of strong physique, did not fall. Instead, he walked up-stairs to the editorial rooms of the *Tribune*, whence he was removed to the Astor House. Police Captain Anthony J. Allaire, who had been a brigadier-general in the army, put McFarland under arrest and he was held to await the result of Richardson's injuries.

No place could have been selected for the shooting that would have aroused more interest. For twenty years the *Tribune* office had been a storm center. To Horace Greeley came all the odd folks developed by a period of social agitation and unrest. All parties concerned in the tragedy were known to him, or to Samuel Sinclair, his partner, while the woman in the case had been a valued contributor to the paper. The victim had been its representative in Kansas and the South before the war, and a correspondent during the conflict, for a part of which time he had been a prisoner in Salisbury Stockade, North Carolina. From this confinement he had escaped with Junius Henri Browne, fellow *Tribune* man, and after months of wandering in the mountains, had reached safety. He was the author of a popular book, *The Field, the Dungeon and the Escape,* detailing his adventures.

The assailant, Daniel McFarland, had, in 1853, met at Manchester, New Hampshire, a rare and precocious girl of fifteen, Abby Sage, of whom he became enamored, and four years later, when she was but nineteen and he thirty-seven, had married her, to begin a very unhappy life. He was of a roaming and intemperate type, but represented himself as possessing a good law practise and considerable property at Madison, Wisconsin. His bride, taken thither, found he possessed no practise, and that the property consisted of small equities buried under large mortgages. They soon returned East and went to live in Brooklyn.

An unsatisfactory existence followed until, through his wife's endeavors, backed by Horace Greeley, McFarland secured a position in the New York Custom House. He held it a number of years and lost it in 1866, when he began to badger his wife into supporting him by elocutionary efforts that led her to the stage. Having some forensic pretense he also gave her instruction, which was supplemented by the teaching of George Vandenhoff, an English actor of talent. It was the age of "elocution," and public readers were in demand. Vandenhoff made a good living from his lessons, and was a sincere teacher.

Mrs. McFarland developed talent and secured some engagements. The couple had had three children. The eldest died, leaving two to the mother's care, plus the idle, morose and drinking husband, almost twice her age. There were many quarrels, the final result of which was a separation. It chanced that McFarland, who had become acquainted in the *Tribune* office, calling for mail, found a tender letter to his wife from Richardson.

Enraged, McFarland hunted Richardson, and meeting him when he was escorting Mrs. McFarland home from the theater on the night of March 13, 1867, fired three shots, one of which took slight effect. Richardson recovered and McFarland was not prosecuted. The strained situation went on for nearly two years, until Mrs. McFarland had secured an Indiana divorce and was free to marry again if she wished. She became noted as a writer for the *Tribune,* the *Atlantic Monthly* and the *Riverside Magazine.* She and Richardson were all this time under the shadow of McFarland's wrath. They did not, however, marry. So matters rested until the end in the *Tribune* office.

Immense excitement followed the second shooting. Greeley, his sister, Mrs. Cleveland, the Sinclairs and many others were deeply concerned and rallied around Mrs. McFarland. It was soon plain that Richardson would not recover, and accordingly he elected to marry the inciting cause of his death. Abby Sage had been united to McFarland in their luckless bond by no less a person than Theodore Parker. Henry Ward Beecher and Octavius Brooks Brothingham performed the next ceremony. Richardson died on the second of December, and McFarland was duly placed on trial before Recorder John K. Hackett. He was feebly prosecuted by District Attorney Garvin, assisted by Noah Davis, who had been retained by Richardson's friends, and was very ably defended by John Graham, Charles S. Spencer and Elbridge T. Gerry. The witnesses called included Horace Greeley, Samuel Sinclair, Whitelaw Reid, Donald Nicholson and Daniel Frohman, all of the *Tribune,* Amos J. Cummings, John F. LeBaron, Fitz Hugh Ludlow, author of *The Hasheesh Eater,* Colonel Thomas W. Knox and Junius Henri Browne.

A very poor witness Greeley turned out to be, becoming much tangled up by Graham, who embarrassed him by making the startling discovery that the great editor sometimes swore!

Making a plea of "emotional insanity," Graham charged Richardson with having seduced the defendant's wife. The long trial ended in a verdict of not guilty, after an hour and fifty minutes of deliberation by the jury. Three hundred people who packed the court room cheered Graham, Spencer and Gerry, while women flocked about the killer and showered him with kisses. The "emotional insanity" was not his alone.

In late September, 1870, Greeley took a tour that carried him through West Virginia, Ohio, Missouri, Kansas and to Greeley, Colorado, the model town which his former agricultural editor, N. C. Meeker, had founded and named in his honor. It was located at the crossing of the Denver Pacific and the Union Pacific railroads. There was no depot at "the new village of Greeley," as he wrote—"youngest cousin of Jonah's gourd." The location "was pitched upon by the locating committee of our union colony about the first of March last," and already seven hundred families were on the ground, who had built themselves three hundred houses. There were scattered about the near-by country, in all, Greeley thought, about two thousand souls. "We have an irrigating canal which takes water from the Cache [à Poudre River] six miles above and distributes it over one thousand acres, as it will do over several thousands more; and we are making another to the north side of the Cache, very much longer, which is to irrigate at least twenty thousand acres. We are soon to have a newspaper (we have already a bank), and we calculate that our colony will give at least five hundred majority for a Republican president in 1872, after harvesting that year a wheat crop of at least fifty thousand bushels, with other crops to match. And we hope to invite the foundation of many such colonies on every side of us.''

Thus he echoed the thought that reached back to Albert Brisbane's luckless phalanxes. He did not dream that in 1872 he would not be so solicitous for a ''Republican majority of five hundred.''

A few months later, in the spring of 1871, he made a long jump to Texas. ''I go to Texas reluctantly,'' he wrote. ''There seems no choice but to be in the world or out of it. I am not sufficiently broken down to refuse to bear any part among men; so I keep on. It will be just the same a hundred years hence.'' His route was by Pittsburgh, Cincinnati, New Orleans and Galveston. The trip took a month and he was much better received than he had expected to be. In November he returned from a strenuous lecture tour to the Northwest, much wearied and depressed. ''I wish it were possible,'' he wrote on November fourteenth, ''for me to find rest this side of the grave, but it seems not to be. Work crowds me from every side. I do not seek it, but it comes. If I could be voted out of the editorship of the *Tribune,* I could limit the rest of my work; but this seems to draw after it incessant applications to do more on every side and there is no escape.''

Reflecting at Christmas that year, with his family absent, he wrote drearily: ''And so my sixtieth Chrismas is going soberly and richer with an abundance of work. I am no richer, unless in friends, for my last ten or twelve years of hard work; and I begin to long for quiet and rest. I have hardly known what home meant for years, and am too busy to enjoy anything.

I most regret the lack of time to read books. I hope I shall not die so ignorant as I am now.''

A keen and constant interest in Greeley's life was Universalism. He used to attend the General Convention Sessions, and is on record as having contributed in 1860 forty dollars toward founding the Theological School at Canton, New York, which is now part of St. Lawrence University. He was present at the proceedings of the Universalist Centenary, held at Gloucester, Massachusetts, September 20-23, 1870, celebrating the formal founding of the Church of John Murray. P. T. Barnum was a fellow delegate. Greeley took considerable part in the proceedings, notably in seating a delegation from Maryland, which sent as many from only one church as other states had sent altogether. There was objection, at which Greeley remarked: ''I move to accept that portion of the report which relates to the Baltimore delegates. It is not their fault that there are no more Universalists in Maryland.'' His motion carried. He also moved a resolution providing for raising a ''John Murray Fund'' of two hundred thousand dollars for church endowment. Supporting it, he said:

''I am very anxious that this two hundred thousand dollar fund shall in no manner be forfeited away, that it shall answer a permanent purpose, and that that purpose shall be such as to bring our views more distinctly and more generally before the public than I think they have yet been brought. I do not feel that our periodicals and our literature command the attention of people outside of our denomination so much, either, as they ought to do or as they might do. For instance, suppose we had a series of from twelve to twenty-four tracts, not merely fly-leaves, as too many tracts are, but tracts of from twelve to forty-eight pages, explaining and enforcing our views of Scripture truth, and our ideas with regard to the Divine governments, as such men as there are among us, such men as our leading men are, would be able to explain and enforce them. If we had a number of such tracts, and then offices in every state, and so far as we are able, in every city, for the distribution of those tracts, at cost, not attempting to give them away, but saying to our friends, 'Here are the best statements we are able to make of our doctrines and our views; you can be supplied with them at cost, whether you want a dozen or a hundred of these tracts,' these tracts handed to your neighbors in exchange for their own, or in answer to their inquiries, would enable the general public to understand our views much better than they do now. Then we have books, which to my view are very important, not now accessible. For instance, Mr. Ballou's *Inquiries*. I asked the other day where I could find them, and was answered, 'They are entirely out of print.' It seems to me that we need to have this and other works of Biblical criticism, which explain points that are not easily comprehensible by persons who only read the received translation,—not, perhaps, in great numbers, but they should be always on hand. In my judgment, the Methodist denomination is to-day nearly twice as large as it would have been had it not been for the Methodist Book Concern, where any person who wishes to know what Methodist views are, as presented by their standard authors, on any important subject can go and find the right book, at a moderate price. I believe the Methodist denomination, for which I have great respect, nay, for which I have admiration, has pushed itself upon public attention, has challenged and commanded public regard, by its publications, even more than by its excellent system of ministerial appointment and reelection.

"Now, such a Publication House we may have. This Murray fund will be a much larger foundation for it than was had by the Methodist Book Concern in its origin. If we could apply it as the basis, as the nucleus of a great Publication Office, under the direction of eminent laymen as well as clergymen, who had a knowledge of business and of publishing, I believe we could make that sum, without any diminution of its amount, do a very important and necessary work. A friend says this fund is intended for education and for missionary work. I answer that publishing provides for both education and missionary work, and I greatly desire that when we have raised the two hundred thousand dollars, as I trust we shall before the end of this year, for the general purpose of advancing our doctrines, we shall put that fund in the shape where it will most extensively and most effectively commend our views to the attention, and I hope also to the approbation, of the general public, who are now to a very small extent, only, reached by our views. There is a very large amount of acquiescence in our views by men who do not know or even do not believe what the Scriptures teach them; the spirit of the age tends toward that acceptance; but a Scriptural and intelligent knowledge of the foundations whereon we rest our views is almost entirely confined to the Universalist denomination. I would have it otherwise. I would have those views so perfectly understood and as perfectly commended as our means will allow.

"I think a plan such as I have rudely outlined would command the attention of many thousands now who do not hear from us, and for that reason I trust this resolution will be referred to some appropriate committee, to present it for action in such shape as will make it acceptable to the great body of the Convention."

The project was carried out, and the Universalist Publishing House came into being and still exists in Boston.

Universalism disregards the doctrine of eternal

punishment dear to the orthodox. Expressing himself on this to a correspondent, Greeley once wrote: "You judge that men will not suffer forever. If to suffer implies pain, I agree with you. In the sense of loss, I think suffering will endure. That is, I believe the very wicked here will never be quite so well off as though they had been good—that they will never make up the leeway they lost while serving the enemy here. I judge that Mary Magdalene is now, and ever will be, in a lower grade than Mary the mother of Jesus."

CHAPTER XIII

IT IS not possible to give an adequate survey of
Horace Greeley's life without dwelling somewhat
painfully upon his domestic relations. No breath of
scandal ever blew upon his fame from the hot furnace
of the times in which he played so great a part. Whatever might be the character of those whom he met
or knew, no stain was ever transferred to his name.
Yet to his domestic circumstances must be laid much
that made his life unhappy and his burden hard. Devotion and distraction make poor company; he felt
the one and was ruled by the other. The combination
made him a poor husband and destroyed the happiness of his wife. She was Miss Mary Y. Cheney, a
charming school-teacher, born in Cornwall, Connecticut, whom he had met through the fatal propinquity of
a boarding-house table in New York. He had taken
early to fads. There was an active belief that Graham
flour contained all the elements of life and the pursuit
of happiness, and sundry practitioners set up foun-
dries, at which the guests were fed on "Graham."
Frequenting one of these, Greeley met his fate. She
was under engagement to teach a season of school at
Warrenton, in North Carolina. Here she boarded with
the family of Squire William Bragg; he had a son in
West Point, who was to become celebrated as Braxton

321

Bragg, Commander-in-Chief of the Armies of the Confederacy.

On his way south to wed, Greeley paused at Washington to take a peep at the Senate, and sent a short account of his observations to the *New Yorker*. His "first impression" of the Senate Chamber was not one of "overpowering admiration." Henry Clay was "the most striking figure on the floor." He was "incessantly in motion" and his "spare erect form betrays an easy dignity approaching to majesty and perfect gracefulness, which I have never seen equaled. His countenance is intelligent and indicative of character; but a glance at his figure while his face was averted would give assurance that he was no common man. Mr. Calhoun is one of the plainest men and certainly the dryest, hardest speaker I ever listened to. The flow of his ideas reminded me of a barrel filled with pebbles, each of which must find great difficulty in escaping, from the very solidity and number of those pressing upon it and impeding its natural motion. Mr. C., though far from being handsome, is still a very remarkable personage; but Mr. Benton [of Missouri] has the least intellectual countenance I ever saw on a senator. Mr. Webster was not in his place, nor was Mr. [Silas] Wright, while I attended the Senate's deliberations. In fact, full one-third of the senators were absent. A civil good-night to them."

Continuing on to Warrenton, the young man found his bride awaiting him, and took her from Squire Bragg's house to the church, returning to New York after the ceremony. The announcement of the marriage appeared at the top of the list of "Married" published in the *New Yorker*, July 16, 1836. It read:

"In Immanuel Church, Warrenton, N. C., on Tuesday morning, 5th inst., by Rev. William Norwood, Mr. Horace Greeley, editor of the New Yorker, and Miss Mary Y. Cheney of Warrenton, formerly of this city."

There was no further mention in the paper—in shining contrast with the flamboyant, ecstatic announcement made by James Gordon Bennett in the New York *Herald* when he committed matrimony.

A house was taken in Greenwich Street which became for the moment a literary center. Esther Greeley came down from Wayne to help adorn it, the schoolma'am not being much of a hand at domestic science. She arrived on a Friday, "the night the *New Yorker* went to press, and brother's reception evening," she relates, and she did not find the house until late, Horace having forgotten to tell her he had moved from 123 Hudson Street to more elegant quarters. "It was half past eleven," Esther continues, "I was trembling with fatigue and excitement and very faint, for I had not eaten since early morning; but all these emotions vanished when I was introduced to my new sister. I had seen no pictures of her, and knew her only through brother's description, and a few letters she had written me since her marriage, and I was quite unprepared for the exquisite and fairy-like creature I now beheld: a slight girlish figure, rather *petite* in stature, dressed in clouds of white muslin, cut low, and her neck and shoulders covered by massive dark curls, from which gleamed out an oriental-looking coiffure, composed of strands of large gold and pearl beads. Her eyes were large, dark and pensive, and her rich brunette complexion was heightened by a flush, delicate as a rose-leaf. She appeared to me like a being from another world.''

The Friday evenings at the Greeley house were very popular. ''Nearly all the men and women of note at that time'' were to be found in the parlors, Esther remarks. ''I can recall General George P. Morris, editor of the *Mirror;* Willis and Lewis Gaylord Clark, editors of the *Knickerbocker Magazine;* Fitz-Greene Halleck, George M. Snow, Professor A. C. Kendrick, of Hamilton College, American translator of Schiller; Mrs. C. M. Sawyer, wife of brother's pastor, then making her début in the literary world; (she was wife of Doctor T. J. Sawyer, Universalist, who lived almost to the end of the century); Elizabeth Jessup Ames, who was writing stories and poems for the *New Yorker;* Mrs. E. F. Ellet, in 1836 a handsome bride, who had come up from the South and was contributing translations from the French and German to the same journal; Anne Cora Lynch, now Madame Botta, and many others.''

This was a swift transition in six years from the tramp printer to goodly company. The Greeleys went about much in their literary circle. Esther even recalls that Horace danced a quadrille on the occasion of a Christmas Eve party, ''and wore such a look of exalted happiness that an old Quaker lady who was looking on remarked to me, 'I didn't think thee could find so beautiful a sight as thy brother's dancing this side of heaven.' ''

In this ecstatic state Horace also wrote poetry. One effort, *The Faded Stars,* filled him with satisfaction. It read:

"I mind the time when Heaven's high dome
　Woke in my soul a wondrous thrill—
When every leaf in Nature's tome
　Bespoke Creation's marvels still;
When morn unclosed her rosy bars,
　Woke joys intense; but naught e'er bade
My soul leap up like ye bright stars!

"Calm ministrants to God's high glory.
　Pure gems around His burning throne!
Mute watchers o'er man's strange, sad story
　Of crime and woe through ages gone!
'Twas yours, the wild and hallowing spell,
　That lured me from ignoble glens—
Taught me where sweeter fountains fell
　Than ever bless the worldling's dreams.

"How changed was life! A waste no more
　Beset by Pain, and Want, and Wrong,
Earth seemed a glad and fairy shore,
　Made vocal with Hope's impassioned song.
But ye bright sentinels of Heaven!
　Far glories of Night's radiant sky!
Who, when ye lit the brow of Even,
　Has ever deemed man born to die?

" 'Tis faded now! That wondrous grace
　That once on Heaven's forehead shone;
I see no more in Nature's face
　A soul responsive to mine own.
A dimness on my eye and spirit
　Has fallen since those gladsome years,
Few joys my hardier years inherit,
　And leaden dullness rules the spheres.

"Yet mourn not I! A stern high duty
　Now nerves my arm and fires my brain.
Perish the dream of shapes of Beauty!
　And that this strife be not in vain

"To war on fraud intrenched with power,
  On smooth pretence and specious wrong,
This task be mine tho' Fortune lower—
  For this be banished sky and song."

Twelve years afterward Greeley wrote a sonnet, *Portrait of a Lady,* which appeared in *The Printer's Book* for 1849. It will be seen that he was then looking backward:

"The blissful June of life! I love to gaze
  On its sweet wealth of ripening loveliness,
And lose the thoughts that o'er my saddening days
  Grim Care has woven clouds which will depress,
In spite of stoic pride and stern resolve:
  Beauty like this the waste of life redeems;
'Round it—their sun—the coldest hearts revolve,
  Warm'd back to youth and gladdened by its
    beams.
But, lady! in that mild, soul-speaking glance,
  Those lustrous orbs, returning heaven its hue,
I greet an earlier friend—forgive the trance!
  'Tis Nature only, imaged here so true
That, briefly, I forgot the Printer's art,
  And hailed the presence of a Queenly Heart."

Matrimony, with its stern realities, evidently soon took the poetry out of him. In many marriages the early years are hardest. Couples have to get used to each other, and as the bliss wears off, disadvantages assert themselves, ofttimes cruelly. The first child brings care and anxiety to the mother and takes her away from the husband, who is apt to relapse into a primordial state. In the case of the Greeleys, all this and much more happened.

The first born in the new household was a boy, who naturally received a warm welcome and was

named Arthur Young Greeley, which was petted into
"Pickie." The mother, in the language of her sister-
in-law, "looked upon his birth in the light of a miracle, as if no other child had ever before been born. He
was Heaven-sent to her, and she sacrificed herself
completely for the better development of Pickie's
individuality; or, to use the language of the reformers
of those days, in illustrating the independence of the
child's selfhood. Nothing could have been more
boundless than her enthusiasm for her baby; and it
was night and day her study to guard his health and
to watch and cherish his opening intellect. No child
prince could have been more tenderly and daintily
nurtured than he was; as his father often said,
'Pickie is a dear boy in every sense of the word,' for
nothing was too rare or too costly for him."

It may be recalled that Mrs. Greeley was a Gra-
hamite, and so her child became an experiment in
pure digestion. His complexion was her pride, and
Esther describes it as "owing in part to his mother's
watchful care of his diet, and to his bathing. An hour
was always allowed for his daily bath, and for brush-
ing out his luxuriant silken hair. No doubt it was
that scrupulous care that gave it so rare a shade. As
for his food, it was quite peculiar. He never ate baker's bread, nor indeed, any bread prepared by other
hands than his mother's or mine, and he was not given
meat or cake—with the exception of oatmeal cake—
while candies, or indeed sugar in any form, butter and
salt were rigidly excluded from his diet, but white
grapes and every choice fruit that this or foreign
markets afforded, he was allowed to eat in abundance.

"His toys, like his meals, were peculiar. One of

the largest rooms in the house was chosen for his nursery, and as his mother would not have a carpet on the floor, it was scrubbed daily. Here his playthings were kept—a singular assortment, one would think them. His mother seldom gave him what would merely amuse him, but sought rather to surround him with objects that would suggest ideas to his mind— on a plan something like the kindergarten system, but more poetic and entirely original with herself. He had lovely pictures and a real violin, while the shops were constantly searched for whatever was curious, instructive or beautiful.''

The result was a sort of hothouse precocity, because of which the child's ''mind and conversation were very unlike those of the children of even our best families, for he never had children for playfellows, and those friends whom his mother permitted to be near him were of the most cultivated and noble character. His language, consequently, was as choice as that of the minds who surrounded him, and very quaint it sounded from a child's lips. At this time Margaret Fuller was with us, and 'Pickie' lived in most intimate relations to this pure-minded woman. In her case, to prevent 'Pickie' from knowing of the existence of wickedness and cruelty in the world, his mother would rarely permit him to converse long with any save the chosen few, lest the innocence of his child mind should be shocked by hearing of war, or murder, or cruelty to animals, while she was ever guarding him lest his eyes might rest upon some painful or disagreeable object.''

The poor little prisoner died of cholera when five years old, July 12, 1848, after an illness of only four hours, the day being, wrote his father, "one of the hottest and longest I have ever known." He, too, had marveled at his boy. In an after visit to Europe he "looked in vain through Italian galleries for any full parallel to his dazzling beauty—a beauty not physical, merely, but visibly radiating from the soul. His hair was of the finest and richest gold; 'the sunshine of picture' never glorified its equal; and the delicacy of his complexion at once fixed the attention of observers, like the late N. P. Willis, who traversed both hemispheres without having his gaze arrested by any child who could bear comparison with this one."

Margaret Fuller, then Marchioness Ossoli, wrote from Italy, August 25, 1848: "No child, except little Waldo Emerson, had I ever so loved. In both I saw the promise of a great future; its realization is deferred to some other sphere; ere long we may follow and aid it there." And "ere long" she did follow.

In the parlor at Chappaqua hung an oil painting of "Pickie" worshiped by the mother as a shrine. It was full length; the charming child held in his hands a cluster of lilies, while his much brushed hair fell upon his shoulders "like a shower of ruddy gold." It was painted partly from life by William Page, but the child died before the sittings were completed, and it was finished from daguerreotypes. Page was a celebrated artist, born in Albany, who, after courses in law and theology, took up the brush with signal success, developing some lines of color that ranked him as a "futurist" in the 'forties.

Six more children—a boy, Raphael Uhland; two infants who died at birth; Mary Inez, Ida L. and Gabrielle—followed "Pickie" into the world. Mary Inez died at six months and Raphael at six years from attacks of croup. Ida and Gabrielle grew to maturity. Raphael was born two years after his brother's death, but never filled his place. He is described as much resembling his father, who was allowed some share in his life. His temperament, according to his Aunt Esther, was "gentle and loving."

Under her bereavements the mother became changed in temperament, neurasthenic and difficult. She lived much in seclusion, and while her husband's devotion to her never failed, they were far apart; he in the world and she out of it. Her housekeeping was the despair of Greeley himself. Servants seldom stayed and the mistress never learned to "keep house." Margaret Fuller, who got along with her hostess better than any other guest, said she did it in "Castle Rackrent fashion." Miss Fuller wrote Mrs. Greeley down as a "typical Yankee schoolmistress, crazy for learning."

Margaret Fuller, Marchioness Ossoli, also was the mother of a precious son, but was accorded the mercy of drowning with him in her arms when the ship upon which she and her husband were returning from Italy was wrecked on Oak Island bar, on the Long Island coast, July 16, 1850, husband and wife refusing to leave the ship separately, when, by so doing, one or both might have been saved. Before sailing she had written a friend in America: "I shall embark most composedly in our merchant ship (the *Elizabeth,* Captain Hasty); praying fervently indeed that it may not be my lot to lose my boy at sea, either by unsolaced illness, or amid howling waves; or, if so, that Ossoli, Angelo and I may go together, and that the anguish

MARGARET FULLER

may be brief." Angelo had been stricken with small-pox, but had been spared, only that the three might die together as she had wished.

Margaret Fuller was always a match for Mary Greeley. Meeting her one day full-gloved on the street, Mrs. Greeley, who had an antipathy to kid coverings, touched Miss Fuller's hand with a shudder and snapped out:

"Skin of a beast! Skin of a beast!"

"Why, what do you wear?" asked Margaret.

"Silk," responded Mrs. Greeley.

Miss Fuller gave a comic shudder and came back with:

"Entrails of a worm!"

October 7, 1871, having returned from a five weeks' western trip, which he described in a letter to a woman friend, Greeley said in that letter concerning his dead sons:

"I only write this because your letter just received intimates a doubt that reference to my son would be agreeable. Two sons, who attained the ages of five and a half and six years respectively, have gone before me, and of whom I cherish none but tender and pleasant remembrances. The older, 'Pickie,' was a poet, the most beautiful child I ever saw. I walked through the great Italian galleries two years after he was called away; but none of the great painters had ever seen a child so lovely. My later son (Raphael) lived to be six months older than 'Pickie,' and was also beautiful in soul and body, but more like me than like his brother, and not a poet at all—only a good, bright, noble boy. I seldom find time to think of either now, but always recall them with sunny memories, and a cheerful trust that they are awaiting me with love and trust."

The Greeleys lived for a long time at Number 35 East Nineteenth Street, New York. William M. Evarts had resided next door, at Number 37, but his growing family caused him to sell the mansion to William Allen Butler, author of *Nothing to Wear*. In *A Retrospect of Forty Years* Butler says:

"During a part of our residence in Nineteenth Street our next-door neighbor was Horace Greeley, who carried his personal eccentricities to some extent into his domestic arrangements. He kept a goat in his backyard, and appealed, when necessity required, to his neighbors to aid him in looking after his gas meter when the lights went out. As the houses in our row were identical in appearance, it was not strange that Mr. Greeley, with his mind intent on great affairs, should mistake one of the others for his own. Returning home one time carrying a box of tea, he made an ineffectual effort to enter my house. My wife, hearing some one at the front door, opened it rather suddenly and the founder of the New York *Tribune* was precipitated, tea chest and all, into our front hall."

This was in the first of the 'fifties. Greeley was a good enough neighbor to defend Butler from a silly charge of plagiarism that followed the wide popularity of *Nothing To Wear,* which had been published anonymously in *Harper's Weekly,* some school miss claiming it for her own.

The next-door neighbor was wrong about the number of goats. Sometimes there were three of them, which Mrs. Greeley, not Horace, kept for the amusement of the children, somewhat crowding the back yard and giving it that shanty-town aspect which much of New York then enjoyed.

A woman acquaintance who had been asked to join

the Greeley family one Sunday morning to attend
Doctor Chapin's church, found them all in the vesti-
bule mixed up with the goats, which, like Mary's
little lamb, seemed to want to accompany the children everywhere they went.

"The question is," she quotes Greeley as saying,
"whether the goats shall go up Broadway with us.
Mother insists that I shan't go to church unless I go
at the head of the procession of children and goats.
That seems more like a circus." They got off at last,
leaving the goats behind, to Mrs. Greeley's great dis-
pleasure, the latter hurling "It's only your cussed
pride" at Horace. The narrator was once in a Broadway stage when Mrs. Greeley, riding in the same
vehicle, pulled a small tin pail from under her shawl
and, handing it to the Reverend Doctor Brett, who was
among the passengers, requested him to "run into the
bakery on the corner and get me two cents' worth of
yeast." He did it while the driver halted the bus.
Doctor Brett amiably turned the episode into a pun:
"Bread is evidently kneaded."

"H-m," replied Mrs. Greeley, "old joke."

The same lady averred that Mrs. Greeley had no
knack of making a home. "She was always clean,
never neat—never neat in appearance, I mean. She
was always washing something and always disheveled. I have seen her take her children without a garment on them out into the street and pump water on
them to wash them."

Beman Brockway, who was a reliable person and
intimate with the Greeleys over a long period, declared that Greeley in his *Tribune* days, that is to say,
the last half of his life, was without a real home.

"He lived at boarding-houses and at hotels, and sometimes in his own home, for he owned one or two houses in the city, as well as the farm at Chappaqua. He permitted Mrs. Greeley to run the domestic establishment and she did it in a way peculiar to herself. I am not inclined to criticize her. She was a female crank, born so, and could not help doing as she did. Some considered her partly insane; others thought she was simply ugly. I do not undertake to decide which party was right. I am satisfied that she did not know how to keep house. She did not have the knack of making a home."

So it was that Greeley stayed away weeks at a time from the Nineteenth Street house. "He was there occasionally," says Brockway, "but he oftener had rooms at some hotel. There were none of the comforts of home and Mrs. Greeley sometimes made things decidedly disagreeable." Some instances in point can be quoted.

"Mrs. Greeley," according to her husband, "in our years of extreme poverty kept her house in strict accordance with her convictions [as a Grahamite]; never even deigning an explanation to her friends and relatives, who from time to time visited and temporarily sojourned with us; and as politeness usually repressed complaint or inquiry on their part, this first experience of a regimen which dispensed with all they dreamed most appetizing could hardly be observed without a smile. Usually a day, or at most two, of beans and potatoes, boiled rice, puddings, bread and butter, with no condiment but salt, and never a pickle, was all they could abide; so, bidding her a kind adieu, each in turn departed to seek elsewhere a more congenial hospitality."

More than one person has stated that when irritated by her husband's abstraction Mrs. Greeley would snatch away his manuscripts and throw them in the fire. To this he bent without reproach, and when the strain became too strong would betake himself to a hotel room and do the work over again. He rarely invited any one to the house for fear of domestic fury. Yet he was never known to utter a word in resentment or reproof. Beyond all doubt he understood how suffering in childbirth and the death of children had warped a delicate and supersensitive mind.

A Washington man who called at the Nineteenth Street house in the fall of 1861 seeking to engage Greeley for a lecture, gives this account of his adventure:

"Inquiry at the *Tribune* office took me to his house on Nineteenth Street. I rang loud and repeatedly, and at last a lady came down-stairs to the door, with sleeves tucked briskly up her arm, and her hair twisted to a knot on top of her head. The following conversation took place:

" 'Is Mr. Greeley in?'

" 'He is not.'

" 'Do you know where he is?'

" 'I do not. He is not stopping here now.'

" 'Can I see Mrs. Greeley?'

" 'You can; I am Mrs. Greeley.'

" 'Do—was—is—does Mr. Greeley come home sometimes?'

" 'Occasionally. He has not come home this week.'

" 'Do you know where he is stopping?'

" 'I do not. He stopped at the Everett House last week.'

"I went down to that hotel and inquired. They said he was at the New York Hotel, and there I found him raging up and down his room and storming over a pile of despatches on the table. I seemed *de trop,* and inquired what was the matter.

"'Matter!' he repeated, in his high falsetto voice, 'enough, I should think. Battle yesterday at Pittsburg Landing; rebels whipped us, of course. Our soldiers are being driven into Tennessee to-day. Our generals are drunk. Buell ought to be shot, and Grant ought to be hung!'

"After a while he quieted down sufficiently to enable me to do my errand and take my leave."

Charles Henry Webb, in pursuit of work, was once asked by the editor to spend an evening at the Nineteenth Street house and "talk it over."

The youthful caller unfolded his ambition to find a place where he could work early and late, to "acquire some object in life and have something to occupy all his time and thoughts."

"Then you'd better get married, young man," said Horace forcefully.

Webb relates that, telling this once to Henry J. Raymond, the latter recounted how, when he had had the job of school-teaching offered him in North Carolina that nearly tempted him away from the *Tribune,* Greeley said earnestly: "Don't go to North Carolina, Raymond. I married my wife there." Writing of the evening spent in Nineteenth Street, Webb says:

"I remember that Mr. Greeley effected a diversion by calling his daughter: 'Come here, Ida, you have not had your grammar lesson yet.'

"'I can't find my grammar, papa,' she said.

"'Oh, never mind,' was the response. 'Bring me the first book you come to; I can teach you grammar out of any book.'"

Contempt for grammar text-books was characteristic with Greeley. He reflected in 1845:

"Grammar came hard to me. I commenced at six years of age, and having but little schooling, wasted the best part of what I had, for it was several years before I discovered authors on that subject knew nothing about it—Lindley Murray especially, the intense blockhead, whose gross blunders I ought to have detected at seven years of age, but did not till ten or eleven. That obtuseness of perception put me back sadly, and I had to learn what I know of grammar after I had devoted more time to it than should have been required in all. Ten weeks with the books we now have are worth more than ten months with such as I learned from."

Like many men who are comfortless with their wives, Greeley enjoyed the friendship of women, but as a rule they were women of high intellectual quality or pleasant companions. He never played with butterflies. Margaret Fuller was a notable example among his friends, though he got a little weary of her somewhat peremptory prominence around the *Tribune* office. Susan B. Anthony and Elizabeth Cady Stanton had his warm friendship. I have heard the lovely Mrs. Stanton tell how, more than once, before a public appearance of his, she had adjusted his unruly necktie and forced his wandering trousers-leg down to the instep. Alice and Phœbe Cary were special favorites. He had met the poetic pair while on a lecture trip and encouraged them to come to New York as a better place to secure reward for their talents than Mount Healthy, Hamilton County, Ohio, in the vicinity of Paddy's Run, where Murat Halstead and Doctor Albert Shaw came from.

The modest venture of the sisters proved a success. Of it Greeley has written:

"Gradually signs of thrift appeared, and eventually they lived in a house of their own, not large or showy, but comfortable and paid for by the labor of their hands. Here they received weekly, without ostentation, literary and artistic guests, and dispensed for many years a quiet, inexpensive hospitality. Their parlor was not so large as some others, but quite as neat and cheerful, and the few literary persons or artists who occasionally met at their informal invitation, to discuss with them a cup of tea and the newest books, poems and events, might have found many more pretentious, but few more enjoyable gatherings. I have a dim recollection that the first of these little tea parties was held up two flights of stairs, in one of the less fashionable sections of the city; but good things were said there that I recall with pleasure even yet, while of some of the company, on whom I have not since set eyes, I cherish a pleasant and grateful remembrance. As their circumstances gradually though slowly improved by dint of diligent industry and judicious economy, they occupied more eligible quarters, and the modest dwelling they have for some years owned and improved, in the very heart of this emporium, has long been known to the literary guild as combining one of the best private libraries with the sunniest drawing-room (even by gas light) to be found between King's Bridge and the Battery."

"The sisters were in striking contrast," recalls the Reverend O. B. Frothingham, who often joined the Sunday evening company at their home. "Phœbe, the jester, was a jocund, hearty, vivacious, witty, merry young woman, short and round; her older sister Alice was taller and more slender, with large dark eyes; she was meditative, pensive and rather grave in temperament, but the two were in most hearty sympathy in every opinion and in all their social and literary aims."

On an occasion at the home of Orville J. Victor, in New Jersey, there was to be a party of literary folk, among them Greeley and the Cary sisters. The festivities included a husking bee. Greeley was prevented from attending and in his annoyance was reported to have used rough language. The next day Phœbe Cary bought an armful of yellow ears to the *Tribune* sanctum and decorated Greeley's desk with them—to "make him acknowledge the corn for swearing," as she put it.

The Carys often visited the Greeleys at Chappaqua, though Alice Cary is recorded as saying that she never went there without being insulted by Mrs. Greeley. Anna E. Dickinson, Mary A. Livermore and other women of note were Greeley's friends.

Because of his relations with the intellectuals, it need not be assumed that Horace could not appreciate women of the softer sort. To one of the latter he wrote: "My friend, I charge you not to disparage yourself, and especially not to regret that you do not, when I have the pleasure of seeing you, talk mainly philosophy or epigrams. I have a large acquaintance with those who are regarded as brilliant women. They appal and fatigue, while you charm and cheer me. I pray you not to be like unto them."

Brockway's account of a visit to Chappaqua was made by him from jottings in his Journal of August, 1857:

"Meeting Mr. Greeley in New York, he asked me to go home with him. He wished me to see his farm, especially the new barn he had just completed. As I did not happen to have other engagements, I consented. He lived at Chappaqua, a station on the Harlem railroad, about thirty-five miles from New York. Arriving at the station, I was somewhat surprised to hear him say, 'I guess we had better register at the hotel; you may want to stay all night.' I assented to the proposition, and entered my name on the hotel register. We then proceeded to the Greeley mansion, a plain story-and-a-half or two-story wood dwelling, standing in a pretty dense forest. It was painted white, and had green blinds. It should not have cost over fifteen hundred dollars to two thousand dollars. Three minutes' walk brought us to the house. A little girl was standing upon the piazza.

" 'I am dreadful glad to see you, Ida,' said Mr. Greeley.

"The child made no response—did not smile—and seemed to regard with entire indifference her father (for the little girl was the daughter of Mr. G.), as well as his pleasant salutation, though he had been absent nearly a week.

"The piazza led into a sitting-room, in which were two domestics, one of them nursing an infant three months old. Mr. G. spoke caressingly to the infant in the nurse's arms, and then disappeared through a doorway in the rear of the sitting-room, and thence up a flight of stairs. In a few moments he returned, accompanied by Mrs. Greeley.

" 'Mr. Brockway,' said Mr. Greeley, when I gave her my hand, which she received solemnly, and, I believe, without speaking.

"Mrs. Greeley was a woman rather below the medium size, thin, with dark hair and eyes. She had thin lips, irregular and somewhat defective teeth. There was little expression in her face, but that little was rather against her. She spoke quickly—not peevishly, nor angrily, as a rule, but her words had a kind of crack like the report of a rifle.

"After the introduction, Mr. G. said he desired to show me over his farm, and thought he would do it before supper. A description of this tour of his premises is here given in my diary, but I will omit it, and bring the reader directly back to the house. Ascending the front steps, we found Mrs. Greeley standing in the doorway.

" 'Things have gone on very well on the farm, mother, since I went away,' said Mr. G., addressing his wife.

" 'They haven't gone well in the house, Mr. Greeley. The roof has leaked; it has rained down all over the house, and—and—wet everything, and everything is—is—being ruined and spoiled.'

"These words and many others of the same purport came from the gentle Mrs. G. like so many electrical discharges.

"A lull ensued, when Mr. Greeley calmly and good-naturedly replied:

" 'No, mother, I don't think everything will be spoiled. I have tried to find Mr. C., whom you desire to fix the house, but he has gone west. When he returns I will see him at once, and have him remedy the difficulty. You know you will not allow any one else to repair the roof.

" 'We shall want supper, mother,' continued Mr. Greeley. 'I haven't had anything to eat since morning, and I am beginning to feel hungry.'

"Recollecting that we had traveled two or three hours through heat and dust, Mr. G. inquired:

" 'Can we not have a basin of clean water, mother? We want to wash.'

"A tin wash basin, half filled with water, was brought and placed on the seat of the piazza; also a clean towel.

"Mr. G. beginning to make preparations to use it, 'mother,' in a rather unmotherly manner, spoke out:

" 'You are not going to wash in that water? One's enough to wash in one dish.'

"Perceiving his dilemma, Mr. G. quickly but quietly observed to me.

" 'You wash here, and I will go up-stairs and wash.'

"In a few moments Mr. G. returned, when he said:

" 'It is growing dark and I think we shall have time to go and see the garden before supper. Would you like to see it?' addressing me. Signifying my assent, we started together for the garden, which was a dozen or more rods from the house, down a rather steep bank.

"When about half-way down the declivity, we heard a pretty sharp voice in our rear:

" 'I thought you wanted supper. It is ready.'

" 'We will be back in a few moments, mother,' returned Mr. G.

"And in the course of ten minutes we did return, and went to supper. By this time it was quite dark in the room, and there was no light on the table.

" 'Where shall I sit, mother?' asked Mr. G.

"Mrs. G. pointed to one of the four chairs around the table, and Mr. G. invited me to have another. Mrs. G. sat opposite her husband and Ida opposite me.

" 'Will you have cocoa or milk?' asked Mrs. G., addressing me.

"I replied that I would have cocoa, whereupon a cup was poured out. Then there was a search—in the dark—for milk wherewith to flavor the same.

" 'Where is the pitcher of milk?' demanded Mrs. G.

"After a pause—'Oh, ah, I have used that, mother,' replied Mr. G., who, it appears, had inconsiderately taken up the pitcher and emptied its contents into a bowl near him, which he was rapidly making way with.

"A further supply of milk was here ordered; my cocoa was tempered and handed me, in the dark. Then came the bread, and then the butter, and afterward a saucer pretty well filled with custard, all of which I partook of, and will do Mrs. G. the justice to say they were good. The custard was specially commended by Mr. G. He 'wished he could obtain such an article in the city. It was never sweet enough there, and he supposed the eggs were not always fresh.'

" 'This was sweetened with maple sugar; that's what gives it its flavor,' returned Mrs. G.; thereupon the qualities of maple sugar were warmly endorsed for the sweetening of custard.

"The writer neither concurred nor dissented, but will say that he has eaten a great deal better custard than Mrs. Greeley's, and when there was no maple sugar used.

"There was apple-sauce on the table—at least, I was asked to partake of it, but declined, and therefore can not speak of it. By the time supper was over—if a meal composed of bread and butter and milk, apple-sauce, custard and cocoa can be called a supper—it was nearly dark; as evidence of the fact, I remark that I tried in vain to determine the hour of the evening by looking at the dial of my timepiece. Still there was no light for at least fifteen minutes after supper was over.

"There was no light, indeed, until I had made repeated efforts to determine the time of night, and was compelled to ask information on the subject, which inquiry resulted in the production of about two inches of tallow candle, which, when lighted, emitted about as much light as one might expect from a tallow dip.

"Mr. Greeley complained that he could see nothing by it, and inquired of 'mother' whether she could not furnish a better one.

"The reply was, that the light was 'good enough.'

"At length we drew back from the table, and uncovering the basket he had brought with him from the city—a large willow market basket—Mr. G. drew up by the side of his wife, with the view of disclosing to her the contents. He said he thought it contained articles that would please her. The first thing taken out was a calfskin nicely rolled up, which was handed Mrs. Greeley.

"She looked at the roll, smelled of it, condemned it as good for nothing, unrolled it, smelled of it again, declared it 'horrid,' stuck it up to her husband's proboscis, and then to her own again, and finally threw it under the table in evident disgust.

" 'Don't you—can't you smell anything disagreeable about it, Mr. G.?' inquired 'mother.'

" 'It smells of tanner's oil, as all new leather does. I don't smell anything else about it. But it is a good skin,' continued Mr. G. 'I went to my shoemaker and told him to send out and purchase for me the very best calfskin he could obtain in the city, and he procured this, and it must be a good one. I don't suppose there are three better ones to be found there. Just look at it and see how fine the grain is.'

"Whereupon it was again examined by Mrs. G., who was forced to admit that it had a fine grain, but she could not endure anything which smelled like that.

"Another package was taken from the basket, which appeared to be a pair of shoes which Mrs. Greeley had ordered made for herself in the city.

" 'Have you paid for them?' was the first interrogatory.

"Being answered in the affirmative, 'What did you pay?' was the next inquiry.

" 'I paid two dollars.'

" 'Why did you pay for them? How did you know they would suit?'

"Continuing to remove the paper in which they had been put up, and at length reaching the shoes, Mrs. G. broke out:

" 'Why, these will never do. They are too large, a great deal too large. They won't fit at all.'

" 'How do you know, mother? You haven't tried them on. You had better try them.'

" 'I don't want to try them. Haven't I got eyes,
and can't I tell whether a shoe will fit me, or whether
it is a rod too large? You can carry them straight
back. I don't want them.'

"This ended the argument touching the shoes, and
a third package was taken from the basket.

" 'Here is a pair of rubbers for Ida,' said Mr. G.,
handing them to 'mother,' minus the paper covering.

" 'What horrible things, Mr. Greeley!' said the
sweet wife; 'why, they are too heavy. They didn't
want to only cover the bottom of the foot, and here
you have gone and got a pair of rubbers suitable for a
boy, to be worn in winter. Why, you know better than
to get a pair of shoes of this sort. Here you have
gone and got a great, heavy pair of shoes, heavy
enough for a man. Why, they'd kill the child; she
shall never, never wear them.'

" 'But, mother, you said you wanted a pair with
broad soles, and I got them. You said you wanted
them to come up high in the instep, and these do.'

" 'These soles are broad all the way from the toe
to the heel, and they are too thick in the instep. They
won't do. Ida shall never wear them. How came you
to get them? I—I wonder that you didn't know better!
You don't seem to exercise the least judgment in buying anything for the family. If you had any sense, you
wouldn't bring anything of this kind into the house;
you can take them back soon as you please.'

" 'Why, mother, I took a great deal of pains in
buying them. I went down to a store in Maiden Lane,
where is kept the best assortment in the city, and I
tried to find just such a pair as you spoke of.

" 'Why didn't you go round to the different stores,
mother? I always go to the largest and best, because
I am more likely to find what I want there. In this
case, I got just the sort of a shoe I asked for, and
thought they would suit.

" 'Come here, Ida, and let me try them on.'

" 'They are too big for me,' said Ida.

" 'But come here and sit on my knee and let me put them on.'

" 'They won't do; I know they won't,' said Ida.

" 'But perhaps they will,' continued the father. 'Come and sit on my knee, and I will try one of them on. Come.'

"After a good deal of coaxing and urging, the child was induced to go to her father and sit upon his knee, which she did very awkwardly, and with evident reluctance. The shoe was tried; result not reported. Then followed a running conversation on the subject of Mr. Greeley's purchases generally—his ability to make them—in the course of which it came out that Mrs. G. had obtained precisely the pair of shoes she had ordered, made, in fact, to order. On all points she was worsted in the argument, and a lull ensued.

"Taking advantage of it, Mr. G. took from the basket a copy of *Putnam's Magazine,* and proposed to read from it.

" 'But first we must have a little more light on the subject. Can't we have a better light, mother? Let us have a better light, and I will read a little. Wouldn't you like that, mother?'

" 'I don't want to hear any reading, and the light is good enough. I believe there are a few sperm or adamantine candles, but the one you are using is good enough—good enough for you.'

" 'But, mother, it is difficult to read by this light. I should complain of it down in the city. Can you not let me have a better?'

"This appeal was successful, and a better light brought out.

" 'Now, shall I read?' inquires Mr. G.

" 'No, I don't want to hear any reading.'

" 'But I have the latest number, and there are several good things in it.'

" 'I don't want to listen to any reading.' And she didn't.

"Then Rufus Wilmot Griswold and others were discussed, and finally the affairs of the farm and its management.

"A garden engine, it seems, had been allowed to remain in the hot sun, and the India rubber hose or pipe connected with it had been impaired. Mr. Greeley remarked that it was difficult to find a man who would take the same interest in another's affairs he did in his own. If he could be at home the whole time things would be looked after more carefully than they were now. His employees did as well as he could expect, but perhaps not as well as they might.

" 'But,' suggested Mrs. G., 'if I had the charge of affairs, I would give my directions, and they should be obeyed.'

" 'Why, mother, you have charge here—in my absence, at least,' rejoined Mr. G.

" 'Damn it, no, I haven't!' was her amiable response. 'I'm a cipher here—a mere slave. I've no rights; no attention is paid me; no respect is shown me. You know this is so.'

"This, and much more in the same strain, was spoken, but so rapidly that it would be hardly possible to report it were it worth while.

"At length I concluded to return to the hotel where the lodgings had been secured.

" 'I guess you had better decide to remain all night, and we will look over the farm more in detail in the morning,' said Mr. G.

" 'He can't stay here!' interposed Mrs. G.

" 'Of course not,' returned Mr. G. 'I thought you understood that lodgings had been engaged at the hotel.'

"Here I took my departure from the house, to the relief of my hostess, probably—most certainly to my own, though I can not say I was altogether displeased with what I witnessed. I pitied, felt incensed, and disgusted, and yet at times I was a good deal amused.

I spent an hour and a half inside the house—perhaps two hours. Only once during that time did Mrs. G. speak kindly and pleasantly, and that was in response to a remark of mine. I said: 'Mr. Greeley, I wonder that you did not build a log house when you came into these woods; it would have been so in keeping with everything else here.'

" 'Oh, yes,' chattered Mrs. G., 'a dear little log house, how cozy and nice it would be! I should like a log house; how pleasant it might be made; I always did like a log house.'

"To her husband she did not speak one gentle, kind, cheerful word. She spoke only to criticize, reprove or berate. On the other hand, he employed only the kindest, most affectionate, most endearing terms. The more frantic her language and manner, the more bland and kind were his expressions. I believe he loved his wife devotedly, and it is not for me to say that she did not love him as well. I can only say, if she did, she had a most extraordinary way of manifesting her devotion."

We get a glimpse of a happier day at Chappaqua in a letter from an unnamed woman friend, who had accepted an invitation, written in these terms: "I am anxious, if the weather should permit, that you should be one of a small party to visit my country home (where nobody lives) and see what a nice place it would be if only good people actually did live there." Accordingly, the lady writes, under date of April 29, 1871:

"Saturday morning at nine o'clock we left the city depot for a trip to Chappaqua. Only Theodore Tilton and wife were of the party besides Mrs. R., Mr. Greeley and myself. Mrs. Tilton I fell in love with at the first glance. She is a frail little creature, about your size, and is just coming back to life after a long sickness. She looks up into your face with such loving, sincere, trustful eyes, that you feel like kissing her every time you meet her glance. The day was one of the happiest I ever spent in my life. Dear Old Horace's face fairly beamed with happiness. We rode all over 'Mother's land,' up hill and down ravines, and over to see his woodland where he spends every Saturday chopping. He and Tilton kept up a fire of jests. . . . There was lots of fun aboard. I'll never say again Mr. Greeley isn't queer. He drove slow, of course, and such driving you never saw. His old horses knew him, no doubt, and they paid not the slightest attention to his chirps and gentle shakes of the lines. He held one line in each hand with elbows sticking out, and his hat on the back of his neck, while his horses went all ways but in the road, and sometimes took us over stumps, to the no small risk of an upset. We visited the cascade last, and drank from the stream as in duty bound. Mr. Greeley has firm faith that this is the very purest and sweetest water in the world. Tilton laughed at him for stepping backward into it in moving, but Horace avowed it did not wet him at all, for he 'drew his foot out so quick the water never found it was there.' From thence we drove up by the field Mr. Greeley is so proud of, which 'used to be the wickedest frog pond you ever saw, all cabbage, and so springy you could not walk over it with safety.' It is a beautiful field now, but the old man's face, beaming in pride of it, was much more attractive to me.''

This visit was made in the absence of Mrs. Greeley in Europe, whither she had departed not long before in search of health, taking Ida with her. The company dined at the hotel. ''Mr. Greeley lamented much that we could not dine at his house, and told me more than

once, in a confidential way, it was 'a sight worth seeing to see Ida get dinner there.' ''

The visitor recites: ''They have built three houses
on the place and only one of them is inhabited, the
man who farms using the back part of that. Besides,
he (Horace) and Mother Greeley each have a barn.
Mrs. Greeley would not have a tree cut, even to trim
it, about the first house. So they left that and built
another in the sunshine to be more wholesome. This
second one was the one we entered, which they propose to use if Mrs. Greeley ever returns, as he thinks
she will in the fall. They have lots of old stock about,
which they keep for the good they have done; as old
cows which 'Mother says shall never be killed while
she lives, because they have given milk to her children.' They 'fell down sometimes and wanted to die,
but Mother would not let them and kept a man to lift
them up and care for them.' ''

Greeley came back with the party to his city house
and read poetry to them all evening, winding up with
Jim Bludso, recently written by his young coadjutor
on the *Tribune* staff, Colonel John Hay. So ended
the perfect day!

With the casual responsibility that seems to have
governed all Greeley family affairs, the youngest
daughter, Gabrielle, then but fourteen, at the close of
school in the late spring of 1871, had set out alone for
Europe to join her mother and sister. She was stricken
with malaria on the ship, went alone to a hotel in
Southampton and finally managed to join the others
in London, where they had hired a furnished house
until September first. ''Both children want to come
home,'' Greeley recorded July twenty-fourth, ''but

will do whatever their mother's health shall suggest as best for her." The London doctors did not know how to treat American ague, but Gabrielle recovered in spite of them. Of Ida at this period Greeley wrote: "Her life has been given to her invalid mother and has been a hard one; but you will see that trial has not hardened her nature, nor soured her disposition. I am flattered when told that she looks like me, though I hardly can see it."

The exiled family decided not to come home, but to try a winter in the south of France. "Perhaps this is best," was Greeley's comment, "as mother is so weak that Ida dare not trust her to cross the ocean. She writes that she is very homesick and means to come in the spring whether or no. I do hope you will yet know Ida. There may have been better among us, but they are gone. She remains to attest the possibilities of our kindred." He feared the family would not find southern France all they had painted. "In the spring," he writes, "they will come home, *D. v.* Ida and Gabrielle take turns in caring for their helpless, suffering mother, who is disabled by rheumatism from walking or even standing, though mind and voice are strong as ever. I grieve for Ida's worn, anxious youth, which never can be regained, though she does not think of it."

The exiles picked on Arcachon as the place to stay. Greeley thought Gabrielle would find it very dull, "with a poor chance of getting that variety of delicate food required by my suffering wife." Later they "threaten to move on six hundred miles or so—perhaps to Nice and perhaps to Italy itself. The children are worn out with travel and thoroughly homesick, but everything bends to the hope of retaining their mother in this sphere, and making her life as bearable as may be." Ida wrote of her desire to run away by herself for three weeks in Italy. Greeley hoped she would, but "I apprehend mother would decline to spare her when the moment came." Mother did not decline, and Ida made the trip in December, 1871. He rejoiced, for "to hear from Ida in Rome is very much to me." Again: "She says her flying trip to Italy cost eight hundred dollars and was worth it. I am very glad she had it and enjoyed it. I wish her to leave Europe next spring content with America forevermore." The girls reported "mother" as very sweet and bright this winter (January, 1872), though unable to walk. The father expressed the wish that Ida "would revere Rome more and the Pope less," a course in a convent school having caused the young lady to embrace the Catholic faith—a strange turn from her liberal forebears.

The family reached Paris about April twentieth, and prepared to return. Mother and Ida delaying, the adventurous Gabrielle set out by herself, to be taken down with typhoid fever on the ship. Her father's account, written on June 3, 1872, reads: "Our dear Gabrielle has come back to me at last, but suffering with typhoid fever. She was seasick for a day or two at the outset of her voyage, and then lapsed into typhoid, which rather increased on the way, as there was no doctor but a German, whom she pronounced an ignoramus, and threw away his medicine. After she landed on Saturday, by mischance after mischance, a full day elapsed before a doctor came to her bedside. I hope she is now doing well, but her eyes have a wild, bad look, and she was wakeful and half delirious through the night." Probably the homeopathic prejudice of the family had something to do with rejecting the remedies.

The political excitement was on, and his "weekly day of exercise and recreation at the farm" had been "spoiled by reporters and interviewers. . . . We had a fine picnic there on the [May] 25th," he continues, "but I do not need picnics and do need sleep, which hates to come near me."

To his surprise, apparently, "my folks came in yesterday morning"—June fifteenth. He had not expected them but on receiving word went down the bay to meet them on the steamer *Rhein.* "My eyesight was so poor I did not recognize Ida among the passengers on deck till long after she had discerned me. Mother, of course, was in her stateroom below. . . . Mother looks older, thinner, if possible, and has lost most of her remaining teeth since she left for Europe, September 1, 1870, but she does not seem to have lost ground essentially. Her mind is as clear and her voice nearly as strong as then." The invalid was taken to Chappaqua after a few days at the Hotel St. Cloud. "It was a sad pleasure," Greeley records, "to us all to see her once more in her own room, in her own bed, where she seemed more contented and satisfied than she had done or could be at any hotel. She has had one or two severe attacks since, with difficulty of breathing, but though she will never walk again, she seems as likely to live for years as at any time since 1865." She did get up and about. In mid-July she took a carriage ride—"looked like a ghost as she reclined in her carriage, but talked as if young and hearty."

Mrs. Harriot Stanton Blatch remembers Ida Greeley, whom she met at Paris and later at Geneva, New York, as very pretty, with a complexion of unusual delicacy. "She told me," Mrs. Blatch recounts, "that she never washed her face, substituting a damp towel for the more liquid form of ablution."

CHAPTER XIV

SYMPATHY for the underdog did not extend with Greeley to the much harassed President Andrew Johnson, quite probably because Johnson retained William H. Seward as secretary of state and presumably as intimate adviser. The Secretary had been severely wounded by Lewis Powell, alias Payne, one of Booth's band of assassins, and was never again his old aggressive self.

Perhaps it was Seward's sly desire to placate Greeley that caused President Johnson to nominate the editor as minister to Austria in July, 1867, to replace John Lothrop Motley, who had resigned. Senator Thomas W. Tipton, of Nebraska, a state for which Greeley had done so much, objected to consideration of the nomination and it was tabled, under the rules, never to be brought up again, the Senate adjourning immediately afterward.

When it came time to select a successor to Johnson the Democrats rallied in the new Tammany Hall in New York, built by William M. Tweed, on Fourteenth Street near Third Avenue, and with much flourish on the Fourth of July, 1868, nominated Horatio Seymour and Frank P. Blair. Seymour had been twice governor of New York, and was much esteemed. Blair had been an active war Democrat. The Republican party had changed its control. Seward had lost his leadership, Thurlow Weed had retired from political activity, and Greeley was out of sorts with all sides. "Practical men" like Zachariah Chandler, of Michigan, Benjamin F. Wade, of Ohio, and William M. Stewart, of Nevada, had circumscribed the influence of Charles Sumner and his high-grade following in the Senate.

Party now took the lead over principles. The problem was to win the election, not to carry out great purposes. To accomplish this Lieutenant-General Ulysses S. Grant was taken from the head of the army and called a Republican, though his only presidential vote had been cast for a Democrat. To the tail of the ticket Schuyler Colfax, of Indiana, popular as speaker of the House, was added. Greeley regarded the ticket gingerly and supported it with misgivings. There is a glimpse of him in the campaign given by John Bigelow in his diary, noting his entertainment of the editor when he came to Highland Falls, New York, where Bigelow resided, late in October, 1868, to speak for the ticket:

"October 29, 1868.—Went to the wharf for Greeley Tuesday evening [27th]. He wore a soft felt hat with an uncommonly broad brim, and the old white coat, bearing in his hand a carpet-bag with an oilcloth covering, so torn as to give the impression of an overloaded package falling through the lining of a coat. I ought here to remark that my acquaintance with Mr. Greeley was almost exclusively confined to what I had learned of him through his paper.

"We shook hands, of course, and I naturally asked him how he was. He said *he* was *cheerful*. Promptly upon reaching my home we had dinner. All my children were at the table, and one of their aunts who was a visitor. Greeley did not address a remark to one of them, but persisted in talking about the value of trees as a crop, advising me to trim out my forest and put in seed to get new kinds, etc., regardless of the expense of trimming and the increased expense of chopping wood that is not taken clean. He talked in a way to satisfy me that, whatever might be his knowledge, his judgment on agricultural matters was simply worthless. He mentioned one thing, however, for which I thank him. He said that after one leaves the Mississippi a few days' journey, one does not find between that and the Pacific a piece of wood of which an ax-valve or two extra could be made. Thus a broken one could not be replaced anywhere on the journey. I asked why they did not plant hickory and ash and other hard woods, which would be more useful on the plains. He said he did not know, but he doubted whether the trees thus planted would have the qualities acquired by those growing in our more rigorous and stormy climate. As evidence of that, he said that the oak of California is good for nothing but fuel.

"As soon as we had finished our repast we went over to the meeting, where I was called upon to preside. On taking the chair I remarked in substance that we were in the midst of a great crisis; that Grant was a great man, and Horace Greeley had come to prove it. He then advanced and spoke about two hours and a half. What he had said was remarkable only for the steady tension of the mind for so long a period. There was no eloquence; he made no striking points; yet the whole told tolerably well upon the audience, which crowded the hall to the utmost. On going home he went at once to bed.

"In the morning while sitting in my library I heard him at the front door coming in. He was bareheaded, though the morning was quite cool. I asked why he did not wear his hat. He said the air felt cool and refreshing; that he had not had so good a night's rest in a long time, at the same time admitting that he was 'but an indifferent sleeper'; that he had not had—to use his own language—'a square night's sleep for fifteen years'; but he said it rested him to lie down.

"I got his hat, put it on him, and took him out to show him a bit of the highland scenery. He began talking about trees and saw nothing. After breakfast I took him in my carriage with my eldest daughter to the steamer *Mary Powell*. He did not speak to any of the family but myself during his stay, nor on leaving, except a word or two to my eldest daughter the previous evening, just before supper, when I was obliged to leave them for a few minutes. When we got on board of the boat he sat down by himself, pulled out a copy of the *Independent,* and read it entirely through, I think, from beginning to end. After a while I joined him. He then showed me the leading article in the *Independent,* which he wanted me to read, saying, 'Here is an article by Tilton on Evarts that is wonderfully well done. I should not wish to have written or published it myself, but it ought to be written and published.' This he said over twice. Perhaps he was thinking I ought to have had it in the *Evening Post.* Then he took it out of my hands. Before he discovered that I had done with his paper my eye had glanced over a gratuitous attack on Motley and Bancroft. I quietly observed to him that Tilton had contrived to make three or four bitter and formidable enemies by those articles, but I doubted whether he would be indemnified for such a result by the pleasure he would give to others. 'Why, yes,' said Greeley, 'the *Herald* made its reputation by its attacks upon people.' He then spoke of Reverdy Johnson's flirtation with Laird and the rebellion fomenters in England, denouncing him violently for something he had said or done. He added that Seward was at the bot-

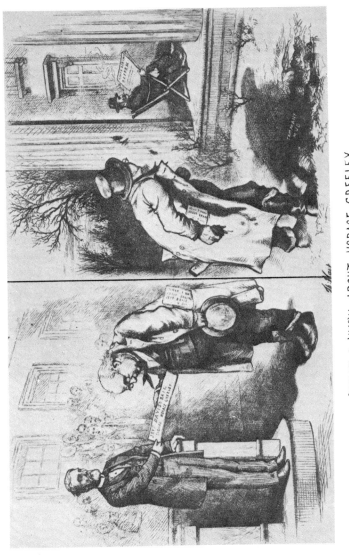

WHAT I KNOW ABOUT HORACE GREELEY.

(From Harper's Weekly, Jan. 20, 1872)

tom of it; it was Seward and not Johnson, for Seward wished to go to England as minister.

"It is a common rumor that Greeley is a declared candidate for the English mission; that he would like to have Morgan secretary of the treasury, in which case he would transfer his aspirations to the vacant seat in the Senate. It is certain that he ran once for the Senate against Evarts, and both were defeated. All these facts taken together account for his zeal in defending the *Independent,* which nowadays seems to be conducted in his interest. Here in a short conversation of half an hour, Greeley, though meaning to be reticent and anything but confidential with me, revealed the furious hatred that was raging in his breast against four or five of the most prominent men of our country merely because they have heretofore stood or may hereafter stand in the way of his ambition. He is now prowling around the state every night making speeches to keep himself in evidence. He is as easily flattered as a child. How strange that a man who loves flattery so much should not treat people more humanely, and should defend such an outrage on public decency as Tilton's article on Evarts."

This is, of course, the ex parte statement of a fastidious gentleman who lived in the upper half of society. Bigelow could hardly be expected to have seen Greeley clearly through spectacles ground in the office of the *Evening Post* of that day, in which he was an owner, and with the editing of which he had much to do. Nothing could have been wider apart than the journalism of the *Tribune* and of the *Post.* Justin McCarthy, about the time Bigelow wrote this lugubrious account of Greeley, found him, "one of the very simplest and one of the very ablest men" he had ever known.

"His intellect," McCarthy wrote, "within its own sphere was originating, broad and keen. He was absolutely without affectation, just as he was without selfish or ignoble purpose. . . . He never cared the least for money, never could be induced to go one step out of his way to make money, hardly ever knew, indeed, whether he had money at the time or whether he had not. It was well said of him that whereas other public men were usually willing to back their money with their opinions, Horace Greeley, as a journalist, was always ready to back his opinions with his money. . . . In the simplicity of his nature and the absolute integrity of his character, he reminded me especially of two men I had known, and who, unlike each other in most ways, were very much like each other in these ways—Father Mathew, the great Irish apostle of temperance, and John Bright."

Both William Cullen Bryant and Bigelow were soon to be allied with Greeley against Grant. Greeley, of course, did not get anything from Grant, nor did any of the old line of uplifting Republicans. Bigelow, writing to Huntington when Grant's election was assured, observed: "Providence takes delight in disappointing people. Greeley, who *loves* Seward, says that the Russian Minister told him that Grant could not get Seward out of the State Department with a file of soldiers." He went, however, without difficulty.

It was soon evident that Grant was in new hands. His Cabinet was a pleasing compound of good and bad, in which the bad had the most influence. Seward's retirement was not accompanied by any appreciation of Greeley on Grant's part. The *Times*, not the *Tribune*, was the recognized party organ, and probably became so automatically, as Greeley could not play party tunes. He had made Whitelaw Reid managing editor, with Colonel John Hay as assistant. The two young men tried to be in accord with their head, but found it no easy matter. Samuel Sinclair, as publisher, had to stand between Greeley and a number of stockholders, who preferred profits to power. The situation after the Jefferson Davis débâcle was not a comforting one. Yet fate favored the *Tribune* and put the *Times* at a disadvantage.

Early on June 19, 1869, Henry J. Raymond died, under strange circumstances. John Bigelow relates: "At a late hour last Friday night [June 18] the body of Henry J. Raymond was brought home in a carriage by two men who immediately disappeared. The servant who opened the door, being in her night clothes, escaped as soon as she turned the key of the door (to admit the party), so that what happened thereafter was not discovered until early in the morning, when Raymond's stertorous breathing was overheard by his daughter Mary."

One of the "two men" who thrust Raymond in through the unlocked door of Number 12 West Ninth Street was George W. Parker, law partner for a time of Chester A. Arthur, later Vice-President and President of the United States. Parker also served as Corporation Counsel of New York City, under Mayor William F. Havemeyer, and was a municipal judge in his last years. I knew him well and he once told me something about the incident. His companion was James A. Booth, State Senator from New York City, 1872-1874, who performed considerable service in helping Samuel J. Tilden clean up Tweed's ring.

Tilden always spoke of him in the highest terms. I also knew Booth, when a boy at Nyack-on-the-Hudson. He was a brother-in-law of Quentin McAdam, a lawyer of some distinction in the mid-'seventies, with whom he spent his summers at Nyack.

Both belonged to the tall hat, frock coat, Republican leadership of the day. In the afternoon Raymond with his daughter had visited in Greenwood Cemetery the grave of his son, Walter J. Raymond, who had died, aged fifteen years, a few months before. In the evening he attended a political conference, where he met Parker and Booth. Taking Major George F. Williams, a *Times* reporter, with them, they adjourned to the Hotel St. Denis, a short distance from Raymond's home, and cracked a few bottles of champagne. Raymond seemed unduly affected, so the two gentlemen called a cab and escorted him to his house, where they rang the bell and saw him inside, as noted by Bigelow. It never occurred to either of them that apoplexy, not wine, was the cause of their companion's uncertainty of gait. They kept still about the facts, however, and so the "mystery" survived.

Raymond had carried on an intimacy with Rose Eytinge, an actress who was the toast of the day, and one of the rumors was that he had been brought from her room much upset by a "scene" due to his severing the relationship, owing to the return of his wife and children from a three-years' absence in Europe. Indeed, Bigelow records the tale as coming from Henry Ward Beecher. This, as I can certify, was not correct. The lady was easily consoled, married a kin of General Benjamin F. Butler. and was mother of Frank Butler, a brilliant and erratic writer on the New York *Morn-*

ing Telegraph. She survived until December 20, 1911, when she died at the Brunswick Home, Amityville, Long Island.

Henry Ward Beecher conducted Raymond's funeral services at the University Place Presbyterian Church. Horace Greeley, Thurlow Weed and James Watson Webb were among the pallbearers, who included besides, George William Curtis, General John A. Dix and Admiral David G. Farragut. Raymond was but fifty years old.

Party schisms now arose. Charles Sumner was soon out of sorts. The split came over the proposed annexation of Santo Domingo, arranged corruptly by Grant's secretary, General O. E. Babcock, which Sumner, as Chairman of the Committee on Foreign Affairs of the Senate, put a stop to. Greeley at the moment rather sided with the President, or at least did not come to Sumner's support. Whitelaw Reid, as managing editor of the *Tribune,* writing apologetically to Bigelow, explained his own reticence in commenting on the paper's course—"because, in my position it is not becoming that I should; but you don't need to be informed that if I had directed it Mr. Sumner would have received from the outset a more continuous, outspoken and hearty support. . . Mr. Greeley has, I fear, a latent feeling of personal dislike for Summer; then he was anxious to avoid a break with Grant or the administration, and specially anxious to prevent what looked for a little while like the ruin of the Republican party." This was written April 10, 1871. Before the end of the year Greeley was espousing independent Republicanism with full vigor and hammering the Grant administration. His own disappointed desires were credited with being the cause. Bigelow wrote Huntington, December 28, 1871: "I fear the presidential bee in Greeley's bonnet is giving the *Tribune* a bad lead. *Timeo Danaos,* etc., and I distrust a candidate that is to depend for his success upon the Democrats nominating no candidate. It is not certain that what has never happened, never will, but there is scripture for saying that what has happened will happen. The Democratic party is in the habit of nominating its own candidate and is not much in the habit of voting for the candidates of other parties—if it knows it."

Two days later, December thirtieth, Reid, writing to Bigelow again, had this to say about his chief's attitude: "With me the course of the *Tribune* has been one of instinctive dislike of men of Grant's character and caliber for our highest positions, and of a deliberate belief that it would be best for a great journal like the *Tribune* to hold itself above party. With Mr. Greeley it has been a dislike of General Grant personally, the belief that he is too small a man for the presidency, and great dissatisfaction with many parts of his management, particularly with his encouragement of disreputable men, and his partisan interferences with the Civil Service all over the country."

John Hay was "doing admirably and becoming corpulent," according to Reid, who voices in the same letter a rumor that the brilliant young colonel was to marry the Swedish singer, Christine Nilsson, which he declared he did not believe. It might be remarked that Whitelaw Reid had no small prejudice against Grant. The feeling had begun at Pittsburg Landing,

CINCINNATUS.

H. G. THE FARMER RECEIVING THE NOMINATION FROM H. G. THE EDITOR.

(From Harper's Weekly, Feb. 10, 1872)

where, as war correspondent of the Cincinnati *Gazette,*
he charged and proved that Grant had been surprised
by Beauregard and Albert Sidney Johnston. He always opposed Grant, and the *Tribune* under him was
a strong factor in breaking Grant's chances for a third
term. He raised the cry of "Cæsarism" most
effectively in 1876.

Revolt had already begun in Missouri, where Carl
Schurz, B. Gratz Brown, Doctor Emil Preetorius and
his young aid, Joseph Pulitzer, had started a movement that ended in the election of Brown as governor
over both Democrats and regular Republicans. It
spread rapidly across the country, being taken up and
argued by all the great editors of the day—Joseph
Medill, of the Chicago *Tribune,* Murat Halstead, of the
Cincinnati *Commercial,* William Cullen Bryant, of the
New York *Evening Post,* Samuel Bowles, of the
Springfield *Republican,* and Greeley. The better-
grade Republicans were shaken out of the Cabinet,
and men more after Grant's heart took their places—
people whom he could understand and work with.
That nothing more than scandal resulted was a tribute
to the President's personal honesty and common sense.
He was certainly surrounded by scamps from the day
he went into office, who sold him shamelessly and
brazened out their frequent failures to "deliver."

Thus supported, the resentment was not long in
taking form, and in season produced the Liberal
Republican party, as it called itself. While Greeley's
evidences of dissatisfaction with Grant were plain
enough, the Republican machine did not seem to have
thought he would leave the party. E. D. Morgan,
Governor and Senator from New York, wrote John

Bigelow, January 27, 1872: "I do not think now that Greeley will bolt the party if Grant is renominated. He is losing some supporters and the paper is more for Grant than any one. It is not certain but that this will induce a change of policy in the *Tribune*." There was ample surface warrant for Morgan's belief. As late as March, 1872, when considering the Missouri call for a national convention at Cincinnati, the *Tribune* had refused to accept its declaration for "a genuine reform of the tariff," which had much of war tax left in it, declaring that, with this cut out, "we will go to Cincinnati." It did not seem probable, with Carl Schurz in the lead, that this would be done. In that same month Greeley wrote to a correspondent: "You see that I am drifting into a fight with Grant. I hate it; I know how many friends I shall alienate by it, and how it will injure the *Tribune*, of which so little is my own property that I dread to wreck it; yet . . . I should despise myself if I pretended to acquiesce in his reelection. I may yet have to support him, but I would rather quit editing newspapers forever." On April sixteenth Bigelow was writing Huntington: "I see no sign of any new defections from Grant for two years past. Every man who now appears in the opposition was ready to knife him two years ago. I cautioned Reid against the dance he was leading the *Tribune*, but I fancy it is old White Coat's freaks, in which he will be indulged until it begins to tell upon the exchequer, which will not be till after election, before which time he will have ample opportunity of hauling his wind."

Although Greeley appeared to be in such an indecisive state, he was steadily being forced into the picture, curiously, not so much by friends as by his foes. So early as January 20, 1872, *Harper's Weekly,* his most potent opponent, was foreshadowing his entrance into the arena, printing a full page cartoon by Thomas Nast, *What I Know about Horace Greeley,* depicting him peering into the White House window at Ulysses S. Grant, who was comfortably ensconced within. February nineteenth, he was lampooned as "Cincinnatus" offering the Democratic and Republican nomination to himself. On March sixteenth, he was again cartooned in the background of a group of independent "conspirators" with "What I Know about Bolting" inscribed on his coat-tail pockets. This sort of thing gave him a prominence that made his candidacy a fact before he knew it himself. Whitelaw Reid was credited with working behind the scenes and Greeley soon became unquestionably receptive.

Yet the foreshadowing of opposition to Grant was in Greeley's mind late in 1871, though he hesitated to drop his party. "Here am I," he wrote on November twenty-sixth, "at the head of a newspaper which is a great property, which others mainly own. If it were all mine I might not mind the risk; but it belongs to others, and I must be seriously damaged by the course I am inclined to take. Moreover, if I take the course, I shall be widely believed to have sacrificed others' property to my own personal resentment,— perhaps to my own personal ambition." All of which came but too true.

In an advertisement proclaiming the merits of the several editions of the *Tribune*—daily ten dollars per annum, weekly two dollars, and semi-weekly four dollars—evidently written by the editor, and published in the *Christian Union* for January 3, 1872, these interesting paragraphs appear:

"A war upon corruption and rascality in office has been inaugurated in our city, whereby the government of our state [New York] has been revolutionized through an instant triumph of Reform which surpasses the most sanguine anticipations. It is morally certain that the government thus inaugurated can not, in its progress, be circumstance to any locality or any party, but that its purifying influence is destined to be felt in any part of the Union, rebuking venality, exposing robbery, wresting power from politicians by trade, and confiding it to those worthiest and fittest to wield it. To this beneficent and vitally needed Reform the *Tribune* will devote its best energies, regardless of personal interests or party predilections, esteeming the choice of honest and faithful men to office is of all New Departures the most essential and auspicious.

"The virtual surrender of the Democratic party of its hostility to Equal Rights, regardless of color, has divested our current politics of half their bygone intensity. However parties may henceforth rise or fall, it is clear that the fundamental principles which have hitherto honorably distinguished the Republican party are henceforth to be regarded as practically accepted by the whole country. The right of every man to his own limbs and sinews—the equality of all citizens before the law—the inability of a state to enslave any portion of its people—the duty of the Union to guarantee to every citizen the full enjoyment of his liberty until he forfeits it by crime—such are the broad and firm foundations of our national edifices; and palsied be the hand which shall seek to displace them! Though not yet twenty years old, the Republican party has completed the noble fabric of emancipation, and may fairly invoke thereon the sternest judgment of Man, and the benignant smile of God. Henceforth the mission of our Republic is one of Peaceful Progress."

The "reform" alluded to went beyond Tweed and included charges of dishonesty in the New York Custom House, to which the *Tribune* gave publicity. In January, 1872, Greeley was called to testify before a Senate investigating committee. This action did not tend to warm up his relations with Grant, who stood behind the rogues in innocent belief that his appointees would do no wrong not warranted by politics. At the same moment Colonel John W. Forney resigned as Collector of the Port of Philadelphia, because it interfered with his freedom as editor of the *Press*. He pleaded with Grant to reconcile himself with Greeley and Sumner, as Lincoln had tried to smooth out kindred political wrinkles. This was beyond Grant's point of view. The inquiry proved the correctness of the *Tribune's* charges.

A Labor Reform party convention took place at Columbus, Ohio, in February, 1872. E. W. Chamberlain, of Massachusetts, presided over delegates assembled from seventeen states, who cast 211 votes on the first ballot, 201 of them for Judge David Davis, of Illinois. Judge Joel Parker, of New Jersey, was named for vice-president. Both gentlemen declined to save the country, and Charles O'Conor, eminent New Yorker, was named by committee. He ran without a companion for vice-president and secured a few votes. The Prohibitionists also appeared for the first time as a national party, nominating James Black, of Pennsylvania, and John Russell, of Michigan, on a platform so long that no newspaper would print it.

"New parties must be born of principles," wrote Henry Ward Beecher in the *Christian Union* of January 10, 1872, with what was in the wind in mind, "and the principle that can attract such Republicans as Sumner and Schurz and Greeley into harmony with the Democracy of the New York *World* and the Louisville *Courier-Journal*—not to speak of the 'unreconstructed' brethren—does not appear."

Whitelaw Reid had gone to Cincinnati, old ground for him, to back the Greeley cause in the convention. "I am fighting a battle at this distance with the Free Traders," Greeley wrote, May 1, 1872, "who want to impose a platform on the convention which will probably defeat its candidates. I am in their way and do not mean to get out of it. They may make the candidate as they please, but not the platform, if I can help it."

To this correspondent he enclosed as "one of the curiosities of the cavern" a telegram from Reid. It read:

"If you are not nominated, I believe we can carry our tariff plank, remanding the whole question to congressional districts [General Hancock's most laughed at 'local issue.'] If you are nominated, the Free Traders are furious and will demand something like language of the Missouri call. Last proposition made to me by [David A.] Wells is that exact language of New York call should be adopted. I have said to [Samuel] Bowles, and others back me in it, that they ought not to ask this of you, but that it is barely possible that you might not object to it. . . . Small Free Trade representation here from New York fighting you bitterly in N. York delegation."

The Liberal Republican party met in convention at Cincinnati on May 1, 1872, pursuant to a call sounded from Missouri on January twenty-fourth, preceding. Things looked formidable. It should be said again that the leading war-horses of American journalism were behind the movement to defeat Grant: Horace Greeley, Joseph Medill, Joseph Pulitzer, Doctor Emil Preetorius, Carl Schurz, Oswald Ottendorfer, Samuel Bowles, Murat Halstead and William Cullen Bryant. They blew up a tremendous breeze. Stanley Matthews, of Ohio, called the convention to order and Carl Schurz, then of Missouri, became permanent chairman. Young Joseph Pulitzer, also of Missouri, was secretary.

The leading candidate appeared to be Charles Francis Adams, of Massachusetts, who had been Lincoln's minister to England, though a number of others were being considered for the place, including Greeley.

The platform adopted was a powerful arraignment of Grant's administration. It read:

"The administration now in power has rendered itself guilty of wanton disregard of the laws of the land, and of usurping powers not granted by the Constitution; it has acted as if the laws had binding force only for those who were governed, and not for those who govern. It has thus struck a blow at the fundamental principles of constitutional government and the liberties of the citizen.

"The President of the United States has openly used the powers and opportunities of his high office for the promotion of personal ends.

"He has kept notoriously corrupt and unworthy men in places of power and responsibility, to the detriment of the public interest.

"He has used the public service of the government as a machinery of corruption and personal influence, and has interfered with tyrannical arrogance to the political affairs of states and municipalities.

"He has rewarded with influential and lucrative offices men who had acquired his favor by valuable presents, thus stimulating the demoralization of our political life by his conspicuous example.

"He has shown himself deplorably unequal to the task imposed upon him by the necessities of the country, and culpably careless of the responsibilities of his high office.

"The partisans of the administration, assuming to be the Republican party and controlling its organizations, have attempted to justify such wrongs and palliate such abuses to the end of maintaining partisan ascendency.

"They have stood in the way of necessary investigations and indispensable reforms, pretending that no serious fault could be found with the present administration of public affairs, thus seeking to blind the eyes of the people.

"They have kept alive the passions and resentments of the late Civil War, to use them for their own advantage; they have resorted to arbitrary measures in direct conflict with the organic law, instead of appealing to the better instincts and latent patriotism of the southern people by restoring to them those rights, the enjoyment of which is indispensable to a successful administration of their local affairs, and would tend to revive a patriotic and hopeful national feeling.

"They have degraded themselves and the name of their party, once justly entitled to the confidence of the nation, by a base sycophancy to the dispenser of executive power and patronage, unworthy of Republican freemen; they have sought to silence the voice of just criticism, and stifle the moral sense of the people, and to subjugate public opinion by tyrannical party discipline.

THE MODERN MAZEPPA—"WHAT I KNOW ABOUT THE ROAD FROM CINCINNATI TO ——."

(From Harper's Weekly, June 1, 1872)

"They are striving to maintain themselves in authority for selfish ends by an unscrupulous use of the power which rightfully belongs to the people, and should be employed only in the service of the country.

"Believing that an organization thus led and controlled can no longer be of service to the best interests of the republic, we have resolved to make an independent appeal to the sober judgment, conscience and patriotism of the American people.

"We, the Liberal Republicans of the United States, in national convention assembled at Cincinnati, proclaim the following principles as essential to just government:

"We recognize the equality of all men before the law, and hold that it is the duty of government, in its dealings with the people, to mete out equal and exact justice to all, of whatever nativity, race, color, or persuasion, religious or political.

"We pledge ourselves to maintain the union of these states, emancipation and enfranchisement, and to oppose any reopening of the questions settled by the Thirteenth, Fourteenth and Fifteenth Amendments of the Constitution.

"We demand the immediate and absolute removal of all disabilities imposed on account of the rebellion, which was finally subdued seven years ago, believing that universal amnesty will result in complete pacification in all sections of the country.

"Local self-government, with impartial suffrage, will guard the rights of all citizens more securely than any centralized power. The public welfare requires the supremacy of the civil over the military authority, and the freedom of the person under the protection of the habeas corpus. We demand for the individual the largest liberty consistent with public order, for the state self-government, and for the nation a return to the methods of peace and the constitutional limitations of power.

"The civil service of the government has become a mere instrument of partisan tyranny and personal ambition, and an object of selfish greed. It is a scandal and reproach upon free institutions, and breeds a demoralization dangerous to the perpetuity of republican government. We therefore regard a thorough reform of the civil service as one of the most pressing necessities of the hour; that honesty, capacity and fidelity constitute the only valid claims to public employment; that the offices of the government cease to be a matter of arbitrary favoritism and patronage, and that public station shall become again a post of honor. To this end it is imperatively required that no president shall be a candidate for reelection.

"We demand a system of federal taxation, which shall not unnecessarily interfere with the industry of the people, and which shall provide the means necessary to pay the expenses of the government, economically administered, the pensions, the interest on the public debt, and a moderate reduction annually of the principal thereof; and, recognizing that there are in our midst honest but irreconcilable differences of opinion with regard to the respective systems of protection and free trade, we remit the discussion of the subject to the people in their congressional districts and the decision of Congress thereon, wholly free from executive interference or dictation.

"The public credit must be sacredly maintained, and we denounce repudiation in every form and guise.

"A speedy return to specie payments is demanded alike by the highest consideration of commercial morality and honest government.

"We remember with gratitude the heroism and sacrifice of soldiers and sailors of the republic, and no act of ours shall ever detract from their justly earned fame for the full rewards of their patriotism.

"We are opposed to all further grants of lands to railroads or other corporations. The public domain should be held sacred to actual settlers.

THE SAGE OF CHAPPAQUA.

"We hold that it is the duty of the government in its intercourse with foreign nations to cultivate the friendships of peace by treating with all on fair and equal terms, regarding it alike dishonorable to demand what is not right or submit to what is wrong.

"For the promotion and success of these vital principles, and the support of the candidates nominated by this convention, we invite and cordially welcome the cooperation of all patriotic citizens, without regard to previous political affiliations."

Reid's labors, it will be perceived, had eliminated the tariff by relegating it to congressional districts.

Adams led on the first ballot with 203 votes. Greeley had 147. Lyman Trumbull had 100, B. Gratz Brown 95, David Davis 92½, and Andrew G. Curtin 62. Greeley had not been seriously considered as a candidate either by himself or others. Adams, Trumbull or Curtin would have been promising, but the two last were war Democrats and the first was not an inspiring person. Before the ballot was announced B. Gratz Brown asked to be heard from the platform. Carl Schurz, the chairman, yielded him the right, and Brown formally withdrew his name. On the second ballot Brown received but two votes. Greeley's total grew to 239; Curtin dropped out and Adams rose to 233. The third ballot gave Greeley 258, Adams 279, Trumbull 156. The fourth resulted: Greeley 251, Adams 279, the others scattering. On the fifth, Adams had 309 votes to Greeley's 258. The Davis and Trumbull factions were irreconcilable and began to give way rather than support one or the other. Adams had 324 votes on the sixth, and Greeley 332. Then delegates began to shift and Greeley received the nomination by 482 to 187 for Adams. A motion to make the choice unanimous failed amid loud dissent. The nomination had been brought about through the Missourians, who were opposed to Carl Schurz, a supporter of Adams, combining with the Illinois factionists. B. Gratz Brown was named for vice-president, and the delegates went home.

Greeley accepted the nomination on May twenty-ninth in terms that recited those of the platform, and closed: "If elected I shall be the president not of a party, but of the whole people. I accept your nomination in the confident trust that the masses of our countrymen, North and South, are eager to clasp hands across the bloody chasm which has so long divided them, forgetting that they have been enemies in the joyous consciousness that they are, and must henceforth, remain brethren."

"There is one annoyance in my present position," he wrote after his nomination, "that I did not quite foresee. Not my having to submit in silence to charges that I could not easily refute; that is no more than I foresaw and was resigned to. But my glorious Saturdays are taken from me. A crowd of interviewers and daguerreotypists infest Chappaqua whenever I am expected there (also, in lesser degree at other times), and make me stand against this tree and on that ladder, and in this, that, and t'other absurd position, which they will soon be transferring to steam presses and sending to excite the laughter of millions, who will, of course, suppose that I wish to be thus depicted and represented. Only one week a candidate, and already counting the time when I shall be out of my misery. . . . You ought to see a few of the letters I am favored with, few of them asking outright

BALTIMORE 1861–1872.
"Let us Clasp Hands over the Bloody Chasm."

(*From Harper's Weekly, Aug. 3, 1872*)

for offices, but a good many asking for hats, as though I were a wholesale hatter. Three dozen assorted, is all they require in the last of these missives I have opened. They are not among those I answer."

The Greeley white hat had been adopted by his more enthusiastic followers as a gonfalon for the campaign.

Naturally, a revolt that had been led by men so eminent and so different made a prodigious stir. The depressed and despised Democrats looked upon it as a happy day. They were smothered in the South by negro votes and they were discredited in the North, yet had they stayed by their guns they might have made an impressive showing. The same might be said of the Independents. But they split almost at once, Carl Schurz, Jacob D. Cox, William Cullen Bryant, Oswald Ottendorfer, David A. Wells and Jacob Brinkerhoff leading a bolt which met in small numbers at the Fifth Avenue Hotel, New York, on June 29, 1872, and put in nomination William S. Groesbeck, of Ohio, and Frederick Law Olmsted, of New York. The excuse was the slaughter of the tariff plank in the platform. This ticket was lost in the shuffle, and the movement vanished as such.

The Democratic Convention, held in Baltimore on July 9, 1872, was a sad affair. Eugene Field, then preparing to cut his milk teeth as a reporter, left this account of it:

"There was a small number of delegates, and the convention was held in a hall of meager proportions and wretched appearance. The proceedings were short; at the time, the writer received the impression that everything must have been fixed beforehand, for the program was pushed at a two-forty rate. There were two incidents of a notable nature. When Delaware was called upon to record her vote, a small, sickly-looking gentleman arose in the body of the delegates and began to speak in a voice so feeble that he could hardly be heard. There were calls for him to take the platform and he did so amid general applause. Standing in this conspicuous wise, emaciation and physical weakness were all the more apparent in him, but this condition and the exceeding pallor of his face, the luster of his eyes, and the weird carelessness with which his long, black, bushy hair was tossed about his head, gave him a certain distinct fascination. He was Thomas F. Bayard, who had risen from a bed of sickness to protest solemnly against the stultification which the Democratic party contemplated. He pleaded earnestly and eloquently, but in vain; his auditors listened respectfully and applauded him heartily; they even extended his time, but voted against him.

"When New York was called, Governor Hoffman answered, and as he stood up his splendid figure, handsome face and noble bearing electrified every beholder. He said little, but what he did say was delivered with rhetorical art and grace. He had a deep, persuasive voice and an ingratiating manner. The convention seemed to go wild with enthusiasm, when, with dramatic effect, he cast the votes of New York for Horace Greeley and B. Gratz Brown, and at that instant a large silk banner bearing upon it a portrait of Greeley was swung out from the gallery in which the spectators sat, whereupon the delegates sprang to their feet, faced the banner and cheered lustily.

"A large number of heelers had come over from Philadelphia to give the independent, or 'liberal' movement their moral support. The writer accompanied them to Philadelphia that night upon one of the wretched boats that ply between that city and Baltimore. As he lay awake that hot miserable night, hear-

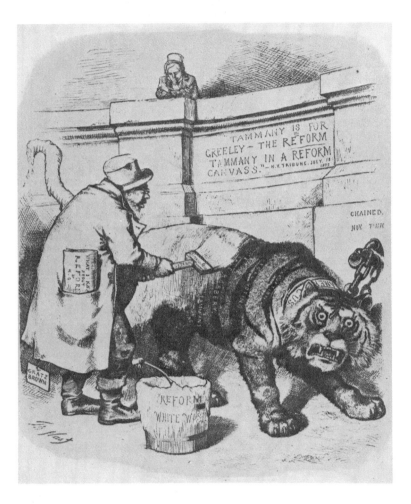

' WHAT ARE YOU GOING TO DO ABOUT IT," IF "OLD HONESTY" LETS HIM LOOSE AGAIN?

(From Harper's Weekly, Aug. 31, 1872)

ing the curses and blasphemies of the drunken mob, he made up his mind that his maiden vote should and would be cast for the nominees of the political party that was happily free from the moral support of the brutal element of humanity.''

In addition to accepting Greeley, the convention approved or swallowed the Cincinnati platform by a vote of 670 to 72. Greeley received 686 out of 720 votes cast, and B. Gratz Brown 713. The Republicans had met in convention at Philadelphia on June 5, 1872, and had renominated Grant. Schuyler Colfax was dropped as vice-president, some scent of the Credit Mobilier scandal having drifted about. His place was taken by Senator Henry Wilson, of Massachusetts.

That Greeley should have welcomed the Democratic indorsement is not strange, though highly inconsistent. He had written to an inquiring Virginia Democrat and free trader, October 18, 1871, saying: ''I am not the man you need. Your party is mostly free trade; I am ferociously protectionist. I have no doubt but I might be nominated and elected by your help, but it would place us all in a false position. If I, who am adversely interested, can see this, I am sure your good sense will, on reflection, realize it.''

Incidentally, Greeley remarked also that the Democrats should have named Salmon P. Chase in 1868, and that their best chances for 1872 lay with B. Gratz Brown, Lyman Trumbull or General Jacob D. Cox— which was true enough. During Greeley's tour of the South in 1871 he had been well received where once he had been proscribed. The newspapers regarded him as openly in the field for a presidential nomination from somebody. No doubt he would have preferred it from the Republican regulars, but the ring around Grant was too strong.

The situation, Greeley felt, was in his hands. Colonel A. K. McClure, of the Philadelphia *Times,* a supporter, wrote: "I never saw a happier face than that of Greeley when I met him. He was then entirely confident of success, and in a very kind and facetious way he reminded me that I had underestimated his strength with the people."

He was soon to be almost alone in this view. Bigelow wrote to Huntington: "Greeley, I think, is destined to learn the differences between notoriety and popularity, and to discover in the course of this canvass from his own experience that it is possible to have one without the other. He may learn, too, that a man may have popularity of a certain sort without being desired for a president. . . . Greeley is an interesting curiosity, which every one likes to see and to show, and in whom we all feel a certain kind of natural pride, but I do not think any one can seriously believe in his fitness for any administrative position whatever. If they do, they know as little of him as he knows of himself."

To the same correspondent on July twenty-fourth Bigelow stated that he could not bring himself to vote for Grant; but "so far as that would help Greeley, I think I should be guilty of promoting the possibility of a result which I can not contemplate without dismay. . . . It is not so much Greeley's eccentricities, nor his ill manners, nor his vanity, that I am afraid of, as the circumstances under which the Democratic and Secession parties have been converted to his support. . . . It is certain that the worst rogues in the country have formed in the Greeley procession, for it includes the New York City ring, and all the secessionists; and it is difficult to believe that, with or without Greeley's knowledge, the Devil does not bear the Cross."

Greeley's own view of the action of the Democrats was voiced in a private letter written July 16, 1872: "I was not much interested in the Baltimore Convention. It did not seem to me probable that I should be nominated at Cincinnati, but I never doubted that Baltimore would accept the candidate of Cincinnati. There would have been no question of this if Cincinnati had nominated Davis, Adams, or Trumbull. It was harder for the Democrats to take me, but there was really no alternative but the utter defeat and probable dissolution of their party. The medicine was nauseous, but the patient was very sick, and could not afford to gratify his palate by the cost of his life. The really astounding feature of the business is the adoption at Baltimore of the Cincinnati platform. . . . It seems scarcely possible to realize that this is the same party that, barely ten years ago, so execrated the Emancipation policy and so howled at me when I addressed to Mr. Lincoln my *Prayer of Twenty Millions*. . . . I grow dizzy when I think of it. And I can imagine no reason for the adoption of our platform unless the Democrats (I mean the controlling majority) mean to stay on it. For they might have endorsed the ticket and spurned the platform. I have done so myself."

"Whatever the result of the contest," he thought, "the Liberal movement is a step in human progress," which he did not believe "can ever be retraced."

July eighteenth he accepted the nomination in a lengthy letter:

"New York, July 18, 1872.

"Gentlemen: Upon mature deliberation, it seems fit that I should give to your letter of the nineteenth inst. some further and fuller response than the hasty, unpremeditated words in which I acknowledged and accepted your nomination at our meeting on the twelfth.

"That your Convention saw fit to accord its highest honor to one who had been prominently and pointedly opposed to your party in the earnest and sometimes angry controversies of the last forty years is essentially noteworthy. That many of you originally preferred that the liberal Republicans should present another candidate for president, and would more readily have united with us in the support of Adams or Trumbull, Davis or Brown, is well known. I owe my adoption at Baltimore wholly to the fact that I had already been nominated at Cincinnati, and that a concentration of forces upon any new ticket had been proved impracticable. Gratified as I am at your concurrence in the Cincinnati nominations, certain as I am that you would not have thus concurred had you not deemed me upright and capable, I find nothing in the circumstance calculated to inflame vanity or nourish self-conceit.

"But that your Convention saw fit, in adopting the Cincinnati ticket, to reaffirm the Cincinnati platform, is to me a source of profoundest satisfaction. That body was constrained to take this important step by no party necessity, real or supposed. It might have accepted the candidates of the Liberal Republicans upon grounds entirely its own, or it might have presented them (as the first Whig National Convention did Harrison and Tyler) without adopting any platform whatever. That it chose to plant itself deliberately, by a vote nearly unanimous, upon the fullest and clearest enunciation of principles which are at once incontestably republican and emphatically democratic, gives trustworthy assurance that a new and more auspicious era is dawning upon our long distracted country.

"Some of the best years and best efforts of my life were devoted to a struggle against chattel slavery—a struggle none the less earnest or arduous because respect for constitutional obligations constrained me to act for the most part on the defensive—in resistance to the diffusion rather than in direct efforts for the extinction of human bondage. Throughout most of those years my vision was uncheered, my exertions were rarely animated by even so much as a hope that I should live to see my country peopled by freemen alone. The affirmance by your Convention of the Cincinnati platform is a most conclusive proof that not merely is slavery abolished, but that its spirit is extinct—that despite the protests of a respectable but isolated few there remains among us no party and no formidable interest which regrets the overthrow or desires the reestablishment of human bondage, whether in letter or in spirit. I am thereby justified in my hope and trust that the first century of American Independence will not close before the grand elemental truths on which its rightfulness was based by Jefferson and the Continental Congress of 1776 will no longer be regarded as 'glittering generalities,' but will have become the universally accepted and honored foundation of our political fabric.

"I demand the prompt application of those principles to our existing condition. Having done what I could for the complete emancipation of blacks, I now insist on the full enfranchisement of all my white countrymen. Let none say that the ban has just been removed from all but a few hundred elderly gentlemen, to whom eligibility to office can be of little consequence.

My view contemplates not the hundreds proscribed, but the millions who are denied the right to be ruled and represented by the men of their unfettered choice. Proscription were absurd if these did not wish to elect the very men whom they are forbidden to choose.

"I have a profound regard for the people of that New England wherein I was born, in whose common schools I was taught. I rank no other people above them in intelligence, capacity and moral worth. But while they do many things well, and some admirably, there is one thing which I am sure they can not wisely or safely undertake, and that is the selection, for states remote from and unlike their own, of the persons by whom those states shall be represented in Congress. If they could do this to good purpose then republican institutions were unfit, and aristocracy the only true political system.

"Yet what have we recently witnessed? Zebulon B. Vance, the unquestionable choice of a large majority of the present legislature of North Carolina—a majority backed by a majority of the people who voted at its election—refused the seat in the Federal Senate to which he was fairly chosen, and the legislature thus constrained to choose another in his stead or leave the state unrepresented for years. The votes of New England thus deprived North Carolina of the senator of her choice, and compelled her to send another in his stead—another who, in our late contest, was, like Vance, a rebel, and a fighting rebel, but who had not served in Congress before the war as Vance had, though the latter remained faithful to the Union till after the close of his term. I protest against the disfranchisement of a state—presumptively, of a number of states—on grounds so narrow and technical as this. The fact that the same Senate which refused Vance his seat proceeded to remove his disabilities after that seat had been filled by another, only serves to place in stronger light the indignity to North Carolina, and the arbitrary, capricious tyranny which dictated it.

"I thank you, gentlemen, that my name is to be conspicuously associated with yours in a determined effort to render amnesty complete and universal in spirit as well as in letter. Even defeat in such a cause would leave no sting, while triumph would rank with those victories which no blood reddens, and which evoke no tears but those of gratitude and joy.

"Gentlemen, your platform, which is also mine, assures me that democracy is not henceforth to stand for one thing, and republicanism for another, but that those terms are to mean in politics, as they always have meant in the dictionary, substantially one and the same thing—namely, equal rights, regardless of creed, or clime, or color. I hail this as a genuine new departure from outworn feuds and meaningless contentions in the direction of progress and reform. Whether I shall be found worthy to bear the standard of the great liberal movement which the American people have inaugurated is to be determined not by words but by deeds. With me if I steadily advance, over me if I falter, its grand array moves on to achieve for our country her glorious, beneficent destiny.

"I remain, gentlemen, yours,

"Horace Greeley.

"To the Honorable James R. Doolittle, Chairman of the Convention, and Messers. F. W. Sykes, John C. Maccabe and others, Committee."

The candidate's Democratic supporters were scandalized by the Tweed ringsters in New York. Nast's cruel pencil put Greeley deep in the Tweed company, as did the one hundred per cent. Republican editors. Among his most bitter opponents was his old associate, Dana, then successfully improving the fortunes of the *Sun* with cynical ability.

E. L. Godkin was chilly in the *Nation*. "The

difficulty,'' he remarked, was ''that men who are enthusiastic about Mr. Greeley are not apt to care much
for reform, while ardent reformers can not be enthusiastic about Mr. Greeley''—just why he did not
make clear. He seemed to think that real enthusiasm
would have been roused by Charles Francis Adams,
who possessed the warmth of a paleocrystic iceberg.
The enthusiasm expected for Greeley, Godkin held,
was of ''the traditional raccoon and log cabin kind''—
a pretty good kind when you come to think of it, but
which he failed to secure. ''We are not now,'' went
on Godkin, ''in a condition to live over again one of
our historic presidential excitements.'' Correctly, he
thought the ''state of mind which the farming population of this country is supposed to entertain toward''
Greeley was ''exaggerated.'' So it proved.

His old friend and fellow paladin in the anti-
slavery cause, Henry Ward Beecher, would have none
of him. ''Mr. Greeley and his friends,'' he said in
the *Christian Union,* ''are fighting General Grant and
we refuse to join them. We believe that Grant will,
during the next four years, make a better president
than Mr. Greeley would, much as we esteem his good
qualities. We see no occasion for changing our candidate and many against it; chiefly and notably, this—
That we should break up a party, that, with all its
faults, is prudent in administration, sound in principles, and safe in the vital point of our affairs—our
fiscal interests; and bring in an inchoate mass of new
men without agreeing among themselves, not cohering
to any central or dominant principles, but subject to
intestine conflicts, out of which no one can tell which
will come into ascendency; whether the advanced no-

"NONE BUT THE BRAVE DESERVES THE FAIR."

MISS COLUMBIA MAY TO H. G. DECEMBER. "Do you see any thing Green in my Eye?"

(From Harper's Weekly, Oct. 26, 1872)

tions of Liberal Republicans or the conservative views of war Democrats, or the malignant reactionary tendency of the old pro-slavery Democratic party. We don't fight Greeley. But we do contend against breaking up the Republican party, and putting the Government into the hands of the Democratic party."

Reproved by Murat Halstead in the Cincinnati *Commercial,* for dropping an old companion in arms, with the taunt that were Beecher running for president he would have had Greeley's support, Beecher replied: "If Mr. Greeley had received the nomination of the Republicans we should have supported him. But what if Mr. Greeley had remained in the Republican party, and Mr. Beecher received the nomination of the Democratic party, would Greeley have supported Beecher then? The *Tribune* would have been a summer threshing floor and no flail would have been long enough or tough enough to beat Beecher small as the very dust."

Twelve years later Beecher left the Republican party and voted and spoke for Grover Cleveland.

The attitude of William H. Seward, who had retired from the office of secretary of state under Johnson and had since made a trip around the world, is cited by J. C. Derby, Auburn man and New York publisher, who was bringing out Seward's new travel book. Derby took proof sheets to Auburn in August, 1872, and the two were sitting together as a Greeley parade went by. "Mr. Seward became very thoughtful," writes Derby, "and said but little; which was to the effect that never in his life had he put any obstacle in Mr. Greeley's way and he certainly should not begin now."

Nor did he. Seward's life ended in the midst of the campaign, on October 10, 1872.

One of the candidate's first acts on opening the canvass was to retire from the editorship of the *Tribune*. The paragraph of announcement read as follows:

"The *Tribune* has ceased to be a party organ, but the unexpected nomination of its editor seems to involve it in a new embarrassment. All must be aware that the position of a journalist who is at the same time a candidate, is at best irksome and difficult—that he is fettered in action and restrained in criticism by the knowledge that whatever he may say or do is closely scanned by thousands eager to find in it what may be so interpreted as to annoy or perplex those who are supporting him as a candidate, and to whom his shackled condition will not permit him to be serviceable. The undersigned, therefore, withdraws absolutely from the conduct of the *Tribune,* and will henceforth, until further notice, exercise no control or supervision over its columns."

Whitelaw Reid then became editor, and J. R. G. Hassard managing editor. John Hay assisted on the editorial page. The paper supported Greeley with exemplary vigor. He opened up the fight at Portland, Maine, on August fourteenth, and kept up a campaign of unparalleled energy. Great receptions were accorded him everywhere and the air was full of hope. The October elections, however, favored the Republicans, and it was clear that Greeley was losing support. Old friends fell away. The partisan press dealt with him severely. George William Curtis, in *Harper's Weekly,* was continuously aided by the grim pencil of Thomas Nast, who unmercifully caricatured the white hat and whiskers.

It had been Greeley's purpose to remain quietly at Chappaqua, but this proved impracticable. During the time it was attempted: "Our Ida is overworked, but I see no help for it. The neighbors offer to help her, but she will accept no help that does not leave her chief director. She is thoroughly in the contest and insists on doing her part in it. It would only annoy and humiliate her to interfere with this. She had about four hundred to feed last Saturday (a special occasion), and she had everything in admirable shape at a little before one P. M."

Taking to the road, the candidate journeyed variously. One trip in September was to New Hampshire, where he climbed Mount Kearsarge. He wrote of it on the eleventh: "I wish you had been at Kearsarge with me. It stands out by itself, in the heart of New Hampshire, with a circle of cultivated hill, valley and woods all around it. Several lakes are visible from the summit. The ascent is very steep and difficult, but two or three young girls, of half my weight and only a fourth of my years, ran up it like goats. I had to rest repeatedly, and lay down on the summit. But the view from that summit is a 'joy forever.' "

On this same day he mentions the election with foreboding: "The Grant folks are full of money and are using it with effect. I shall do my best to defeat them and hope to succeed. But defeat, should that occur, will have many consolations. I like my home better than any spot in Washington: wouldn't you? And while there are doubts as to my fitness for president, nobody seems to deny that I would make a capital beaten candidate."

Greeley's attitude on the stump had been marked by spirit and breadth of view. Daniel W. Voorhees, Democrat, of Indiana, said that "for elevation of thought, propriety of sentiment, for broad philanthropy, for general benevolence, and for Christian statesmanship, the speeches of Mr. Greeley . . . have no parallel in American history."

By the eve of the early state elections, October first, Greeley was only anxious that, after all was over, his friends should be able to say, "He did not throw his chances away by any blunder." He was willing to go to defeat under such a verdict—"But I am not yet beaten." Alas, but he was!

He had been vigorously campaigning for six weeks when the results of the state elections showed his fate was sealed. He wrote, October fourteenth:

"You must not take our reverses to heart. I may soon have to shed some tears for my wife, who seems to be sinking at last, but I shall not give one to any possible result of the political canvass. I shall fight on to the end; but for you, please say, with King Augur of old, 'The bitterness of death is past,' and think henceforth of less melancholy themes."

The strain told heavily, yet his speeches continued strong and convincing. They held forth sound promises, but these were not wanted in a land of prejudice and partisanship. What was really the greatest unselfish independent movement in American history was going down in defeat. Greeley had nothing of Democratic ideas in his system. He was protectionist and federal. The wonder is that he came out so well. In the popular vote he received a total of 2,834,125

to 3,597,132 for Grant, who had 286 electoral votes
to Greeley's 66. Grant's vote gained nearly 600,000
over 1868, and Greeley was 130,000 in his total ahead
of Seymour. Georgia, Kentucky, Maryland, Missouri,
Tennessee and Texas alone were for Greeley. Congress, in counting the vote, rejected the Greeley electors from Louisiana and Arkansas, and three of those
cast in Georgia. In the final count, 63 electors were
counted against Grant, 42 for Thomas A. Hendricks,
Greeley being dead, 18 for B. Gratz Brown, 2 for
Jenkins and 1 for David Davis.

CHAPTER XV

Two weeks before election, Greeley had been called from the field to the bedside of his wife, whose long illness suddenly took an acute form. She was cared for at the home of a family friend, Doctor Alvin J. Johnson, in New York. Here for a fortnight her husband watched and waited in supreme anxiety. He said to an acquaintance: "I am a broken old man [he was but sixty-one]; I have not slept one hour in twenty-four for a month; if she lasts, poor soul, another week, I shall go before her."

She died on October 30, 1872. Five days later election fell, November fifth. On the sixth the *Tribune* announced defeat. On the seventh appeared this announcement in the place on the editorial page usually occupied by the leader:

A CARD

"The undersigned resumes the editorship of the *Tribune,* which he relinquished on embarking on another line of business six months ago. Henceforth it shall be his endeavor to make this a thoroughly independent journal, treating all parties and political movements with judicial fairness and candor, but counting the favor and deprecating the wrath of no one. If he can hereafter say anything that will tend to heartily unite the whole American people on the

"SAVE ME FROM MY TOBACCO PARTNER!"

"OLD HONESTY." "Do, Somebody. arrest him, or I shall never get to the White House!"

broad platform of Universal Amnesty and Impartial Suffrage, he will gladly do so. For the present, however, he can best command that consummation by silence and forbearance. The victors in our late struggle can hardly fail to take the whole subject of southern rights and wrongs into early and earnest consideration, and to them, for the present, he remits it.

"Since he will never again be a candidate for any office, and is not now in full accord with either of the great parties, which have hitherto divided the country, he will be able and will endeavor to give wider and steadier regard to the progress of science, industry and the Useful Arts, than a partisan journal can do; and he will not be provoked to indulgence in those bitter personalities, which are the recognized bane of journalism. Sustained by a generous public, he will do his best to make the *Tribune* a power in the broader field it now contemplates, as, when Human Freedom was imperilled, it was in the arena of political partnership.

"Respectfully,

"HORACE GREELEY."

New York, November 6, 1872.

In the same issue, a few columns away, appeared a jocular editorial, *Crumbs of Comfort,* of which John Bigelow records, as of November sixteenth: "Reid breakfasted with me and told me a great deal about Greeley and the *Tribune.* Seems to think his position there depends upon Greeley's being there. Says Greeley was very indignant at the article entitled *Crumbs of Comfort,* that appeared a day or two after election. He projected an article correcting it— it was written by Hassard—which, if printed, would have sent every editor out of the office. Reid sup-

pressed it. Greeley even then whined and cried and
went on like a baby. He called himself over and over
again 'a black fraud,' said he was ruined, the *Tribune*
was ruined, turn Reid out, turn any one out, to save
the paper.''

To the casual reader the ''Crumbs'' were merely
amusing, the pertinent parts reading:

''There has been no time until now, within the last
twelve years, when the *Tribune* was not supposed to
keep, for the benefit of the idle and incapable, a sort
of Federal employment agency, established to get
places under government for those who were indisposed to work for their living. Any man who ever
voted the Republican ticket believed that it was the
duty and privilege of the editor of this paper to get
him a place in the custom-house. Every red-nosed
politician who had cheated at the caucus and bought
at the polls, looked to the editor of the *Tribune* to secure his appointment as gauger, or as army chaplain,
or as minister to France. . . .

''The man with two wooden legs congratulated
himself that he could never be troubled with cold feet.
It is a source of profound satisfaction to us that office-
seekers will keep away from a defeated candidate who
has not influence enough at Washington or Albany to
get a sweeper appointed under the sergeant-at-arms,
or a deputy sub-assistant temporary clerk into the
paste-pot section of the mailing-room. At last we
shall be let alone to mind our own affairs and manage
our own newspaper, without being called aside every
hour to help lazy people whom we don't know and to
spend our strength in efforts that only benefit people
who don't deserve assistance. That is one of the results of the election for which we own ourselves profoundly grateful.''

The next day, November eighth, appeared Horace Greeley's last contribution to the page he had made so powerful. It said:

CONCLUSIONS

"The general result of our late presidential election indicates that

"I. The objections to General Grant's rule originally urged by Senators Sumner, Schurz, Trumbull, etc., were forcible and well grounded. Many of the most respectable of the journals which, on either side of the Atlantic, vigorously urged the President's reelection now insist that the abuses thus proclaimed must be acknowledged and corrected; some of them demand, in addition to the reforms specifically promised at Philadelphia, others still more radical and thorough.

"II. But, where thousands admitted that the criticisms aforesaid were just, far fewer were ready to accept the only alternative presented. They say they would have supported Adams, or Davis or Trumbull; but not Greeley. Hence the vote is quite light even in states and districts where the contest was spirited.

"III. The great mass of our people felt no sympathy for those they still regard as rebels. On the contrary, they hold that these have been treated more leniently than they deserve. The majority will tolerate, but not approve, the gift of office to a Longstreet, an Akerman, a Settle, who has been baptized into the Republican church, but they are not willing that any others shall hold office where they can prevent it.

"IV. Whichever party carried in October two of the three Central States—Pennsylvania, Ohio and Indiana—is morally certain to choose the President in November. There has been no exception to this rule, save in 1824, when Jackson carried Pennsylvania and Indiana, and had a plurality of the electors chosen, but Adams was elected by the House.

"V. These two states having gone for Grant in October, not only was the contest virtually given up in the North, but thousands of the so-called Rebels went over to Grant, believing this the shortest way to perfect Reconstruction—that is, to secure for themselves a practical equality of rights with other citizens. Thus General Kershaw, of South Carolina, at one time urged his fellow rebels to run no ticket against Grant, as this would enable them to appeal with effect for Federal sympathy as against their rascally state rulers.

"VI. The Republicans have won a perilous triumph. John Randolph said that one was the best possible majority. When the old Republican party had chosen Mr. Monroe President, with only one elector dissenting, it dissolved and ran four candidates at the next election.

"VII. Though the Democratic party broke into fragments, not one of these has distinctly proposed a return to the anti-negro policy of other days. On the contrary, the Bourbons, who urged all manner of objections to Greeley, said nothing of his devotion to Equal Rights, regardless of color. We may fairly conclude that there will be no further formidable, systematic opposition to Impartial Suffrage.

"VIII. There is little or no complaint from any quarter of violence or terrorism at the polls. Blacks and whites swarmed around a thousand polls, but scarcely a blow was struck and no serious riot occurred. It is thus settled that Whites and Blacks can vote together without a breach of the peace—'rebel' and 'nigger' treating each other with forbearance and consideration.

In the meantime something had happened in the *Tribune,* and for the first time Greeley learned that a movement was under way to unseat him. Greatly discomposed, he wrote bitter letters to intimates, con-

"HOME-STRETCHED."

NOVEMBER 5TH HIS BORROWED STEED WILL HOME-STRETCH HIM.

(From Harper's Weekly, Nov. 9, 1872)

demning Whitelaw Reid, most unjustly. One of these was to Miss Mary Norton, of Hightstown, New Jersey, who once gave me the substance of the plaint, which was that Reid had betrayed him and that he was to be ousted from the editorship of the paper. He also commented on the results of the election in this fevered correspondence, saying to one correspondent, C. A. Haviland, of Chicago: "My misfortunes do not come 'single files, but in battalions.' I grieve that you are also a sufferer from our disastrous cause. I can not say that I see any light ahead. Indeed, there is none!"

To another he sent the message: ". . . Nor do I care for defeat, however crushing. I dread only the malignity with which I am hounded, and the possibility that it may ruin the *Tribune.* My enemies mean to kill that; if they would kill me instead, I would think of them lovingly. And so many of my old friends hate me for what I have done that life seems too hard to bear."

To Caleb Lyon, of Lyonsdale, New York, who met him on Broadway after the smash, he said this: "I was an abolitionist for years, when it was as much as one's life was worth, even here in New York, to be one; and the negroes all voted against me. Whatever of talent and energy I have possessed I have freely contributed all my life long to protection, to the cause of our manufactures; and the manufacturers expended millions to defeat me. I even made myself ridiculous, in the opinion of many whose good wishes I desired, by showing fair play and giving a fair field in the *Tribune* to Women's Rights; and the women have all gone against me."

All this was as nothing to the true trouble, the prospective loss of the paper. The real "betrayer," if he could be fairly so called, was Samuel Sinclair, the publisher, who had sold his twenty shares for two hundred thousand dollars, because of pressing personal needs, and so enabled William Orton, president of the Western Union Telegraph Company, to secure an option on enough *Tribune* stock to give him control. Schuyler Colfax, having been excluded from being the country's vice-president, needed a job. It was Orton's purpose to make Colfax editor, as a handy aid to those corporate interests incidental to regular Republicanism. When the full force of the Credit Mobilier scandal fell on Colfax, he was no longer eligible, and Orton could not swing his options. He therefore turned them over to the wily Jay Gould, who could. Neither Orton nor Gould was mentioned in the office situation described by Reid. "There has been," wrote Bigelow to Huntington, "a formidable combustion among the stockholders of the *Tribune* led by Sinclair, to unhorse Reid, but thus far unsuccessful. Sinclair, I believe, wants Schuyler Colfax to be the future figurehead of the paper. . . . Hay wants to sell a share of the *Tribune,* and Greeley has borrowed, I am told, an inconvenient amount on his shares. The stock has fallen from ten thousand dollars to about six thousand dollars a share, at which price I should think it an excellent purchase. Reid and all the rest, I believe, mean to make a Republican paper again of the *Tribune,* and I have no doubt, when Greeley is well and notoriously out of it, it will be as prosperous as ever, if not more so." This prophecy never came true.

Greeley fluttered in and out of the *Tribune* for a few days. His sleeplessness grew. On November thirteenth he made his last visit to the office, remaining thereafter at Doctor Johnson's. The weary brain again flamed into fever. All sorts of reports of madness flew about. Bigelow on the twenty-fourth wrote Huntington: "The disaster has been too great for Greeley. I think he has been crazy for many years. Now, alas, the fact can not be disguised. I was told a week ago he was out of his head. Yesterday it was currently reported upon good authority, that application had been made for his confinement at Bloomingdale. That institution, not wishing to have its administration again brought under public discussion so soon after its recent arraignment by the press, declined to receive him. Therefore he was consigned to the charge of a private establishment. This I hear from excellent authority, and I am the more disposed to credit it, as Reid and Hay both had quite prepared me for such a catastrophe. I fear a similar fate is in store for Sumner."

The private "establishment" was the home of Doctor George S. Choate at Pleasantville, New York. Here the best medical advice was secured from brain specialists, including the famous Doctor Brown-Séquard and Doctor E. Krackowizer. The first public mention of its editor's condition appeared at the head of the *Tribune's* first editorial column on November twentieth. It read:

"Mr. Greeley's correspondents must excuse him if their favors receive less prompt attention than has been the custom. He has been seriously unwell, since his wife's death, from nervous prostration, resulting mainly from the severe strain upon his nervous system, through want of rest and sleep, during the last month of her illness. Nothing but his remarkable strength of constitution has enabled him to give attention to his recent duties, but it may be safely trusted to restore him speedily to his usual vigorous health.''

This fair hope soon became untrue. Gabrielle and Ida kept close to their father's bedside, as did numbers of faithful friends. In another week his condition had become so alarming as to produce this from the *Tribune* on November twenty-eighth:

"We are deeply pained to say that in the last thirty-six hours Mr. Greeley's condition has changed greatly for the worse. Throughout yesterday he remained nearly all the time unconscious. In a counsel of some of the most eminent physicians of the city, only one was without hope, but all regarded the case as critical and alarming.''

The sick man had fallen into a stupor, from which he never fully rallied. The files of the *World* give this story of his last hours:

"Miss Ida Greeley, who through all the sad moments preserved a wonderful self-control, sat at the bedside through it all, supporting, when needful, her father's head. At half past five Mr. Greeley was lying unconscious, when an old and dearly loved friend, whom he and his family knew as 'Auntie' Lamson, entered the room and approached the bed. Mr. Greeley did not stir until Mr. Stewart roused him and asked, 'Do you know who this is?' He feebly said 'Yes,' and stretched up his hand in greeting, and then relapsed into his reverie. . . . Later he was asked,

'Do you know that you are dying?' and in the same manner, without tremor or apparent emotion, he answered, 'Yes.' The pulse at this time was gone and the breathing so quick and faint that it seemed that every gasp were the last. . . . When asked if he was in pain he laid his hand upon his breast, but without otherwise replying, and returned to his semi-unconscious state, lying now with closed eyes and hands sometimes twitching nervously, but generally still. Doctor Choate then said that death would probably ensue in half an hour, though possibly not in two hours. The former opinion proved correct. At half past six Mr. Greeley stirred uneasily, and began to mutter indistinctly something which the friends around him could not catch. His daughter Ida, Mr. and Mrs. Stewart, Mr. Carpenter, Doctor Choate, and Auntie Lamson were all in the room, and anxiously bent over the bed to interpret if possible what they feared, with good reason, were the last words. Mr. Greeley still indistinctly murmured for a while. Then there was a relapse into quiet for a time. After a silence of some minutes the muttering was again heard, but was all unintelligible. Miss Greeley, however, bending close to the couch, thought she distinguished a request from her father that his head be lifted higher. The pillows were accordingly arranged in such a way as to render the faint breathing as easy as possible, and a hush fell upon the room. There was no more murmuring. The pulse had died out long before. The breath was caught shorter and shorter and heard fainter and fainter, and three and four times within the last fifteen minutes the attendants believed it had come and gone for the last time. The eyes were closed, and as the last breathings came, the right hand was stretched out again in the familiar gesture, and death almost instantly followed. There was no evidence of pain in the last moments, and indeed the nature of the disease forbids its supposition.

The face hardly changed, only setting a little into a look of perfect peace.''

The day was November 29, 1872. Last words have been accorded Greeley, as breathed with satisfaction and resignation. What he really said in his waning moments was quite as different as *"La Garde meurt, et ne se rend pas,"* was from what Cambronne really said at Waterloo. It need not be repeated.

They took the poor burned-out body, whence the great soul had fled, from Pleasantville to the New York City Hall, opposite the office of the *Tribune* in which the man had labored so long and so well. Here it lay in state while thousands of mourning people passed the bier and looked for the last time upon the dead. Then the coffin was closed and borne to the house of Samuel Sinclair, to await the last ceremonies on December 4, 1872.

The funeral was held in the Church of the Divine Paternity at Fifth Avenue and Forty-fourth Street, services being conducted by its pastor, Doctor E. H. Chapin, Henry Ward Beecher and Doctor Thomas Armitage. Clara Louise Kellogg, then greatest of American singers, sang, *I Know That My Redeemer Liveth*. President Grant and Vice-President Colfax came from Washington, as did Henry Wilson, the Vice-President elect, whose own funeral was to be the next great pageant in New York. The Governors of New York, New Jersey and Connecticut attended with their staffs. Chief Justice Salmon P. Chase, Thurlow Weed, William M. Evarts and Lyman Trumbull headed the eminent pallbearers. A great procession followed the body to its grave in Greenwood, where another Universalist clergyman, the Reverend James

M. Pullman, brother of the car builder, committed dust to dust.

There was an immediate and nation-wide revulsion of feeling. Horace Greeley had done so much for liberty, so much for human welfare, had done it so tirelessly, so unselfishly, and at such sacrifice, that all the land went into mourning over the man it had lately covered with odium. There were no enemies left.

"Since the assassination of Mr. Lincoln," wrote George William Curtis in *Harper's Weekly,* which had so strongly opposed Mr. Greeley, "the death of no American has been so sincerely deplored as that of Horace Greeley; and its tragical circumstances have given a peculiarly affectionate pathos to all that has been said of him. The tone of the public comment reflects the enthusiasm of his own nature, and is characteristic of the kind as well as the extent of the impression he had produced upon the country. He was not, however, a simple character. The general and distant impression was often modified upon nearer approach; but the accepted estimate is undoubtedly that which will pass into the history of these times. The most striking fact in regard to Mr. Greeley is that he was considered peculiarly representative of the American genius and spirit, so that he was often regarded as the typical American. He was born poor. He rose by his own talents and labor. He was conscientious, and a natural democrat. He founded a great newspaper, and befriended the poor, the laborer and the oppressed. He distrusted all but what is called practical education. He condemned the social conventions. He was an ardent and sincere politician. Is not all this Amer-

ican? we are asked. And was there any such conspicuous representative of all this as Horace Greeley?''

"When Horace Greeley died," wrote Henry Ward
Beecher in the *Christian Union,* "unjust and hard
judgment of him died also. More than this, it is
given . . . to see a leader who had taught his followers so true a love of liberty for its own sake, so
dire a hatred of oppression and tyranny, that, when
they thought him deceived and wandering, they could
follow his counsels rather than himself."

"The poor white hat!" exclaimed Harriet Beecher
Stowe. "If, alas, it covered many weaknesses, it covered also much strength, much real kindness and
benevolence, and much that the world will be better
for. . . ."

Bigelow, writing to George Von Bunsen, on
December twenty-fourth, cruelly but clearly made this
point: "The Greeley force, terminating, as the most
famous forces always do, in tragedy, was really one
of the most dramatic events in all history. The traitors of 1860 got possession of this poor man, whose
mind had been disordered for many years, but who
had accumulated a vast amount of political power in
a long life of laborious journalism, and tried to ex-
ploit him. They hoped, through the weakness of his
character and the ballot box, to get control of the
government, which they had tried unsuccessfully to
secure with the sword. But God makes the wrath of
men ever to praise Him. Nothing of all that Greeley
ever wrote against slavery and its ultimates (violence
and tyranny) did one-half as much to annihilate its
champions and abettors as his consenting to be their
candidate for the presidency. In the eyes of the angels

MR. GREELEY'S LAST PORTRAIT

that was the great benefaction of his life to his country.''

The New York *World* rendered Greeley deep tribute. Twice in succession its editorial page overflowed with praise of the great career that had come to such a cruel close.

Charles A. Dana, in the *Sun*, had this to say:

"His attitude as a reformer also gained for him the reputation of a humanitarian and philanthropist, one bent chiefly on assuaging the woes of mankind. This distinction he repeatedly disclaimed. He was not a philanthropist, he said; his purpose was only to establish justice and equal rights among men. There was truth in this disclaimer. His sensibilities were uncommonly quick, but mere benevolence, or the purpose of simply doing good to others, did not control him. Though he hated to witness any scene of misery, he had no skill in personally administering to distress. Besides, his ruling motives were of the intellect more than of the heart. He contended against slavery, not because he cared particularly for the negroes—on the contrary he rather disliked them—but because it was contrary to that democratic equality which was the fundamental principle of his political creed, and because he understood that slavery was not only an aristocratic but an intolerant element in our politics; and that under its rule neither he nor any other northern man could hope for preferment, except as the reward of a servility and self-abasement; and for this he was too upright and too proud. So with his lifelong advocacy of temperance; it did not proceed from any sympathy with men governed by the passion for liquor. Such men he looked upon with disgust and contempt; and in the possibility of their reformation he habitually disbelieved. Temperance in his view was a branch of political economy, a sort of public hygiene tending to promote the general happiness and increase the wealth of the community; and his views were similar in respect of every reform and every philanthropic cause which he advocated.

"As a man Horace Greeley was, first of all, a sincere thorough-going democrat. He met every one as an equal, and was free alike from snobbish deference and social presumption. He was also exceedingly generous and charitable. While he was still poor we have known him to respond to a demand for pecuniary assistance, made by some person to whom he was under no obligations, by sitting up late at night and writing an article for some magazine, by which he could get twenty-five dollars or fifty dollars to give away. According to the necessity of his profession, his personal friends were comparatively few; but though he was too much occupied with his thoughts and his professional avocations to give much time to social intercourse, they could always count upon him in any time of need. His purse and his credit were theirs; he hastened to their assistance often before they asked it; and he died comparatively a poor man; the fact is chiefly due to his lavish and persistent benefactions toward them. But those who cultivated his society most were not always such as could best appreciate him. He was fond of admiration and open to flattery; and flatterers too often deluded him. He was an affectionate rather than an attentive husband and father. His feelings were easily touched; but his attachments were not deep. In his private relations to his public opponents he retained none of the bitterness of controversy, and was always ready to meet them out of the arena with genial courtesy and kindness; and yet he was jealous rather than confiding, and suspicious rather than tolerant."

William Cullen Bryant, the "villain" of old controversial days, spoke these words in the *Evening Post:*

"The honors shown his remains, then, are honors done to his profession; but they are also an evidence of the consideration in which he was himself held. They prove that whatever opinions we may have individually formed of the intellectual or personal merits of the subject of them, the great body of the people discovered in him grounds for admiration, attachment and gratitude. They saw in his efforts to enlighten and guide the sentiments of his fellows something more than a paltry pursuit of wealth or a vain ambition of power and fame. They saw in them an earnest desire to do good, to help forward the better interests of the community, and to maintain that spirit of justice and freedom which in our hot and reckless enterprises we are apt to forget, but which constitutes the very bond and cement, as it does the life and glory, of civilized society.

"With Mr. Greeley's political and philosophical views of things, we were not in entire accord; his manner of presenting his convictions did not always meet our approval; but for some objects, and these among the most momentous that ever divided the nation, we labored long in common, and we can bear witness to the zeal, the fearlessness, and the vigor with which he battled for the right. In the slow but intense and bitter controversy against slavery, which has filled our history for nearly fifty years, we found him always a powerful coadjutor, and we doubt whether any single instrument used against the gigantic wrong was more effective in the work of its gradual overthrow than the press which he managed with so much courage and determination. So far as the history of that conflict has been written, and so far as it is yet to be written, one of the most prominent places must be given to the sturdy, unflinching and persistent assaults of the *Tribune* newspaper. The more zealous abolitionists were sometimes apt to criticize the peculiar methods of its warfare, but none, we think, will at this day deny the efficiency of its services.''

Following Horace Greeley's death, Whitelaw Reid and John Hay prepared to step down and out of the *Tribune*, when the former learned the fate of Orton's option. By quick work he was able, with the help of others, including especially William Walter Phelps, to acquire these options and the control of the property. He wrote Bigelow, February 18, 1873, giving what he called some details concerning "our revolution and counter-revolution in the office," the "upshot of it all" being that "I succeeded in seeing so far into Orton's hands as to be able to play better cards than he, and won the game. I made a concession which smoothed things somewhat at the close, leaving him one share out of the fifty-one, and agreeing to make him one of the nine trustees, as I immediately arranged to have Hay buy another share, which gives us the fifty-one and enables us to control the paper absolutely as we please, trustees or no trustees. The concession does not amount to much, but it enlists Orton's cordial cooperation in business matters, which, owing to his position at the head of the telegraph, is valuable. . . . One of my first acts was to turn Sinclair out and at the annual meeting of the stockholders in January to have myself elected publisher as well as editor for five years, the contract to that end having heavy penalties attached.''

The astute young Reid does not mention Gould in the matter, but the savor of Gould's share in the transaction was retained in the public mind as long as that cunning financier lived, and did the *Tribune* great and undeserved harm.

Horace Greeley's friends, the printers, did not forget him. Typographical Union No. 6 caused a bust to be erected over his grave in Greenwood, and placed him in bronze at the triangle made by Sixth Avenue, Broadway and Thirty-third Street, which is known as Greeley Square. Another statue blocked the entrance to the Tribune Building at Spruce Street and Park Row, until the paper moved up-town to West Fortieth Street. Then it was shifted to City Hall Park, where it rests in a little grove, and the tender leaves of young trees shade the figure of the great and good man who loved their kind so well.

THE END

INDEX

INDEX

413